GLIMPSES INTO HAYWOOD COUNTY'S

CARROLL C. JONES

Glimpses into Haywood County's Past
Carroll C. Jones

Published November 2025
Little Creek Books
Imprint of Jan-Carol Publishing, Inc.
All rights reserved
Copyright © 2025 Carroll C. Jones
Book design: Tara Sizemore

This book may not be reproduced in whole or part, in any manner whatsoever, without written permission, with the exception of brief quotations within book reviews or articles.

ISBN: 978-1-970471-11-3
Library of Congress Control Number: 2026932286

You may contact the publisher:
Jan-Carol Publishing, Inc.
PO Box 701
Johnson City, TN 37605
publisher@jancarolpublishing.com
www.jancarolpublishing.com

For my wife, Maria, who took a huge risk many years ago when she blessed me with her love and companionship. She has truly made my life special and worthwhile.

Also by Carroll C. Jones

Non-fiction:

The 25th North Carolina Troops in the Civil War

Rooted Deep in the Pigeon Valley

Captain Lenoir's Diary

Thomson's Pulp Mill:
Building the Champion Fibre Company at
Canton, North Carolina – 1905 to 1908

East Fork Trilogy fictional series:

Master of the East Fork

Rebel Rousers

August's Treasure

AUTHOR'S ACKNOWLEDGMENTS

Over the past couple of decades, I have been blessed with significant support and inspiration for my writing projects, including the articles that have been selected and included in Glimpses into Haywood County's Past. Thanks to all including family members, friends, readers, and newspaper editors for sharing valuable information, ideas, praise, and constructive critiques.

Almost every paragraph of the many articles collected in the new book underwent my wife's scrutiny, first seeking understanding and then judging whether the written words possessed the style and interest sought by readers like herself. A nodding head or certain facial expressions usually let me know if revisions were in order. Thanks, Maria, for your patience and willingness to share honest feelings and helpful thoughts, among the other valued gifts you have given me.

Another family member's creative ideas were also routinely sought. My Double-Second-Cousin Edie Burnette—a former newspaper journalist and teacher, as well as an accomplished author in her own right—has regularly perused my articles over the years and shared judgements of history content, accuracy, and grammatical issues. So, understandably, I am truly grateful for Cousin Edie's support and the meaningful contributions she has made.

Several local historians have been forthcoming with information and even old maps and photographs which have been extremely useful in my renderings of the past. Of course, I have endeavored to give formal recognition to all contributors in the footnotes and afternotes, but I would especially like to acknowledge two of these individuals—Evelyn Coltman and Jerry Ledford. Both are extremely well-informed on our local history and, over the years, have been quite generous in sharing their thoughts along with historical resources they have gathered and written about. Many thanks, Evelyn and Jerry.

One other important resource for local history information cannot go unmentioned. The Canton Area Historical Museum is loaded with all sorts of old documents related to the histories of Canton and Haywood County, the paper mill, and local citizens from the past. With assistance from the museum's curator, Caroline Ponton, I have been able to discover and use historical information from these sources, including old "Champion Log" newsletters and magazines, hundreds of old photos and maps, diaries, letters, drawings, and paintings. Thank you, Caroline, for the assistance you have given me over the years in finding and utilizing the museum's extensive resources.

Finally, I would like to thank Jan-Carol Publishing's team for their superb work editing and combining all my articles into a book titled *Glimpses into Haywood County's Past*. They took the project on when others were unsure or simply overwhelmed with the challenge. Now you are about to discover what a wonderful job Jan-Carol has done in organizing the many stories and photos of Haywood County's past and presenting them in a manner that history lovers will appreciate.

Best regards and good reading!

COMMENTS FROM LOCAL AUTHORS

A few notable western North Carolina authors/historians have shared their own critical comments and opinions about author Carroll C. Jones and his glimpses into Haywood County's history. You can read what they had to say below.

Edie Hutchins Burnette:

"Carroll Jones lives among fertile hunting grounds for writers and history buffs like us. His stories are taken from the mountains of western North Carolina's Haywood County, with some of the tales actually reflecting early life throughout the Southern Appalachians. Readers can choose from a varied menu of meticulously researched stories or opt to be immersed in a pleasant journey of meeting people, of exploration, and occasional adventures.

"Carroll's mission has always been one of accurately gathering historical facts worthy of preservation. For example, he writes about our shared great-grandfather whose obituary described him as being 'a useful citizen,' and for good reason. The man's lifetime endeavors included being a Civil War soldier, a farmer, teacher, surveyor, public servant, insurance salesman, and a newspaper editor, to name a few.

"Carroll, also, recounts strenuous hikes that sometimes resulted in amazing discoveries. For example, he searched for and found an abandoned reservoir that once supplied water to George Vanderbilt's distant vacation lodge. On another occasion, he discovered the site of a rare funicular railroad along with old artifacts hidden amidst a dense forest in the Middle Prong Wilderness.

"His carefully chosen words paint accurate pictures, whether it be a personal experience, a description of a long-ago logging village, treks along mountain streams in search of elusive native trout, the life of a prolific mountain inventor, or Haywood County's beautiful Pigeon Valley.

"I am proud of the fact that we are double-second Hargrove cousins, and we can still share numerous childhood memories of our adjoining family farms on the 'back-side' of the Pigeon River. With similar interests and recollections, we will continue to strive to be 'useful citizens' by sharing a desire to accurately record details from long-ago times for readers interested in such things."

Edie Hutchins Burnette is a native of Canton, North Carolina, and a descendant of pioneering families of Haywood County. She is the widow of Charles R. Burnette and has one daughter, Alison (Ray) Frazier, and two grandchildren. In addition to her work as a newspaper journalist and schoolteacher, Edie wrote and published the book *Mountain Echoes*, a compilation of many stories she has written about the history of western North Carolina.

Evelyn Coltman:

"Historians who descend into dungeons at library archives to retrieve rare tidbits of data, ferret out original documents, unearth relevant files, and research singular records for their next book or project are to be commended for their focus on tracking primary sources that either corroborate or refute an understanding of the subject at hand. Carroll Jones is an expert at this level of historical research.

"Researchers who pore over secondary analyses to ascertain the impact of a historical figure, a prior event, or a notable trend lend credence to their topic by their willingness to assess the subject from a variety of perspectives. Carroll Jones is adept at analyzing historical context by studying the opinions of those who preceded him.

"Pursuing primary and secondary source studies is as far as many historians go in their quest to learn the truths hidden under layers of dust, neglect, and time. Fortunately for those who focus on the importance of understanding our past with an accurate and sensitive perception, there are rare historical researchers who go the extra mile beyond tracking original sources and beyond reading what others have written about the topic. These unique scholars reach the pinnacle by visiting original sites with the intent of gaining a visceral, intuitive, almost spiritual connection to their subject. Such a viewpoint allows the reader to gain an understanding, not only of the facts, but also of the heart of the matter.

"Carroll Jones is the epitome of the pinnacle scholar because, whenever possible, he actually visits the locations he studies. He writes about Buck Spring Lodge, the kaolin mine, Boomer Inn, the pea vine railroad, the funicular railroad, Garden Creek archaeological site, Bethel Community Cemetery, Garden Creek School and swinging bridge, Three Forks, the Phoenix-column truss bridge, and other subjects with a firsthand familiarity that allows the reader to gain an accurate, intimate, even poetic perspective because Jones has visited the locations—even on sometimes treacherous terrain.

"Fortunately, Jones is also a readable writer who permits us the luxury of learning about history—not with a dull, dry recitation of dates and data—but with the same comfort and anticipation we experience when we curl up with a well-written novel whose pages we cannot wait to turn."

Evelyn Coltman has guided Bethel Rural Community Organization's Historic Preservation Committee during Cold Mountain Heritage Tours, the publication of her six award-winning *Legends, Tales & History of Cold Mountain* books, the release of three award-winning DVDs and two CDs, the collection of 30 award-winning historic art prints, the erection of six local historic markers, and the presentation to 10 worthy citizens of Pigeon Valley Awards for Historic Preservation.

Gerald Ledford:

"Lifeguard Carroll Jones taught me how to swim at the Robertson Memorial YMCA in Canton, N.C., in the mid-1960s. I had no idea at the time that Carroll and I would one day write and publish articles and history books about eastern Haywood County, where we both grew up. In addition to teaching me how to swim all those years ago, I'll always be thankful for the generous help he gave me as I was preparing the second edition of *If Rails Could Talk...Volume 2, Sunburst & Champion Fibre* for publication.

"So often, I have been disappointed with regional histories that tend to be filled with inaccurate information. Sometimes the chronology and flow of ideas in some of these books are difficult to follow. Carroll's writing style is precise, factual, and easy to read. His books will hold your interest. When Carroll's book *Thomson's Pulp Mill* came out, I and many others realized that it was the definitive early history of the largest industry ever seen in western North Carolina. If you don't own it, get a copy now while you still can.

"Carroll and I both have a love for history. You'll enjoy reading this newest book of his, *Glimpses into Haywood County's Past*."

Gerald (Jerry) Ledford is renowned for his knowledge of railroading history in western North Carolina. To his writing credit, he co-authored *If Rails Could Talk*, a six-volume series that offers a comprehensive history of logging and railroads in the mountains of western North Carolina.

TABLE OF CONTENTS

Dedication	iii
Author's Acknowledgments	v
Comments from Local Authors	vii
Table of Contents	xi
Preface	1

Before Settlement

The Pigeon River Once Emptied into the Atlantic Ocean	5
The Pigeon Valley's Garden of Human Culture	10
When an Army Invaded the Pigeon Valley	17

Forks of Pigeon (or Bethel)

A "Turn-O-Meal" at Cathey's Mill	23
Haywood County's Phoenix-Column Bridge	29
Haywood County's Forgotten Inventor	39
A Matter of Graveyard Sleuthing	53
The Sonoma Kaolin Mine	60
The Old Garden Creek School... and the Swinging Bridge	67
Memories of Mountain Thanksgivings	78

Sunburst (or Spruce)

The Canton-to-Sunburst Pea Vine Railroad	83
An Illuminating Panorama of Three Forks (Sunburst)	99
Ghosts of an Old Funicular Railroad	109
My Middle Prong Passion	120

Searching for Boomer Inn	129
A "Pioneer Site" on the West Fork of the Pigeon River	140
Remembering Lake Logan	149
George W. Vanderbilt's Buck Spring Lodge—and the Ram-Jet Pump	163

Following Great-Grandfather's Footprints

Captain Hack Hargrove—A Useful Citizen	183
When a Trip to the Market Took a Month's Time	213
Captain Hargrove's Diary Discovered Among Attic Plunder	222
Confederate Flag Waving	227

Canton Memories

How, Why, and When Did Canton Really Get Its Name?	231
Colonel Silas A. Jones' Pipeline Dream	238
Canton's Old Dam Blown to Kingdom Come	248
Champion Paper and Fibre Company's Tabulating Office	253
Canton's Original Bucket Factory	259
Champion YMCA's Gra-Y Program	264
A Canton Boy Through and Through	274
Plumb Proud of My Mountain Dialect	280
A Canton Boy's Hometown Memories	287

Preface for *Thomson's Pulp Mill*	297
A Glimpse of the Author	303

PREFACE

Some may have wondered about my late plunge into literary endeavors, or more specifically, writing books and shorter articles about local history. Certainly, this retired civil engineer has not undertaken a new pursuit for financial gain. Trust me, hopes of a bestseller or even monetary rewards were never motivational factors. My dives into the past were mainly driven by a want to learn more about western North Carolina's history, preserve the history for generations to come, and share this knowledge with others.

Initial works of non-fiction, including *The 25th North Carolina Troops in the Civil War* and *Captain Lenoir's Diary*, were founded on extensive research of primary and secondary sources, as well as focused studies of related published works. Both books, in my opinion, are extremely valuable additions to our written knowledge base of western North Carolina's history. Although extremely time-consuming and requiring laborious writing and re-writing, these projects filled me with purpose and, eventually, a strong feeling of satisfaction and accomplishment.

More recently, I delved off into historical fiction efforts that might require some explanation. Turns out, it was a rather impulsive notion that got me started down this path of make-believe. The true circumstances that drew a young man named Thomas Isaac Lenoir into the Haywood County mountains prior to the Civil War—as covered in meticulous detail in *Captain Lenoir's Diary*—intrigued me greatly. In fact, I was inspired to invent and write a fictional story based somewhat on the challenges Lenoir faced while trying to survive and make a living on the East Fork of the Pigeon River. This story became the first novel in my *East Fork Trilogy* series.

Seemingly out of the blue, my pen—actually, my computer—created a young character named Basil Edmunston who was turned loose in the rural East Fork region of the Pigeon River Valley in the years preceding the Civil War. Neither Basil nor I looked back after that as we conceived and crafted the pages of the following three books comprising a trilogy: *Master of the East Fork*, *Rebel Rousers*, and *August's Treasure*.

It was indeed a learning experience to develop interesting characters, write dialog for the first time, and dream up meaningful stories. The fact that I became so emotionally caught up in these tales was truly unexpected. For example, *Rebel Rousers* tells a story about two young Rebel soldiers who could not stay out of trouble during the Civil War. I became quite attached to both of them when writing the book, and there was one scene that really got to me.

During a fierce battle with the Union troops, Confederate Private Hartgrove dropped his Mississippi Rifle and ran as fast as his skinny legs would carry him toward the fallen banner of his regiment. Ignoring the lethal gunfire whizzing all around him, he reached down and took up the tangled flag from the dead flag bearer's corpse. Raising it high into the air, he overcame fearful instincts and began moving directly toward the enemy lines. Upon seeing their flag advancing once again, the Confederate colonel and his re-inspired troops began following behind Private Hartgrove as he led a successful charge against the Yankee line.

While writing this intense scene, I was overcome with emotion and respect for the bravery demonstrated by the young soldier. Indeed, it was so emotional that more than once I had to stop writing and wipe away the teardrops on my computer's keyboard. Please believe me, it truly happened!

After satisfying myself with that three-year, or so, immersion into fiction, I did not have to look far to uncover another subject of interest regarding Haywood County's history. A friend shared with me a trove of old photographs taken during the construction of Canton's original paper mill (Champion Fibre Company) between 1905 and 1908. These wonderful photos that had been passed down through his family kindled a fire in me, and there was only one way it could be doused. I had to learn and tell the true story of how

Canton's paper mill came to be, through these photos and my writing.

The resulting book is titled *Thomson's Pulp Mill: Building the Champion Fibre Company at Canton, North Carolina: 1905 to 1908*. By writing this story, that burning fire inside of me was very effectively extinguished. For a Canton boy, whose great-grandfather helped build the mill, whose mother and father worked there and who himself worked at the mill, nothing could have been more fulfilling than helping Mr. Peter Gibson Thomson build that mill again.

Unfortunately, five years after the book's publication, a much more significant fire in Canton was apparently extinguished forever. Pactiv Evergreen, the owner of the paper mill in Canton at the time, made the fateful decision to shut the mill down after 115 years of continuous operation. Never in my own lifetime did I expect this would happen. But it has happened, and there is no doubt the impact of the mill's closure on Canton and Haywood County's citizens is significant. Somehow, those of us who have chosen to live here will have to find a way to patch this huge hole in the road and continue life's journey. Afterall, it is up to us to make sure our futures and that of our children and homeplace remain bright.

News of the mill's shutdown had more than a sobering effect on me. This event reinforced a truth we should all never forget. One cannot control everything in their life and life is short. So, it convinced me to stop procrastinating and get to work on another book I have been thinking about publishing before it is too late.

Between the seven books I have written over the past 20 years, there have been intervals when I sketched out shorter articles that are mostly related to the history of Haywood County. Some were published in local newspapers while others I deemed to be too personal or were too lengthy for the newspapers. These encompass a variety of subjects including a tale about the time, eons ago, when the Pigeon River emptied into the Atlantic Ocean, discovering my Great-Grandfather Hargrove's footprints, logging at Sunburst in the early 20th century, an old Pea Vine railroad, George Vanderbilt's Buck Spring Lodge, the Bethel community's forgotten inventor, Haywood County's 19th-century Phoenix-Column iron-truss bridge, graveyard sleuthing, and stories about Canton and its huge paper mill, to name just a few.

For posterity and for those readers who might enjoy my dives into Haywood County's history, I have assembled some favorite articles into this book titled *Glimpses into Haywood County's Past*. Hopefully, you will find reading them to be an interesting and memorable learning experience.

Best regards and good reading!

The author,
Carroll C. Jones

BEFORE SETTLEMENT

One of many markers along General Griffith Rutherford's war trace

The Pigeon River Once Emptied into the Atlantic Ocean

Introduction

Today, there is a gap in the Newfound Mountain Range where the town of Canton, North Carolina, straddles the Pigeon River. This natural geologic breach provided the most viable way for the first explorers and pioneer settlers to reach the interior of North Carolina's western mountains. It was essentially an eastern gateway into the mountains, one that General Griffith Rutherford exploited in 1776 when he led a Revolutionary War army on a punitive campaign against the Cherokee Indians.

A century later, engineers would take advantage of this same opening to route the first railroad deep into the remote fastness of Haywood County. However, millions of years before these relatively recent historical events occurred, the gap in the Newfound Mountains served yet another significant purpose.

The late author and historian W.C. Allen maintained that eons ago, a monster river drained all the waters of Haywood County and the extreme western region of North Carolina. However, this ancient river flowed not toward the west and the Mississippi River and subsequently to the Gulf of Mexico, as the Pigeon River does today. Instead, it coursed in an eastward direction through an opening in the Newfound Mountains near Canton. This "old Canton water gap," as Allen and others have referred to it, facilitated a giant river's escape from its mountain confines to the Atlantic Ocean.

Formation of the Appalachian Mountains

To understand how the old Canton water gap was likely created requires some mental exercise. Also, the past geologic events and weathering forces that occurred over hundreds of millions of years to form the Appalachian Mountain Range must be considered. That is right—hundreds of millions of years, an unfathomable length of time that is extremely difficult to comprehend.

Publications by the United States Geological Survey and National Park Service indicate that the birthing of the Appalachian Mountains began more than four-hundred-million years ago as a result of plate tectonics. Those being the 16 massive plates that make up the earth's crust, forever floating and moving around on the molten mantle which lies deep underneath.

When one oceanic plate began sliding under another passive plate, a zone of subduction at the interface of contact was created. The extreme pressures and heat generated by the forces of the planet's crust plates colliding spawned volcanoes in the zone of subductions. These volcanic eruptions formed peaks and spewed lava and ash, blanketing the landscape with layers of igneous rock.

In addition, the sedimentary rock deposited in previous ages on the top passive plates began to be uplifted as the underlying oceanic plates continued to push and fold. Thus, more mountains were built up. Subsequent extreme weather events created streams and torrents of water which gradually eroded the mountains away. Rock, debris, and sediment were carried to lower elevations and deposited, creating new layers of sedimentary rock. And it was in this relentless and violent manner, longer ago than we can fathom, that the early Appalachian Mountains were born.

After the Appalachians began to form, the mountain-building plate tectonics continued as continent after continent collided and melded together to create a single supercontinent named Pangea. It is thought that the Appalachian Range grew to Himalayan proportion by the time Pangea was completely developed, approximately 240 million years ago.

Then, sometime around 220 million years ago, the supercontinent began to break apart, and the land mass that would ultimately become the continent of North America rifted and drifted away from Pangea. As a result, the tectonic forces that created the Appalachians were stilled and another cycle of weathering and erosion prevailed, ferociously wearing the rock and mountains away again.

By the end of the Mesozoic Era some 65 million years ago—which was about the time of the great dinosaur extinction, the Appalachian Mountain terrain had been worn down to an almost flat plain. Thence and until the present day, uplifting caused by ongoing plate tectonics, with one plate sliding under another, and extreme weathering and erosion forces have been constantly working to produce the distinctive topography we recognize as the Appalachian Mountains.

Birth of the Pigeon River

Western North Carolina was a broad flat plain with sluggish meandering rivers when the above-mentioned Mesozoic Era ended. It was marked then, as it is today, by two areas of higher elevation—the Great Smokies to the west and the Blue Ridge Range in the east. These mountain ranges, which ran parallel with one another in a northeast to southwest direction, were comprised of only low rounded hills with the loftiest points reaching no higher than 3,000 feet above sea-level. During that age, as now, the Great Smokies were slightly higher than the Blue Ridge Range, thus forming the continental divide of streams flowing to the western interior waters and those seeking the Atlantic Ocean.

The expansive and relatively flat valley between these two mountain ranges was drained by two main rivers. One had its source in the northern Appalachians and ran along a southwesterly course, through the vicinity where Asheville is located today. The other river originated in the extreme western end of the present state of North Carolina and flowed in a northeasterly direction, eventually passing through an opening in the Newfound Mountains—the Canton water gap—and then joining up with the previously mentioned stream near Asheville.

Consider this second river that falls out of the Great Smokies in the far west and gathers up enormous volumes of water on its route out of the mountains. Topographic features visible today and geological evidence reveal that its ancient course passed through the modern areas of Topton, Bryson City, Sylva, and Balsam Gap. From there it flowed through the Haywood County regions of Waynesville, Lake Junaluska, Clyde, and then, after collecting the Pigeon Valley drainage, made its escape through the Newfound Mountains at the Canton water gap.

This monster river then continued along its bed toward Asheville to merge with the other river draining from the north. Their combined waters ultimately escaped the Blue Ridge Range and meandered southeasterly through the piedmont and coastal plains before emptying into the Atlantic Ocean.

For millions of years, the waters of Haywood County were gathered up by that second ancient river and carried over a now extinct riverbed through the Canton water gap in today's Newfound Mountains. Only after more gradual uplifting of the region occurred and the resulting swifter mountain streams devoured significant portions of the softer rock of the Great Smokies did the drainage patterns begin to change.

Near a point now known as Waterville, Tennessee, ruthless streams finally succeeded in cutting a small breach through the Great Smoky Range. It was an opening that presented a more favorable gradient for the waters on the eastern side of the divide to flow into another drainage basin—one that drained to the west. Over a very long period of time, the waters of that ancient monster river were gradually tapped to flow through this new path of less resistance. Thus, the river renowned in these modern times as the Pigeon River was born, its waters flowing to the west and finally into a mega-stream that would later be known as the Mississippi River.

Similar paths were carved elsewhere in the Smokies, giving rise to other newly formed rivers, such as the Hiwassee and Little Tennessee Rivers. The creation of the Pigeon River and several other mountain waterways eventually reversed the course of that old monster river.

Conclusion

With the birth of the Pigeon River came the demise of the Canton water gap. Presently, there is a small creek whose headwaters spring from the eastern slopes of the Pigeon River basin near the old Canton water gap. Known as Hominy Creek, this stream still flows east into Buncombe County, generally following the bed of the ancient monster river on a meandering course toward Asheville and the French Broad River.

Interestingly, W. C. Allen noted that the passive Hominy Creek stream is gradually, little by little, eroding and cutting its way backward through the eastern flank of the Pigeon River basin. One might surmise that someday, perhaps a million years in the future, the Pigeon River will be tapped by the Hominy and diverted from its present course. It could very well escape again through the old Canton water gap and join Hominy Creek in the run to the French Broad River and, possibly, the Atlantic Ocean.

Note: Research material for this article was taken from multiple sources, including *The Annals of Haywood County, North Carolina* by W.C. Allen, *Western North Carolina: A History from 1730 to 1913* by John Preston Arthur, publications by Garrett A. Smathers for the Town of Canton, and *Rooted Deep in the Pigeon Valley* by Carroll C. Jones.

In this aerial photo looking eastward over Canton, the old Canton water gap can clearly be seen. It was through this gap that the waters of western North Carolina may have flowed to the Atlantic Ocean. (author's collection)

The Pigeon Valley's Garden of Human Culture

Introduction

Memories of childhood automobile trips from our home in Canton, North Carolina, to my grandmother's farm in the rural community of Bethel remain vivid in my mind. The highway (Hwy 110) was paved and ran along the "frontside" of the Pigeon River, unlike the "backside's" dirt road (today's paved Hwy 215) that hugged the river. One of the landmarks that my brother and I looked for, while peering out the windows of our family's 1950's-era Dodge, was the drive-in movie theatre. Its colossal outdoor screen was truly magnificent and never failed to catch our attention. However, it was the farm fields surrounding the drive-in movie site that always aroused my youthful fascinations.

Mother told us that in this expansive Pigeon Valley bottom, less than a mile south of Canton where a small stream known as Garden Creek spills into the Pigeon River, there were once Indian settlements. She explained how earthen mounds protruding from the farm fields had been excavated and studied by archaeologists. Arrowheads, pottery sherds, post molds, and other evidence had been discovered proving Indigenous people once lived there, thousands of years ago.

Reading about archaeology topped my interest list back then—besides playing ball. All I could think about was plodding through those plowed fields along the river and searching for Indian artifacts. Certainly, I failed to comprehend the cultural importance of the Garden Creek archaeological site or realize how far back in time the earliest people had occupied that Pigeon Valley bottom.

The First Haywood County Dwellers

Today, the Garden Creek archaeological site is a fertile bottomland that lies on both sides of the Garden Creek stream and is sandwiched between Hwy 110 and the Pigeon River. Part of the site has been covered by residential development. Perched on high ground amidst this modern conglomeration is the Plott house, which was constructed in about 1904. The beautiful old farmhouse seemingly still presides over the surrounding historical land that was once formerly attached to it.

However, before much of the residential development occurred, the significant cultural legacy that was buried on the Garden Creek site for thousands of years was unearthed and interpreted by archaeologists. A chipped-stone artifact named the Palmer Corner-Notched point was one good example. These unique spearpoints were found in concentrations of cultural refuse known as middens and suggest the Garden Creek site was occupied intermittently as long ago as 8000 B.C. It is thought that the early hunter-gatherers who fashioned these lithic tools inhabited the valley of the Pigeon River on a seasonal basis, traveling in small groups and using game trails and water gaps to penetrate the mountain wilderness.

The heavily forested mountains certainly held abundant quantities of quartz and other varieties of rock that could be used for making stone tools and weapons. Wild game including beaver, turkey, deer, bear, elk, bison, and freshwater fish would have been hunted and butchered for food and clothing. Also, dietary supplements such as fruits, nuts, berries, and roots were easily gathered and eaten. But each fall, these bands of hunter-gatherers would likely have retreated to warmer environments. The harsh winter climate that prevailed in the mountains following the last ice age would have driven them to more comfortable homesites located in the lowland regions of present-day North Carolina, South Carolina, Georgia, and Tennessee.

Over several millennia of the Archaic Period, the archaeological era dating from 8000 B.C. to 1000 B.C., the mountain climate continued to warm. As a result, more favorable animal and plant resources became available to the nomadic hunter-gatherer families. Sophisticated artifacts recovered from the Garden Creek site and linked to the late Archaic Period indicate aboriginal people were beginning to adapt and develop strategies that allowed them to live year-round on the upper Pigeon River flood plain.

Through the Millenia in the Pigeon Valley

Exploration of three Garden Creek mounds and contiguous village middens revealed even more evidence that enabled archaeologists to better understand the history of the early aboriginal dwellers who occupied the site during the Archaic and subsequent archaeological periods. These later periods included the Woodland (1000 B.C. to 1000 A.D.), Mississippian (1000 A.D. to 1650 A.D.), and Euro-American (1650 A.D. to Removal). Many thousands of artifacts were discovered, charted, studied, and cataloged, helping define the cultural stratigraphy of these different periods.

Associated with the Woodland Period are very small chipped-stone points indicating the introduction of the bow and arrow, as well as ceramic sherds marking the beginnings of pottery-making. Also unearthed at Garden Creek was evidence of advanced ceramic crafting, a movement to a stratified social structure, and maize/bean/squash cultivation that can be traced back to the Mississippian Period.

During the more recent Euro-American Period, contact and trade with

European settlers is demonstrated by unique objects found in the upper layers of the mounds and middens. These include European-made trade items such as glass beads, glassware, and iron implements.

It is believed that by 1776, the Garden Creek site was no longer inhabited. In that year, General Griffith Rutherford led an army through the Pigeon Valley on a punitive campaign against the Cherokee People. There are no accounts from soldiers' diaries or historical records that suggest an encounter with the Cherokee at Garden Creek, located just below the spot where Rutherford's army crossed the Pigeon River.

Nevertheless, when Joseph and John McDowell acquired this land in 1789 (situated within Burke County's borders at the time), the deed's property description located it as lying "below where Rutherford's army crossed (the Pigeon River) including some Indian Town houses." This old deed seems to confirm that some Indian structures were still standing at Garden Creek when Rutherford's army marched through in 1776. It is strong evidence that the last Indigenous people to occupy the Garden Creek site had not been gone very long.

Conclusion

Investigations at Garden Creek were on-going from 1880, when the Valentine Museum of Richmond, Virginia, began mining mounds, through the late 1960s when the Research Laboratories of Anthropology of the University of North Carolina conducted several years of intensive exploration of two of the three mounds and selected village middens. The site has proven to be an extremely rich one. Many artifacts, ancient human burials, and other evidence have revealed much about the history of the people and cultures of the Appalachian Mountains' summit region.

Today, the mounds at Garden Creek have largely disappeared as a result of residential growth and agricultural activities. Yet, before that occurred, we know these man-made earthen platforms and the surrounding middens were a veritable garden of human culture, giving up many important secrets. One of them being that the upper Pigeon Valley has been host to humans for the last 10,000 years.

Note: An apology is offered to readers for the brevity of the article. Any dive into the extremely interesting and complex details of this subject would have made the piece lengthy and, likely, a little tedious for some to read. Sources include *Garden Creek Indian Mounds Archaeology Site at Canton, N.C.* by Garrett A. Smathers; *Cherokee Prehistory* by Roy S. Dickens, Jr.; and *Cherokee Archaeology* by Bennie C. Keel.

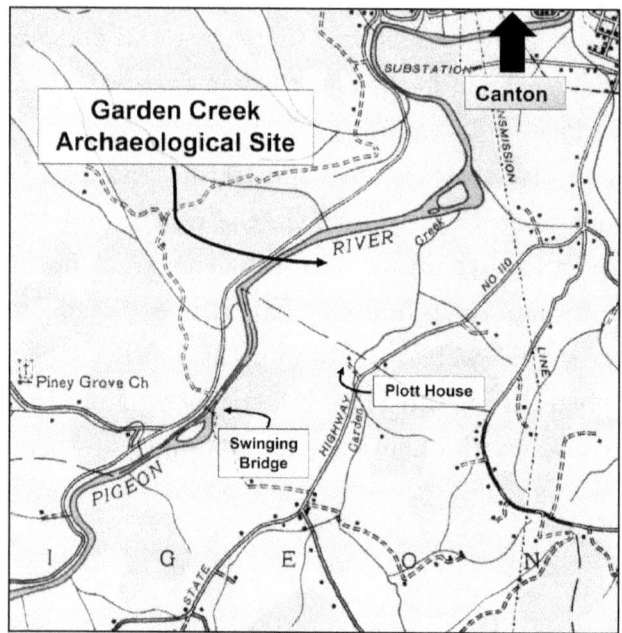

Left: The Garden Creek archaeological site indicated on this map lies just south of Canton, N.C. Note the location of the old Plott house as well as a swinging bridge that once spanned the Pigeon River. (1935 USGS map)

Below: The Garden Creek archaeological site is captured in this panoramic view, bordered by the Pigeon River along the bottom of the photo (to the north) and Hwy 110 at the top. A tree-lined Garden Creek runs through the middle of the site, and residential development occupies the grounds on the west side. (drone photo by Doug Barnes)

The beautiful James Henry Plott house still stands today on a hill next to the Garden Creek archaeological site. It was built in 1904 and overlooks the Pigeon River and the fields first inhabited by Indigenous people 10,000 years ago. (author's collection)

This Palmer Corner-Notched projectile point was found at the Garden Creek archaeological site. The chipped-stone point was once attached to the end of a spear shaft and used by ancient hunters in the Early Archaic Period, between 8000 to 6000 B.C. (UNC website: ancientnc.web.unc.edu)

When An Army Invaded the Pigeon Valley

Introduction

In the year 1776, an army penetrated the rugged and remote mountains of western North Carolina on a punitive campaign against the Cherokee Indians. The path of this invasion snaked from the eastern frontier slopes of the Blue Ridge Range across high ridges and through deep river valleys to the furthermost western mountains of the state. Some 2,400 soldiers and Catawba Indians led by General Griffith Rutherford blazed their course smack through Haywood County's Pigeon Valley wilderness.

Today, ubiquitous highway historical markers indicate the location of Rutherford's old "war trace," or route, through strategic mountain gaps and along water courses. Most curious onlookers reading these signs are left to ponder the condensed message and wonder what in the world is a "trace," or why North Carolina's militiamen were fighting Indians and not the British during the Revolutionary War (also known as the American Revolution). In fact, very few will comprehend the importance of General Rutherford's bold action and the role it played in the American Revolution, the eventual removal of the Cherokee Indians to the West, and the settlement of western North Carolina's mountain frontier.

General Rutherford's Campaign

The significance of the year 1776 will not be lost on most Americans. It marked the beginning of the Revolutionary War—the year that the original 13 colonies declared their independence after years of oppression and dominance by an English colonial government. The Cherokee Indians, who in 1754 had sided with the French against Britain during the French and Indian War, chose to ally with the British at the outset of America's revolution. Their frustration at continuing encroachments by white settlers into their mountain lands, even though King George's Proclamation of 1763 prohibited white trespass west of the Blue Ridge, drove them into England's welcoming arms.

Empowered by the Crown's treaties, the Cherokee began demanding the withdrawal of all white settlers from the lands west of the Blue Ridge Mountain Range. When these demands went unheeded, the Indians initiated a series of raiding actions in May of 1776 against the white settlements along the mountain frontier fringes. The result of these aggressive acts was the killing of some 37 pioneer men and women. Soon, news of these atrocities reached General Griffith Rutherford in North Carolina's Rowan County. One of six brigadier generals commissioned by the state's new Provincial Congress, Rutherford commanded the militia in the Salisbury District. Immediately, he began raising an army and preparing to take retaliatory measures against the Indians.

After assembling a force of 2,000 fighting white men, several hundred Catawba Indians, and the necessary supply resources for a 40-day operation, General Rutherford struck out westward on September 1, 1776, from Davidson's Fort near present-day Old Fort. Not unexpectedly, the Indians fled before the imposing American forces and were not easily brought to battle. The armed troops systematically destroyed numerous vacated Indian villages, granaries, and crops in the fields along the river valleys including the Pigeon, Tuckasegee, Hiwassee, Valley, Oconaluftee, and Little Tennessee rivers. Everything of import to the Cherokee was either burned or ruined to further their depredation and destroy their ability to wage war.

General Rutherford and his men met with little opposition and, as a result, casualties were light on both sides. There were several skirmishes, however, with perhaps the fiercest of these occurring at Wayah Bald Gap near today's town of Franklin. After about a month of this scorched-earth warfare and believing their mission accomplished and the Cherokee severely punished, General Rutherford's weary band retraced their pathway out of the mountains and back to the safety of Davidson's Fort. Orders were given for the route to be marked, and the "Rutherford Trace" was soon to become a crucial gateway for white settlers moving into the remote mountain fastnesses.

The Indians had indeed suffered an enormous loss and were greatly weakened and demoralized by Rutherford's stunning action. They would become disillusioned, as well, with broken English promises to restore their lost lands. Eventually, the Cherokee treated with the American Republic, ceding more rights and giving away additional Indian land to the fledgling nation. Consequently, there would be no stopping of the American pioneer migration into western North Carolina's frontier wilderness. Appetites for the verdant bottomlands and virgin forests in the Cherokee territory were whetted; and the Indians and English were powerless before the relentless onslaught of Scotch, Irish, German, and English settlers who were hungry for new land to homestead.

Rutherford's Trace Through the Pigeon Valley

The Pigeon Valley was among those pristine river valleys that Rutherford's army encountered on its destructive incursion into the Cherokee territory. The soldiers and "friendly" Indians reached it by initially penetrating the Blue Ridge through a breach in the range now known as the Swannanoa Gap. Trudging over and down the steep mountain walls until encountering the Swannanoa River, the legion followed this meandering water course through the area lying south of today's Asheville to its confluence with the French Broad River.

General Rutherford's army proceeded to ford the French Broad at a point described as the "War Ford." On the far west bank of the grand river, the expeditionary train of soldiers, Indians, and pack horses came upon a tributary stream which was later named Hominy Creek. They followed this lazy watercourse through unspoiled woodlands, meadows, and hillsides that have since been transformed into today's communities of Sand Hill, Enka, and Candler.

Near Hominy Creek's origins in today's Haywood County, General Rutherford and his troops abandoned the small creek and crossed a low ridge into the drainage area of the Pigeon River. Accounts vary as to where the large army crossed the Pigeon. One early land deed in the county records has a property boundary description which reads, "to a point at the Ford of Pigeon where a great army once crossed." In the late 1800s, a small settlement known as "Ford of Pigeon" actually existed where the town of Canton is located today. This reference in the early deed could indicate the point where Rutherford's army waded across the river in the town's vicinity. Certainly, today's citizens of Canton would be surprised to learn that a "great army" may have roamed along its riverbanks during the Revolutionary War.

However, another earlier deed description dated 1809 describes a tract of land obtained by Joseph and John McDowell in the year 1789 "lying in the county of Burke when granted, afterwards in Buncombe, and now Haywood County." It further locates the land as being about three miles "below where Rutherford's army crossed, including some Indian Town houses." This is the same property that was later acquired by James Henry Plott in the Garden Creek area between Canton and Bethel. So, it seems more likely that General Rutherford's troops did not ford the Pigeon River in the Canton vicinity but proceeded up the lush Pigeon Valley bottomland to where the farming community of Bethel thrives today.

The great army eventually crossed the river just below the juncture of its east and west forks and soon escaped the Pigeon Valley through a break in the mountains. Interestingly, this location is now called Pigeon Gap—the same place where today's US Highway 276 passes and connects Waynesville with the Bethel community. Leaving the Pigeon Valley behind, General Rutherford continued his hunt for the Cherokee along Richland Creek and across Balsam Gap into the wild river valleys and highlands beyond.

Conclusion

General Griffith Rutherford's military expedition did not destroy the Cherokee Indians, but it did serve to undermine their fighting capacity and break their spirits. Afterward, the Cherokee Nation would cease to be a major force to reckon with during the Revolution and their leverage at future treaty tables was significantly diminished. They were compelled to relinquish vast areas of ancient tribal lands through one treaty after another with the American Government, until their final expulsion to Indian Territory west of the Mississippi River.

This Cherokee exodus from the western North Carolina mountains in 1838 and 1839—often referred to as the "Trail of Tears" —has gained considerable notoriety over the years. It is considered an example of the United States government's mistreatment of the Native American People in pursuit of territorial expansion and its Manifest Destiny.

Undoubtedly, many of General Rutherford's men were struck with the natural beauty and enormous potential of North Carolina's western mountains. Some of them would return just a few years later, at the conclusion of the Revolutionary War, to lay claim to vast plots of fertile farming ground along the Pigeon River. Jacob Shook was among these pioneers, becoming one of Haywood County's very early white settlers and prominent citizens. Shook built a prosperous farm close by the banks of the Pigeon River and near today's town of Clyde. It was where he is reputed to have constructed the first frame house in the county.

Descendants of Jacob Shook still abound in Haywood County. As it turns out, this Rutherford militiaman and pioneer settler happens to be the author's fourth-great grandfather.

Note: Research material for this article was taken from multiple sources, including *Western North Carolina: Its Mountains and Its People to 1880* by Ora Blackmun, *The Early History of Haywood County* by W. Clark Medford, and *Rooted Deep in the Pigeon Valley* by Carroll C. Jones.

Many highway historical markers illuminate General Griffith Rutherford's war trace through western North Carolina. This one is located at the Pigeon Gap on Hwy 276. (author's collection)

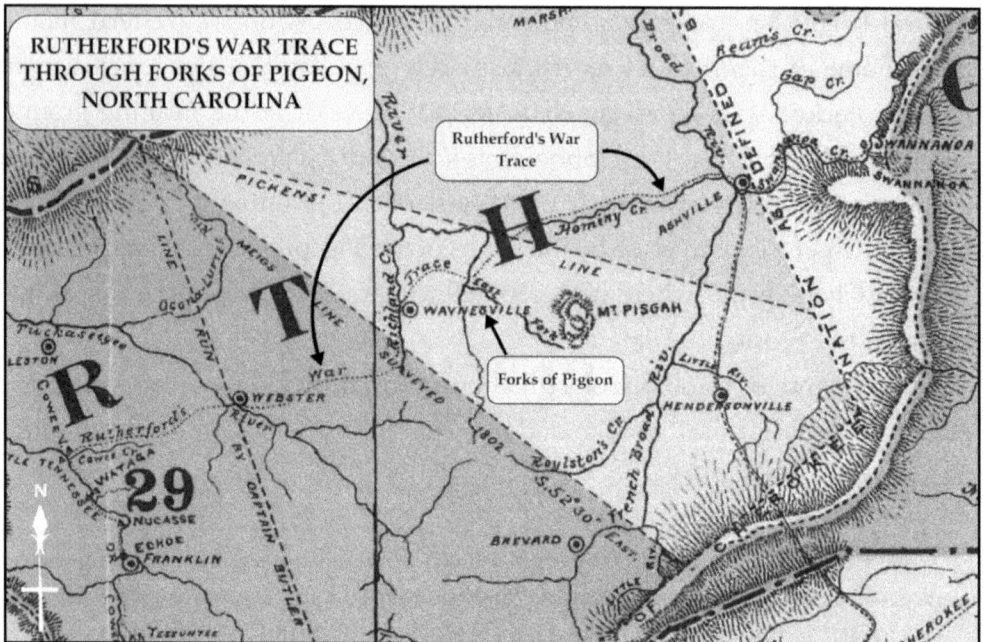

In September 1776, General Rutherford's army followed the trace shown on this map (dotted line) that ran through Asheville, up Hominy Creek to the current Canton area. From there it tracked up the Pigeon River and across the river at Forks of Pigeon, then tracing beyond Waynesville to the western wilderness of North Carolina. (a cropped section from a map of the former territorial limits of the Cherokee Nation, published ca. 1884)

FORKS OF PIGEON (BETHEL)

A Glimpse of Bethel's Rural Countryside (Painting by Mary Jo Owen)

A Turn-O-Meal at Cathey's Mill

The term "turn-o-meal," or "turn-of-meal," was an expression the old timers often used that simply meant one's "turn." It was so-called because at the grist mills "each man's corn was ground in turn—that is, he waited his turn."[1] Of course, one hardly ever hears this idiom used today, but back when my Great-Grandfather William Hartgrove was a young boy growing up in Haywood County's Pigeon Valley, he anxiously awaited the miller's pronouncement that it was his father's turn-o-meal to have his corn ground. That would have been at Cathey's Mill in the community

---
1 Horace Kephart, *Our Southern Highlanders*, 1913, p. 366

of Forks of Pigeon in the 1850s.

Cathey's general mercantile store and grist mill were vital businesses for the pioneers who lived and farmed in western North Carolina where the east and west forks of the Pigeon River are joined. These enterprises, owned by Colonel Joseph Cathey, who was a well-respected and prominent citizen in the area, were the hubs of the community for the Pigeon Valley settlers as well as important centers of commerce.

All young boys would have been thrilled at any opportunity to go to the mill and see the marvelous workings of the huge water wheel driving wooden-geared mechanisms and huge grinding stones. The Colonel's facility was driven by water diverted from the East Fork of the Pigeon River into a 14-foot diameter waterwheel. The vertical wheel worked much like a turbine and was powered, or made to turn, by the force of water flowing under the wheel and against blades mounted on the wheel's periphery.

This undershot design, as it was called, was simpler to build than the overshot method where the water is sluiced over the top of the water wheel. Although the undershot design was less powerful, it was especially suited for conditions where the riverbed was relatively flat. Moreover, it was the next best option when the difficulties of obtaining a source of water high enough to flow over the top of an overshot wheel could not be reasonably overcome.

Dred Blalock is said to have built the mill for Colonel Cathey sometime in the 1840s while he was still a relatively young man—probably not yet 30-years old.[2] This native mechanic and builder, who later served as a lieutenant in the Confederate 25th North Carolina Infantry Troops during the Civil War, constructed a three-story building to house the milling machinery.[3] It is not

---

2   Evelyn Coltman, *Legends, Tales & History of Cold Mountain: A Pigeon Valley Heritage Collection Book 4*, "Mills, Milling, and Millers," 2008, p. 78. Coltman's research indicates that the original mill, owned and operated by Colonel Joseph Cathey, was built by Dred Blalock sometime in the 1840s.

3   E. H. (Dred) Blalock was listed as a 33-year-old "mechanic" in the US census of 1850 for Haywood County, North Carolina. In June 1861, at the age of 44-years, he enlisted in Company F of the 25th N.C. Infantry Regiment. These facts indicate that he would have been about 28-years old in the mid-1840s when the Cathey mill is thought to have been built.

See *The 25th North Carolina Troops in the Civil War: History and Roster of a Mountain-Bred Regiment* by Carroll C. Jones for more details of Blalock's Civil War service.

clear how many sets of millstones were used with the operation. However, it is known that the gearing which transferred the energy and torque from the water wheel's main horizontal rotating axle to the vertical shafts that turned the heavy granite millstones was hand-crafted from wood. Certainly, it took the combination of Blalock's innate mechanical and crafting genius and Cathey's supreme intellect to conceive and construct this processing mill, which was capable of grinding corn and the other grain products grown in the region.

Drawn to the machinery of the mill with a boy's insatiable curiosity, the wide-eyed, youthful William Hartgrove would have taken in everything about the unfolding scene. He surely watched and listened to the miller bark directions to men unloading and hefting baskets of corn and wheat to the hoppers located high above the sets of grinding stones. The miller was the boss of the mill's operation, and although not known for certain who William might have observed, it very well could have been John Mann. Mr. Mann is listed in the 1850 Haywood County census as a "miller" and is enumerated directly below the immediate family of Joseph Cathey. It is suspected that he was employed as the miller and boss of the Colonel's grinding facility and was the object of William's fixed gaze.

If the youth could have followed John Mann inside, he would have seen the miller throw a lever to open a sluice gate and begin feeding the Hartgrove's corn into the middle of the round groaning millstones. With a practiced eye and trained ear, miller Mann set the gap between the top runner stone and the lower bed stone to grind the corn to the exact texture ordered by William's father. As the runner stone slowly turned against the stationary bed stone, the shells of corn were ground between the hard stone surfaces into finer and finer particles. Grooves cut into the millstones' faces facilitated the movement of the ground corn—or meal—outward to their perimeters, where the meal fell over the edge of the bed stone into a wooden vat enclosing the stones. Once collected in the vat, the meal spilled through a spout—the meal spout—into waiting sacks below where the farmer's treasure was captured.

After measuring out a portion of the meal in a toll dish, or toddick, to compensate the miller for his services, the father and son would have latched hold of their precious sack of meal and loaded it aboard whatever means of conveyance they employed on that particular day—wagon, sled, or an ol' mule.[4] Before heading off for home, however, they may very well have stopped off at the store to pick up some vital domestic necessity. Cathey's general store, located in the vicinity of the mill, was where folks from the Forks of Pigeon area came to buy or barter for goods that could not be grown at home or were not easily crafted.

As William's keen eyes perused the store's contents, he would have been overwhelmed by the exciting sights and aromas to be found there. The counters, tables, and floor were filled with all manner of things including farm tools, hand tools, hardware, rope, dry goods, spices, coffee, produce, foodstuffs, flatware, silverware, colorful calico materials, clothing, hats, boots, and medicines. Hard and soft candies with wonderful fragrances and colors were also displayed in great abundance to tease William's senses.

Of course, there were always Cathey family members about that William knew and visited. As a matter of fact, he would one day marry Colonel Cathey's granddaughter, Nancy Louisa Cathey. It would not be overly presumptuous to believe he might have bumped into that pretty little girl on occasion, as she mingled with her grandfather's customers. Who can say what thoughts or sparks were initiated upon those first innocent encounters.

Also located in the store building was the Forks of Pigeon post office where letters were received and posted. And for a small fee the Colonel or one of his employees wrote letters for the customers whose literary skills might understandably be lacking. Somewhere upon the grounds of those Cathey enterprises, William's Uncle Alfred Franklin Hartgrove and Uncle John Hartgrove plied their blacksmith skills. Through their extraordinary abilities to heat, beat, shape, and weld iron over hot forges into useful implements and hardware, they provided a vital service for Colonel Cathey's customers and the community.

Eventually, William would get the dreaded nod from his father that broke the strange spell which the store held over him. He would then know for sure it was time to go. Tired and hungry after a long day at the

---

[4] Horace Kephart, *Our Southern Highlanders*, 1913, p. 366

mill, young William Hartgrove strode over to his father's side and set out for home. His weariness did not expel fervent hopes that another turn-o-meal at Cathey's would be a short time in coming. And, certainly, the thought of laying eyes on that pretty Nancy Cathey again did not escape him.

The Cathey mill can be seen in this old photo with the flood waters of the East Fork of the Pigeon River raging by. Just upstream from the mill, an iron-truss bridge span allowed pedestrian and horse and wagon traffic to cross the river. This bridge was built in 1891 by the same company and at the same time another iron truss bridge was constructed over the nearby West Fork of the Pigeon River. (collection of Charles Cathey)

An artist's rendering of the Cathey mill shows the dam and bridge across the East Fork of the Pigeon River. (painting by Nettie Vance Penland from collection of Eula Rigdon)

Haywood County's Historic Phoenix-Column Bridge

Setting

Spanning the West Fork of the Pigeon River in western North Carolina's Haywood County is an old Pratt Truss Bridge bearing the State DOT's label "Bridge No. 79." This mountainous region, which is primarily drained by the Pigeon River running from south to north into Tennessee, is host to a rural farming community known as Bethel. Situated five miles south of Canton and six miles east of Waynesville, Bethel is the home of Bridge No. 79.

The river is relatively flat and shallow at the bridge site next to Lake Logan Road (State Road 1111), where the stream's cold, clear water flows slowly northward. Some 20 feet above the rocky riverbed, the bridge decking spans 80 feet between steep embankments covered with low undergrowth and lined with hardwood trees.

Working farms and well-kept houses, dating mostly from the middle to the latter half of the 20th century, are scattered throughout the bridge's picturesque rural valley setting. Within view is a well-preserved farmhouse, whose construction features suggest it likely dates to the late 19th or early 20th century. When standing in the center of Bridge No. 79, one can look in any direction and see the surrounding forested mountains with Cold Mountain looming just five miles off to the southeast.

Historical Background

During the decades following the Revolutionary War, pioneers began finding their way through the mountain passes and establishing homesteads throughout the wild river valleys of western North Carolina's Buncombe County. In the early 1800s, settlers populating Buncombe's former Cherokee

Indian territory lodged an appeal with the state's General Assembly, declaring the distance to the county courthouse in Asheville too great and inconvenient. Moreover, they pleaded that the roads were frequently impassable, especially during the winter season. Thus, in 1808, the state legislators established the new county of Haywood, with its county seat in the small village of Waynesville, 30 miles west of Asheville. At the time, Haywood included all the land along the Pigeon River and its tributaries and encompassed the region extending from the Pigeon watershed to North Carolina's border with Tennessee.

By about 1850, a stagecoach and wagon road known as the Western Turnpike had been completed, joining Waynesville and points further west with the largest town in the region, Asheville. Present-day US Highway 19-23 connecting Asheville to the east and Waynesville to the west generally follows the original path of the old turnpike, directly through Canton. For many years Haywood County's farmers used the rough Western Turnpike to drive their livestock and haul produce such as corn and apples to markets outside of the mountains. Not only did these drovers have to negotiate the rutted and ofttimes muddy road, but they were also forced to wade small streams and ford the wider Pigeon River at the small settlement called Ford of Pigeon—later to be formerly named Pigeon River in 1891, and then Canton in 1893.

Once reaching Asheville, the travelers encountered yet another heavily used turnpike road. The Buncombe Turnpike, which ran north and south, was a graded road with some sections improved and paved with logs. It coursed through the French Broad River valley, offering access to Tennessee and Virginia to the north and the southern markets in Greenville, South Carolina, and Augusta, Georgia. Until the arrival of the railroad in the early 1880s, these two turnpike roads were the primary commercial arteries used by Haywood County's farmers and merchants to escape the mountains.

The railroad finally reached Waynesville in 1882, its tracks first passing through the tiny settlement of Pigeon River (present day Canton), located astride the river with the same name. These two Haywood County communities immediately gained an importance beyond all anticipation of the locals, becoming rail hubs where livestock, timber, and produce could be shipped to markets outside of the surrounding mountains. It was not long before wealthy outlanders began to converge there to enjoy the majestic mountains and soak up the healthy climate, while lounging and recreating in the hotels and hot springs.

Another important county road at this time connecting Waynesville and Pigeon River (Canton) passed through the community of Forks of Pigeon (present-day Bethel). The "Forks" was an old farming settlement that had developed in the first half of the 19th century on land surrounding the confluence of the east and west forks of the Pigeon River. These streams that brawled out of southern Haywood County's mountain wilderness areas, flowed much more languidly by the time their waters joined to form the Pigeon River. Since there were no bridges in Forks of Pigeon, the farmers had to ford the East and West Fork Rivers to get to the schools, churches, county court, markets, mills, and their neighbors' farms. The closest bridge was the railroad bridge located at least five miles downstream in the bustling rail hub village of Pigeon River. So, when the rains came and the fording spots became too dangerous to cross, daily activities were interrupted and considerable hardships imposed upon the local folk.

As a consequence of the increasing prosperity brought about by the arrival of the railroad in the early 1880s, the county was able to fund road improvements and infrastructure projects. Aware of the dire need of not one but two bridges at Forks of Pigeon, the county commissioners contracted to build two "wrought iron bridges"—an "80-foot span" across the West Fork near the Terrell ford and a "100-foot span" over the East Fork, just a quarter of a mile to the northeast next to Blalock's Mill (formerly known as Cathey's Mill). Wood Brothers & Company was hired to build the stone foundations and abutments, and Dean and Westbrook Engineers of New York was selected to supply and erect the wrought iron bridges.

Acting as an agent for the Phoenix Bridge Company in Phoenixville, Pennsylvania, Dean and Westbrook selected a Phoenix-column bridge from the bridge company's catalog to span the West Fork. The Phoenix order no. 613, dated May 16, 1891, specified "1-80' Rdwy Thro' Span" for Haywood County, North Carolina. Fabrication began on the West Fork bridge's two 80-foot-long Pratt trusses in June, and the structures were ready to be shipped in September of 1891. The weight of the bridge components totaled 12,058 pounds and Phoenix's material and labor costs were $3,944.

It is unknown what price Dean and Westbrook passed along to Haywood County for the purchase and shipment of the Bridge No. 79 components. However, the minutes from a May 1891 Haywood County Commissioners' meeting reveal that a contract for $4,675 was awarded to "Dean and Westbrook, bridge contractors, and Wood Brothers & Co., stone masons" to build the West Fork and the East Fork bridges: "the super and sub structure compleet [sic]... in first class style." Judging from the May date of the meeting minutes and the September completion date given on the Phoenix order, the contractors would likely have erected the bridge over the West Fork by the end of the year 1891.

For more than 30 years thereafter, pedestrians, horses, livestock, wagons, and later automobiles, trucks, and tractors crisscrossed the West Fork of the Pigeon River over the single-lane Bridge No. 79. As a result of growing traffic, State Road No. 284 passing through Forks of Pigeon and connecting Waynesville with the booming pulp mill town named Canton (formerly Pigeon River) was eventually improved and upgraded after the Champion Fibre Company began operations in 1908. These highway upgrades in the early 1920s included construction of new spans across the West Fork and the East Fork Rivers in essentially the same locations as today's bridges.

Local tradition has it that in 1925, a band of men from up the river disassembled the outmoded Bridge No. 79, hauled it piece by piece in horse and wagons to the present site, and reassembled it on foundations made of handmixed concrete. The utility of the relocated bridge was immediately appreciated and exploited by the many valley farmers who lived and worked on the fertile lands along the banks of the West Fork, as the traveling distance required to safely cross the river was shortened by several miles.

In 2013, more than one hundred and twenty years since Bridge No. 79 was built and at least 85 years since it was relocated, a new vehicular bridge was installed approximately 700 feet farther upstream. At that same time, the entire structure of Bridge No. 79 was sandblasted and painted, and a new timber and plank flooring system with an asphalt deck was added. Following the installation of new wooden guard railing and timber bollards to block automobiles, the bridge was repurposed for the use of pedestrians and cyclists only.

Bridge No. 79

Although currently relegated to light-duty service, Bridge No. 79 retains its original structural integrity. Two 80-foot long, five-panel Pratt trusses still incorporate the Phoenix Bridge Company's patented wrought iron Phoenix columns—the only remaining example of this 19th-century breakthrough technology in a North Carolina bridge. These distinctive built-up columns, which have an outside diameter of approximately four inches, are used for the vertical compression members, portal inclined end posts, top chords, and lateral struts. Pairs of square-shaped, forged eye-bars work in unison to carry the tensile forces in the lower and diagonal chords, as well as the hip verticals. Original cast-iron compression fittings join the Phoenix columns and accept the tension bars and lateral bracing in pinned connections. Suspension loops attached to the lower panel points support the old built-up iron floor beams, which carry a refurbished timber stringer and plank-flooring system covered with a two-inch layer of asphalt.

Rare decorative elements—reported to be the only ones left on a North Carolina truss bridge—continue to adorn the portals, including iron starburst motifs, urn-shaped finials, and recognition plaques at each end. The plaque on the southeast portal memorializes the county commissioners who authorized the bridge construction: "Haywood County Commissioners - E.H. Howell, C.B. Roberts, J.M. Gwynn." On the northwest end, another identically shaped plaque presents the name of the bridge builder: "Built 1891 by Dean & Westbrook Engineers, New York."

No more than two dozen bridges incorporating Phoenix columns are thought to survive today, with the greatest concentration being in New Jersey, New York, and Pennsylvania. Haywood County's Bridge No. 79 is the only remaining example of the Phoenix-column truss bridge technology in North Carolina. Importantly and of national significance, it is the only known survivor of the 19th century in the United States.

Today, more than one hundred and thirty years since its original iron elements were puddled and formed, Bridge No. 79's Phoenix-column trusses look as fresh and strong as they did when the first horse-drawn wagons loaded with corn and apples rolled through them. The survival and presence of Bethel's historic bridge is just one more reason that locals can take pride in their beautiful community.

Note to reader: The information presented in this article is taken from the author's research and submittal to the National Register of Historic Places. In the year 2019, Bridge No. 79 was officially placed on the National Register of Historic Places.

This is a current view of Bridge No. 79 looking downstream, with the waters of the West Fork of the Pigeon River flowing under it. (author's collection)

The upper corner of a bridge portal is shown here with original ornamentation intact and a "PHOENIX" foundry marking visible on the angle iron bracing. (author's collection)

This is one of the bridge's original Phoenix columns with the foundry marking "PHOENIX IRON CO" plainly showing. (author's collection)

The builder of Bridge No. 79 is recognized by this plaque located on the upper side of the northwest portal. (author's collection)

Shown here is a photo of the actual Phoenix Bridge Company order #613 for Haywood County's "80' Rdwy Thro Span" Phoenix-column bridge. (Haywood County, N.C., archives)

FORKS OF PIGEON (OR BETHEL) | 37

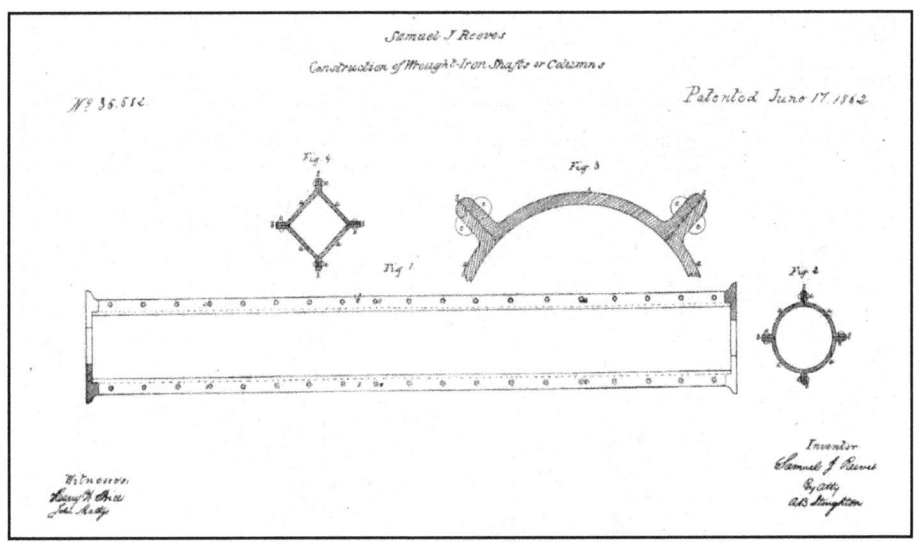

Details of the Phoenix Column construction are shown on this 1862 patent application drawing. Note that the iron structural members are identified as "Wrought-Iron Shafts or Columns" on this drawing. (Haywood County, N.C., archives)

An early photo shows a horse-drawn carriage rolling across Bethel's Phoenix-Column bridge. (Bethel Rural Community Organization collection)

Shown in this photo is the surviving stone abutment that once supported the east end of Bridge No. 79 at its original location. The old stone foundation can be found on the eastern embankment of the West Fork of the Pigeon River, just downstream of Hwy 276 and alongside Hwy 110. (author's collection)

Haywood County's Forgotten Inventor

Calvin Filmore Christopher was touted as North Carolina's "most prolific inventor" by one reporter writing for *The State* magazine in 1935.[5] At the time of the Pigeon River inventor's death in 1940, another journalist noted "although he is one of the greatest inventors ever to live in this part of the world, he is practically un-talked about in his own county, Haywood."[6] Regrettably, almost a century later, the creative genius who lived and worked in the Bethel Community is not only an obscure memory—but he is a forgotten one. How could that be?

By some accounts, Christopher registered more than a hundred inventions with the US and Canadian patent offices. A "Googling" dive into the internet world has uncovered and verified more than 30 patents registered in Calvin F. Christopher's name. His new and improved ideas included stock tethers, a railway turntable lock, railway switch, a driving mechanism for traction road engines, various improvements to steam engines, several varieties of merchant scales for computing prices of weighed objects, churn gearing, a swinging crib, motors, power transmitting mechanisms, a collapsible wheel rim to facilitate changing tires, a unique turfing (or tufting) needle, computing machine, portable calculating device, a measuring instrument for fabrics, a filling station machine that computed the price of gasoline delivered, a fly trap, and a dinner pail, among other things.

Contemporary accounts reveal that one of Christopher's most profitable inventions was a machine that could dig a ditch four feet wide and two feet

---

5   *The State* magazine article, *Our Most Prolific Inventor*, Nov. 2, 1935; Pearle Justice Yates (Yates)
6   *The Waynesville Mountaineer* newspaper article, *Noted Inventor Passes*; May 16, 1940 (Noted Inventor Passes)

deep in one minute. The patent and all rights to the invention were sold to the French government, who employed this equipment extensively digging ditches and shallow trenches during World War I. Among the other inventions credited to Mr. Christopher that have thus far eluded the author's patent search efforts are a compressed brick machine and a monkey wrench with sliding adjustment—not screwed.[7]

Incredibly, the legacy of this veritable mechanical genius who imagined, designed, and built these wonderful things is now lost to us—swept away by the ages as surely as his old Bethel homeplace was eventually carried away by the flood waters of the Pigeon River. It is high time to resurrect the memories of this North Carolina inventor and bring due recognition to his name and accomplishments.

Calvin Filmore Christopher was born around 1859 to parents of Dutch descent. In or about 1862, he moved with his family from Pittsburgh, Pennsylvania, to North Carolina's Haywood County, where he spent his early years in the Beaverdam Township near present-day Canton.[8] [9] As it happened, this period coincided with the American Civil War and the difficult reconstruction era that followed. Calvin's father was too old to fight for the Rebels or the Yankees. Instead, he earned a living making shoes and farming a piece of land he did not own. Given the timeframe and family circumstances, it is likely that Calvin, his parents, and eight siblings suffered the same hardships and pains of hunger and poverty that their highland neighbors and most southerners experienced during the war.

The 1870 Federal Census reveals interesting facts that speak to the youthful Christopher's early education, or lack thereof, in the aftermath of the Civil War. Enumerated as 12 years old and a farm worker at the time, Calvin could

---

[7] *The Waynesville Mountaineer* newspaper article, *Haywood Man is Noted Inventor*, Sept. 9, 1937; W.C. Medford (Medford)
[8] Medford
[9] The *Waynesville Mountaineer* newspaper article, *Recognition Drive for Bethel Inventor*, March 12, 1969; John Roper

neither write nor did he attend school that year. Family lore holds strong to this day that he enjoyed very little formal schooling and was self-taught.[10] Yet, his lack of scholarly training could not stifle the innate cleverness and creative genius which would spawn a steady stream of sophisticated and technical innovations in the years to come.

When Calvin—or Filmore, as he preferred to be called—had reached his early 20s, he was married to Martha Poston of Haywood County and employed as a fireman on the Southern Railway's Asheville to Spartanburg line.[11] According to the 1880 census data and United States patent records, the young Christophers were living in Spartanburg, South Carolina, at about that time. And it seems that Filmore's imaginative mind was already turned toward improving and inventing contraptions.

In 1882 and '83, he and another man from Spartanburg obtained patents for two tether mechanisms. Although different in appearance and construction, both devices served the same purpose of tethering cows or other animals to a rope, pulley, and weight system—one that was self-winding and that secured the animals while grazing in unfenced pastures. The latter patent, which was more practical in construction and simpler to set up, was sold for the tidy sum of $13,000.[12]

Filmore's railroad experience likely inspired two other early inventions. He and a couple of associates from Asheville, North Carolina, patented a railway turntable lock, an apparatus that enabled a person standing on the huge turntable or within the table pit to lock the tracks securely in line and in place. Another railroad invention, which came later, was an automatic "Railway-Switch." It allowed the motorman or any person operating the approaching railroad car to shift the rail switch without exiting the car, thereby directing the car to either track. Christopher's improved switching mechanism was first put into operation in 1908 by the Asheville

---

10   *Legends, Tales & History of Cold Mountain, Book 2; Chapter 4, Calvin Filmore Christopher;* Evelyn Coltman (Coltman)
11   *Legends, Tales & History of Cold Mountain, Book 2; Calvin F. Christopher—Master Inventor;* Lois Davis, Christopher's great-granddaughter (Davis)
12   *Finis and Farewell; Filmore Christopher, Haywood's Inventive Genius;* p. 51; W.C. Medford

Electric Company on the city's streetcar lines.[13] It was tried out in one or two other cities as well but apparently did not meet with overwhelming success. The patent was eventually sold for $3,500.[14]

Filmore appears to have abruptly re-directed his mechanical genius sometime around 1890. In the short span of two years, between 1892 and 1894, he is credited in the patent registry with four inventions—all involving the steam engine. One of these bore the official title "Driving Mechanism for Road Engines" and was his attempt at improving the gearing of the steam-driven road tractors of the day. Two other patents related to the steam engine introduced modifications to the slide valve arrangement of piston engines, as well as provided certain other improvements to allow the pressure of steam to be utilized to its greatest capacity. Yet, it was another of Christopher's engine inventions that was to provide one of the greatest opportunities of his career.

The title on the patent was simply "Steam Engine" and the literature claimed it to be new and useful improvements in rotary steam engines, whereby the pressure of steam is used to its fullest extent. Actually, it involved Christopher's very complicated and novel combination and arrangement of parts to not only use steam efficiently, but to use the steam to actuate valves, cylinder heads, gates, etc., in order to secure the proper feed of steam to and from the cylinder. This original rotary steam engine design obviously represented a leap from Filmore's days designing stock tethers a few years earlier.

One reporter who witnessed an exhibition of the Christopher Rotary Steam Engine in January 1894 was indeed impressed with what he saw. He wrote that "the engine is surely destined to revolutionize the motive power of the world. It is extremely simple in construction, without piston rods or valves, and has no dead center. It reverses with great ease and its power is just double that of the old piston rod engine."[15] Calvin Christopher was as enthusiastic as this journalist of the benefits of his new steam engine, and he must have thought the invention would lead to riches.

Other venture capitalists were convinced as well, and a new company named

---

13 The *Greensboro Daily News* newspaper article, *New Switch for Street Railways*; July 2, 1908
14 Medford
15 *The Watchman and Southron* newspaper article; Jan. 10, 1894 edition

C.F. Christopher & Sons was founded in Spartanburg for the manufacture of the engine.[16] A factory was hastily built and equipped at the expense of $90,000; and just when things were about to take off, fate reared its ugly head. Tragically, the factory caught fire and burned down, destroying everything. To make matters even worse, there was no insurance to cover the loss; hence, the entire enterprise was abandoned. Years later, when asked about the ups and downs of his career, Filmore would have indeed reflected on this catastrophe when responding, "No, it wasn't all easy sailing—not by a jug full."[17]

Still another tragedy occurred not long afterward, just before the arrival of the 20th century. Filmore's wife, Martha, died in 1899, leaving behind six children for him to care for: Knox, Maude, Pearl, Robert Edgar, Clementine, and Bertha. As was generally the case then, given similar circumstances, another marriage was hastily arranged. And so it was that less than five months after Martha died, Filmore married Louisa Jane Pless, a native of Haywood County's Pigeon Valley. More commonly known as "Lula" or "Lu," this good woman would become a devoted and lifelong partner and friend for her husband.[18]

In or about the year 1900, the Christophers took up residency in Washington, D.C., where Filmore helped establish a company to manufacture, market, and sell what was to be his most successful invention—the merchant's price scale. This company, known as the Columbian Automatic Computing Scales Company, began to produce two types of Christopher scales which were patented in May and September of 1900.[19] Both models were called "Price Scales" in the patent literature, the second one apparently being an adaptation of the first with platform improvements.

Christopher conceived his price scale to improve on the construction of existing scales in use and to provide a simple and comparatively inexpensive one capable of simultaneously indicating the weight and price of an object. Also, he desired to provide a means for the scale to be readily rotated so that

---

16   Davis
17   Medford
18   Davis
19   *The Washington Post* newspaper article, *Bill of Complaint Dismissed*; April 14, 1905 (*Bill of Complaint Dismissed*)

the buyer and seller could alternately see the price and the weight. This, of course, is all inventor and patent speak, but when asked about his inspiration for the new-fangled scale, Filmore toned the language down a bit.

He explained, "One day at a local store I bought some meat. The grocer threw the purchase on some old-fashioned scales and then got out pencil and paper and began multiplying the weight by the price per pound. It was a rather tedious process, in as much as the man was not much of a mathematician. As I watched him with growing impatience and observed his ciphering ineptness, the notion of the price scale came over me then and there."[20]

The computing scale for merchants was a nationally recognized major invention at the time.[21] In fact, one *Raleigh Morning Post* correspondent identified Christopher as the "inventor of the famous computing scales."[22] But turning fame into fortune proved to be a "jug full" of rough sailing, just as before when the steam engine factory burned to the ground. This time, another scales company—the Computing Scales Company of Dayton, Ohio—brought forth a lawsuit against Calvin Christopher and the Automatic Computing Scales Company, claiming patent rights infringement.[23]

The case was heard in Washington, D.C., in or around 1902, and it was a long, drawn-out, and hotly contested legal affair.[24] Witnesses were rounded up from Haywood and Buncombe County, Spartanburg, and other places to testify and prove that the idea for the computing scale was Christopher's own. Many folks traveled to the nation's capital and provided testimony before the court that they had either seen Calvin Christopher's diagram for the scale or his completed model long before the year 1901. In the end, Christopher and his scales company prevailed when the District Supreme Court ruled to dismiss the complaint.[25]

---

20 Yates
21 Medford
22 The *Raleigh Morning Post* newspaper article, *Reward of Genius: A Successful Inventor Will Reside in Asheville*; April 4, 1905 (*A Successful Inventor Will Reside in Asheville*)
23 *Bill of Complaint Dismissed*
24 Medford
25 *Bill of Complaint Dismissed*

The young inventor, Calvin Filmore Christopher (Bethel Rural Community Organization)

Wasting little time, Calvin sold all his interests, patents, and pending patents for approximately $87,000 and moved back to the North Carolina mountains.[26] In the spring of 1905, he and Lula and the children—the ones who still remained with them—moved into one of the "handsomest properties" in West Asheville. This is not surprising, given that one reporter affirmed Christopher had earned more than $100,000 at that point in his career as a "reward of genius."[27]

Interestingly, while residing in Asheville for a decade or so, Calvin F. Christopher was listed in the city directories as a boarding house proprietor, grocery store owner, a barber, and an inventor.[28] Clearly, Filmore's tinkering invention work was not occupying all of his time. Nor would it be a stretch to deduce that these other pursuits were supplementing his already ample income from inventions and patents.

---

26 Medford
27 *A Successful Inventor Will Reside in Asheville*
28 Davis

The Asheville period proved to be a fruitful one for the inventor, producing a steady flow of patents over the years while he and Lula lived there. These included the automatic "Railway-Switch" patent mentioned previously, three more counter "Computing Scales" which offered new improvements over the original patents sold to his former company, an innovative "Metallic Clothes-Line," and a "Dinner Pail" containing a multitude of storage compartments.

Obviously, Christopher's obsession with the merchant computing scale remained as strong as ever, and he continued to strive toward its perfection. He even helped establish another company—the Independent Scales Company—and a small manufacturing plant in Asheville to produce and sell these new computing scales.[29] But just as he had done before, Filmore eventually sold his patents and company interests and removed to Haywood County's Pigeon Valley.[30]

By about 1915, the patent records suddenly show Canton, North Carolina, as Calvin Christopher's official address, although he resided in the nearby Bethel Community. The property along the East Fork of the Pigeon River where Filmore and Lula lived and worked was situated just upstream from the confluence of the East and West Forks of the Pigeon River. Known in earlier times as Forks of Pigeon, Calvin Christopher allowed a more suitable name for his place and its surroundings might be, of all things, "Arc Park." This brand seemed both logical and appropriate to him, given the property's proximity to the Pigeon River and the mountain stream's proclivity for unleashing biblical flooding events. Well, believe it or not, the name stuck![31]

Arc Park became the center of Calvin Christopher's world as he entered the final stage of his remarkable inventive career. He and Lula's comfortable white frame home was situated close to his workshop and waterwheel-powered millhouse. There was even a turbine-generator plant to provide electricity for not only Arc Park but also to a county home for indigent

---

29 *The Tradesman* magazine notice; Sept. 26, 1912
30 Yates
31 Coltman

people located nearby.³² It was quite the set-up for an inventor.

These utilitarian facilities provided ample opportunity and convenience for Filmore to carry on with his experimentations with electricity, mechanical power transmission, perpetual motion, and whatever schemes or fantastic notions his genius could hatch. And, of course, there was always more work to be done perfecting his several types of merchant computing scales.

Over the next 15 years or so, Christopher cranked out at least 14 more inventions that earned him patent rights for the ideas. Listed below are the ones that have come to light so far.

- Two patents offered new and different mechanisms for transmitting power effectively and efficiently through mechanical means.
- Another patent titled a "Motor" was essentially a different mechanism for more effectively transmitting power from a prime mover to the driven element.
- A patent was obtained for a wheel rim that could be disassembled to facilitate the changing of automobile tires. Although the idea later proved to be impractical, this patent was sold for $10,000.³³
- One patent provided a novel means of mounting a crib or cradle for superior swinging and vertical movements.
- A "Collapsible Box" patent provided a solution for storing or transporting a piano or an organ.
- A patent for the "Turfing (or tufting) Needle" presented a unique design to allow for quick threading of cord or yarn. The idea was immediately assigned to the National Needle Company for an undisclosed amount of money.³⁴
- The "Churn Gearing" patent offered folks a unique gearing arrangement to transfer the rotary motion of their laborious churn cranking into a vertical up and down movement of the paddle or stirring device. This equipment was eventually manufactured in Knoxville, Tennessee.³⁵

32	Coltman
33	Davis
34	*Official Gazette of the U.S. Patent Office, Vol. 283*: Feb. 1921; p. 442
35	Medford

- A "Car Badge" patent provided an enhanced security measure for automobile owners. Certainly ahead of his time with this notion, Filmore's unique badge could theoretically prevent theft when attached to a car. However, should the car be stolen, the badge could assist in locating the car and apprehending the thief.
- The "Measuring Instrument" patent provided a novel device that could measure the length of a flexible article—cloth, ribbon, rope, string, surveyor's tape, and the like.
- A novel "Calculating Device" was patented and promoted as The Christopher Time and Dial Machine.[36] The chief aim for this portable calculator was to provide a means to mount the mechanism so that calculations could be carried on and noted readily.

And the patent for a "Filling Station Machine" offered automobile filling stations a novel contraption whereby the cost of any number of gallons of gasoline, at any specified price, could be ascertained readily. Also, it could compute quickly and accurately the amount of change due to the seller out of a bill or coin of a specified value.

In addition, two more patents were obtained that expanded on his merchant computing scale, or price scale. One was named the "Combination Computing & Paper Roll Machine." Apparently, the major advancement with this invention was the additional wrapping paper holder that was mounted conveniently next to the computing scale. The other patent was called the "Revolving Computing Scale," which presented a computing scale that could be reversed on a vertical axis, allowing the purchaser as well as the merchant to see all the computations and the like.

---

36   The Greensboro Daily News newspaper article, *Time and Dial Machine Is Made by Tarheel Inventor*, Jan. 26, 1926

FORKS OF PIGEON (OR BETHEL) | 49

Christopher's "new and useful Dinner Pail," as described in US Patent No. 1,093,110, is pictured above in its closed and open positions. (courtesy Canton Historical Museum)

Shown in the photo above is one of Christopher's many scale inventions. This particular scale was designed to compute the price of a weighed object. (courtesy of Canton Historical Museum)

Various accounts have publicized even more Calvin Christopher inventions that were unique and commendable, although they have yet to be gleaned from the patent records. These included the previously-mentioned ditch-digging machine that was sold to the French government at the onset of World War I, a monkey wrench with sliding adjustment—not screwed, a compressed brick machine invention, a "Lumber Lightning Calculator," and a cotton weighing and computing machine.[37]

---

37   *Mountain Echoes; Obscure Haywood Inventor's Vision;* p. 311; Edie Hutchins Burnette

Filmore continued fiddling with his violin and laboring away on his innovations at Arc Park until about 1937. It was then that his health began failing and he became unable to stand the daily physical and mental rigors of his profession. His workshop was locked up and, at once, all those pipe dreams and experimentations with magnetism, electricity, sustained flight, and perpetual motion became just that—dreams. Three short years later, in 1940, the Pigeon River inventor passed on from this world, leaving behind a body of work that can hardly be contemplated today.

At the time of Christopher's passing, a reporter reminded readers that "the world's grocers and butchers today never have to take pen and paper to figure the cost of weighed purchases. Millions of us save labor, time, and money with 100 other devices. They owe it to an obscure Pigeon River inventor, but they don't know it."[38]

No matter his obscurity, the utility of Calvin Filmore Christopher's several computing price scales alone changed countless lives for the better—the lives of citizens of North Carolina and all across the country. Few people in Haywood County and North Carolina had heard of him during his lifetime. Today, more than 80 years after his passing, Christopher is an all but forgotten man. One can only wonder how that can be—how can North Carolina's most prolific inventor be forgotten?

---

38 Noted Inventor Passes

FORKS OF PIGEON (OR BETHEL) | 51

Calvin Filmore Christopher and his wife, Lula, are shown standing next to several of his inventions. (Bethel Rural Community Organization collection)

Calvin Christopher is pictured here in his later years sitting on the porch and likely contemplating the wonderful things he had imagined and invented. (Bethel Rural Community Organization collection)

The Bethel Rural Community Organization erected a highway historical marker in 2017 to recognize and remember Haywood County's forgotten inventor. It is located at the intersection of Hwy 110 and Max Thompson Road in Bethel. (author's collection)

A Matter of Graveyard Sleuthing

Introduction

On a recent visit to the Canton Area Historical Museum, I had an opportunity to examine a vintage photograph that had come to light from the James Henry and Flora Kinsland Plott collection. It was a wonderful pastoral scene of a farming bottomland hosting a cluster of buildings and scattered haystacks, not unlike the familiar Pigeon Valley settings in today's rural community of Bethel, North Carolina.

There was a large, multi-story brick residence clearly depicted in the dated photo. This exceptional building was surrounded by a good-sized barn, smaller outbuildings, and an unusual two-story, seemingly windowless structure that had a chimney poking up at one end. But where exactly was this impressive-looking farm located—and whose was it?

Getting to the Bottom of Things

A cemetery with grave markers visible in the foreground of the picture could not escape notice, giving me a notion of where the old farm might have been. On an instinctual whim and with the old photo in hand, I later found myself prowling the Bethel Community Cemetery amongst my own ancestors' gravestones. I thought there was a chance the photo might have been taken from somewhere on the cemetery property. It was certainly an elevated hillside offering similar views of a beautiful river valley with mountains in the background.

Very quickly, I was able to match up the mountain profiles that could be seen off in the distance with those in the background of the photograph. It was obvious that a photographer had once stood on top of this cemetery hill and aligned his camera in an eastward direction, up the valley of the East Fork of the Pigeon River and directly at Mt. Pisgah.

However, there was no grand farmhouse in sight. Instead, the observable modern targets in the early photograph's field of view were a paved road named

Market Street (formerly Terrell Lane), an active Hwy 276, a Dollar General Store and another convenience store, the Jukebox Junction restaurant, and several other unremarkable structures here and there.

Thankfully, there exists today in Bethel a group of dedicated and concerned citizens known collectively as the Bethel Rural Community Organization. One of their missions—along with benevolence projects and rural farmland preservation work—is historic preservation. A query to this group about the old photo and farm yielded quick and intriguing results.

Community club member Bill Terrell was able to identify the farmhouse in question as being the very one his ancestors, William Stewart Terrell, a Civil War veteran, and wife Mary Lucinda Kirkpatrick built in the 1880s. Bill Terrell was, also, able to offer more clues to the photograph's mystery. During that same 19th-century decade when the beautiful farmhouse was built, the railroad had reached Haywood County, bringing prosperity to the region with it. Consequently, William Terrell was able to realize increased profits from his general store, allowing him to construct an exceptional two-story brick house that included Italianate decorative elements.

In 1893, the Terrell's general store across the road from the new house was washed away by the flood waters from the West Fork of the Pigeon River. It was soon replaced with a more substantial building—a two-story brick building with a single chimney and similar Italianate architectural features as the house in the photo. Both extraordinary buildings can be recognized in the old photo, with a road (Market Street) running between the house and store and then toward the river in the distance.

It is not known precisely when this photograph was taken. Yet, if one looks closely at the image, a railroad track can be detected running along the bottom of the cemetery hill. These rails would have belonged to the Tennessee & North Carolina Railroad which linked the Champion Fibre Company's pulp mill in Canton with the logging and sawmill enterprises at Sunburst.

Construction work began on the railroad in 1907, and it was completed in about 1913. In the early 1930s, the tracks were removed after Champion Fibre impounded the waters of the West Fork of the Pigeon River to form Lake Logan. Therefore, the photograph of the Terrell farm was made sometime during the railroad's operational period, likely the 1920s based on the dates found on gravestones visible in the photo.

According to Bill Terrell, the house and store survived until about 1980 before being razed. Although the exact site of these former buildings is difficult to determine today, Bill's memory places them just on the south side of Hwy 276, across from where Market Street joins the highway. Evidently, when the new highway was constructed in the 1930s, the surveyors carefully laid out the road to barely miss the Terrell house and store before bending to cross the West Fork of the Pigeon River over a new bridge at the old Terrell's Ford.

A Matter of Graveyard Sleuthing

Certainly, Bill cleared up the mystery regarding that amazing Terrell farm photo, but there was one thing that still vexed me. I wanted to discover precisely where the camera had been set up to capture the original photographic image. In order to do that, it was necessary to find those same cemetery gravestones that are shown in the foreground of the old photo, all of them situated and aligned exactly as they appear in the photo.

So, a friend and I went back to the Bethel Community Cemetery to do some more sleuthing. We began searching across the entire cemetery, back and forth, looking at every stone, while trying to find the ones whose shape and position relative to each other perfectly matched those shown in the old image.

Alas, the one particular grave marker that we were looking for could not be found. It was this distinctive shaped stone, with an unusual, curved top and pointed cap, that was needed to align things just right to establish the photographer's position.

For more than an hour, we walked among the tombstones while reading familiar names and imagining times gone by—times when people like Joseph Cathey, Augustus C. Hartgrove, Pinkney Inman, Etheldred Blalock, and James Sheffield were living members of Bethel's society. Then, suddenly, these fascinations vanished upon the lifting of a single toppled stone marker.

There was no telling how long ago that gravestone had broken off from the base it was carefully propped against. But my friend and I immediately saw it was the exact size and shape we were searching for. Studying the photo, we could also see that this stone was in the correct position relative to another unique yet fallen grave marker just below it. There were no doubts now—we had found what we were looking for. One hundred years ago, a man with a camera had worked from a nearby spot to photograph the Terrell farm.

Gazing out from that vantage point on the cemetery hill, I could imagine a train passing by below, headed for Canton. Black smoke billowed from the locomotive's stack as it tugged a train of railcars loaded with lumber and pulpwood.

Then, I envisaged wagons rolling up the narrow dirt lane toward the Terrell house and store, where several people were loitering and walking about. And in the expansive bottom fields along the river, I could even conjure a scene of a mule-drawn mowing sickle cutting the hay that would soon be raked and piled in stacks.

Those were the real secrets hidden in that old Terrell farm photo. As you have learned, it took a Bethel community organization's involvement and an imagination bent toward history to see things in the picture clearly. Oh—and there was that matter of graveyard sleuthing that helped.

Note: Research material for this article was taken from *Legends, Tales & History of Cold Mountain: A Pigeon Valley Heritage Collection, Book 6* by Evelyn Coltman of the Bethel Rural Community Organization.

This Terrell farm photograph was taken a century ago from atop the Bethel Community Cemetery. The Terrell's impressive farmhouse, general store, and barn stand out in an expansive field beyond the cemetery gravestones. In the far distance, Mt. Pisgah's profile can easily be spotted. (from Plott Collection held at the Canton Historical Museum)

Evelyn Coltman of the Bethel Rural Community Organization is holding up the broken gravestone which was the key to unravelling the mystery of where the original Terrell farm photo was taken. (author's collection)

The William and Mary Terrell farmhouse shown here was constructed of brick and adorned with Italianate decorative elements. Built in the 1880s, the house survived for a century until falling victim to the ravages of time. (from Bill Terrell collection)

After its predecessor was destroyed by a flood in 1893, the second Terrell general store building shown here was constructed. The substantial brick structure possessed similar Italianate ornamentation as the Terrell's new house located close by. (from Bill Terrell collection)

A young Clifton Terrell poses on horseback next to the former Terrell's general store. (from Bill Terrell collection)

The Sonoma Kaolin Mine

Introduction

A few years ago, Norman Long escorted me and a few other Bethel Rural Community Organization members to the top of a ridge above his house in Long's Cove. This setting in Haywood County, North Carolina, was once known as the Chinquapin Grove community. While rubbing bloody briar pricks and huffing and puffing from the strenuous hike to the hilltop, we all managed to gaze into an enormous yawning crater in the ground. I grasped a tree limb and peered down in amazement into the deep hole, taking great care not to fall in while trying to understand what I was looking at.

Norman allowed that this giant hole, which appeared to be a hundred feet deep and maybe two hundred yards long, was made by miners one hundred years ago. Although overgrown with trees and underbrush, we onlookers could barely grasp the enormity or understand the significance of what we saw. Little did we know that Bethel, North Carolina, was once host to a substantial mining operation!

Claiming the Rights to the Kaolin

Local lore credits Mrs. Mary Long's foraging pigs with discovering the kaolin deposit on a ridge well above her home in the Chinquapin Grove community. A white powdery substance covering the pigs' snouts was tested and it proved to be kaolin, a soft white clay used in manufacturing china and porcelain.

Called the "Sonoma kaolin prospect" in one trade bulletin, the deposit was located about one mile southeast of Woodrow, North Carolina, and a short distance from the Tennessee and North Carolina Railroad (T&NCRR). This was the branch line which connected the logging and sawmill enterprises at Sunburst with the Murphy Branch of the Southern Railway system at Canton.

In 1916, Dr. C.J. Hand of Swain County purchased the rights to mine the kaolin from the widower Mrs. Long and several other heirs-in-law of her deceased husband T.B. Long. Dr. Hand secured rights to "all the kaolin clay in and under a certain piece or parcel of land" where members of the Long family then resided. He agreed to mine 40 tons of kaolin clay per week and pay the Longs 50 cents per ton in royalties. At the end of each 52-week period, the Longs would also receive an additional four thousand dollars, less the previous royalties paid.

Further bargains between Dr. Hand and the Longs were made for the property rights of portions or parcels of land upon which buildings could be erected for the purpose of washing, pressing, and drying the kaolin clay and housing the machinery to do so. Allowances were made as well for the sidetracks, flumes, ditches, tram roads, coal bins, roads for ingress and egress, and such other buildings and work as might be necessary for the most economical mining operation. Interestingly, in a matter of only a few months, Dr. Hand signed over all these legal agreements to the Hand Clay Company, a corporation he formed with its principal office in Canton, North Carolina.

Dr. Hand anticipated the need for tram cars to transport kaolin from the mine to the T&NCRR, where it could easily be loaded in rail cars and transported to customers. In fact, he negotiated a deal with Mrs. Mary K. Terrell, wife of the deceased William Stewart Terrell, acquiring the rights to run his tram line across the large Terrell farm lying on the far side of the West Fork of the Pigeon River and between the mine and the railroad.

In consideration of these tram rights granted by Mrs. Terrell, Dr. Hand agreed to designate the W.S. Terrell & Sons Co. —a general merchandise business—as the exclusive commissary of the Hand Clay Company. Time tickets printed and issued to the clay company's employees would be redeemable in merchandise at the Terrell's store. In turn, the Hand Clay Company would pay cash to purchase back these same time tickets held by the W.S. Terrell & Sons Co.

The Kaolin Mining Operation

A contemporary trade bulletin reported that in 1907 the "Sonoma prospect consisted of a single pit 15 feet deep on the top of a ridge, three-fourths mile south of Sonoma." As previously mentioned, in 1916, Dr. C.J. Hand purchased this kaolin clay deposit, which was located above the homes of Mrs. Mary Long and other members of her family in the Chinquapin Grove community.

During the first year or so of operation, miners worked exclusively in an open excavation using picks and shovels to dig the raw material from the ground. The crude kaolin was then loaded in minecarts and pushed over rails to the head of a water flume nearby. The higher elevation of the mine afforded a convenient grade for sluicing the kaolin down a wooden trough to a processing plant in the valley below.

By 1918, the deposit was being worked in two open cuts, each about 20-feet deep and 90-feet wide. Two tunnels, approximately 55-feet and 125-feet long, were excavated through the walls of the open cuts to facilitate the passage of minecarts to the water flume. According to one source, the tunnels had lights installed in them to illuminate the passageway.

In order to reach deeper into the ground to access the clay, two vertical shafts were also opened to extract the material. These shafts—or vertical holes—were 15 to 20 feet in diameter and sunk in approximately four-feet-high lifts to extract the kaolin clay. Timbers were used to form and support the earthen wall of the shaft as the excavation work proceeded deeper and deeper. A horse-powered hoisting apparatus and buckets were used to lift the excavated material out of the shaft. By 1919, one of the shafts had reached a depth of almost one hundred feet.

Once the kaolin material was excavated, it was conveyed downhill by a water flume to the valley below, where the refining processes were installed in huge sheds. The first steps in the process were removing impurities from the kaolin, such as fine sand, quartz, and mica. To accomplish this, the Hand Company used specialized equipment that was identified as washers, sand wheels, sand and mica troughs, and screens. After being run through these different stages that utilized large quantities of water, the purified kaolin was then concentrated in tanks using alum as a flocculator.

Early on, it was determined that the water demands of the flume, the kaolin refining process, and the personal drinking and hygienic requirements of the mining employees exceeded the quantity of water being provided by a pumping station located next to the West Fork of the Pigeon River. Therefore, in early 1917, the Hand Clay Mine purchased rights to use the water from springs located on the property owned by Joseph Decatur Justice and his wife, Etta Justice, heirs of the deceased T.B. Long.

For the relatively low sum of 30 dollars, the Justices granted the water rights and agreed "not to in any manner whatsoever interfere with the flow of the water from said Springs or to in any manner whatsoever contaminate the water from said Springs..." This appears to be an example of how well the Justice and Long families cooperated with the mine company in order to keep the mine running as efficiently and productively as possible. Of course, they had a stake in the operation. The royalties they earned, based on the mine's production, were an important income source for the family.

Getting back to the kaolin mining process, after being purified and concentrated, the thickened kaolin was conveyed into an agitator before being pumped to a press. The heavy steel and cast-iron pressing equipment squeezed the kaolin into cakes containing only eight to twenty percent water. These cakes were then placed on steam pipes in the drying shed to dry. When sufficiently dried, the kaolin was scraped off the steam pipes and loaded into tram cars.

The tram line ran from the refining plant along a downhill grade to an iron-truss bridge that spanned the West Fork of the Pigeon River. After crossing the bridge, the tram followed the public road (today's Market Street) that passed through the Terrell property to the foot of a hill below the Methodist Episcopal Church. From there, the narrow wood rails were laid along the bottom of the hill to reach a railroad sidetrack on a lot owned by the W.S. Terrell & Sons Co. At this spot, the kaolin could be transferred to rail cars and shipped to Canton and beyond.

A wonderful account published by Bethel Middle School students in 1992 describes how the loaded tram cars were pulled by two mules in single file, one in front of the other. Upon leaving the processing plant, where there was a good downhill grade, the men would sometimes unleash the tram car from the mule team and let it run by gravity all the way down to the river crossing. This source explains how the men would have to pile sand on the tracks to keep the tram car from running away and jumping the tracks.

After hooking the mules back up to the cars, the kaolin was hauled across the bridge and over the wooden rails to a sidetrack near the Woodrow depot, where the kaolin was loaded into a waiting railcar. From there, the kaolin was hauled by the T&NCRR to the Southern Railway's tracks in nearby Canton. At that junction, the carload of kaolin product was transferred to the Southern's domain and shipped to customers who manufactured porcelain, china, and other types of whiteware products.

Another intriguing tidbit of information uncovered by the Bethel Middle School students in their excellent expose of the mining operation reveals that the tram cars did not return to the mine empty. Instead, they were loaded with coal from a depot yard before being hauled back to the kaolin refining plant. The coal was then used to fuel the two boilers associated with the plant. These boilers provided steam to generate electricity and to dry the compressed kaolin over steam pipes.

A scientific bulletin published in 1925 and titled "The Kaolins of North Carolina" states that the Hand Clay Mine located at Sonoma was purchased by the Harris Kaolin Company out of Dillsboro, North Carolina. Although it does not confirm when this transaction occurred nor has the Haywood County records revealed the sale, it would likely have taken place in or around the winter of 1918-1919 when modifications were made to the kaolin refining plant. At the time of the bulletin's publication in 1925, the Sonoma clay mining operation appears to have still been an active concern.

Conclusion

On the way back from the mine, Norman Long took us by his brother J.M. Long's house for a brief chat. Both Long brothers still lived in the Chinquapin Grove community where their grandparents T.B. and Mary Long settled. While growing up there, they saw evidence of the mining operation and heard plenty of stories about it from their parents, kin folk, and neighbors.

J.M. recalled that in or about 1955, when he built his present house in the vicinity where the kaolin refining plant had been located, there were still large quantities of white sand spread across the field. It was everywhere, he said, and so thick that it had to be removed. Undoubtedly, this would have been the fine sand that had been washed and removed from the kaolin clay over the several years the refining plant was in operation.

He also said there was a boarding house near where he lives, and he seemed to remember that the mining employees who stayed there with their families were from "out west." By that, he meant they were from territories west of Haywood County, probably from Swain and Jackson counties where there were older mica and kaolin mining operations. It is likely that the Hand and Harris mining companies brought in several experienced miners to run and work their Sonoma mine and plant.

An old frame house stands today just below the ridge where the kaolin mine was worked. The house's dormers, eave bracketry, and plain style date it to the era of the kaolin mining operation. Norman explained that this was the old Justice house, built for his Aunt Etta Justice and her husband, Joseph Decatur Justice. He was not at all hesitant when stating that the income from mining royalties allowed his grandmother and the Justices to build such a fine home.

All in all, it was a great learning experience—that little chat with the Long brothers about the kaolin mine and, also, the arduous trek to the old mining scar that looms above their homes. I am extremely grateful to Norman and J.M. for their time and for sharing cherished memories. They opened my eyes to something I knew absolutely nothing about—a once active mining industry in Bethel, believe it or not.

Note: Research information for this article was taken from the following sources: a publication titled *Pigeon Valley: Hand Mine* compiled by Bethel Middle School students (1992), and two trade bulletins: *Mining and Treatment of Feldspar and Kaolin* (1913) and *Bulletin No. 29: The Kaolin's of North Carolina (1925)*.

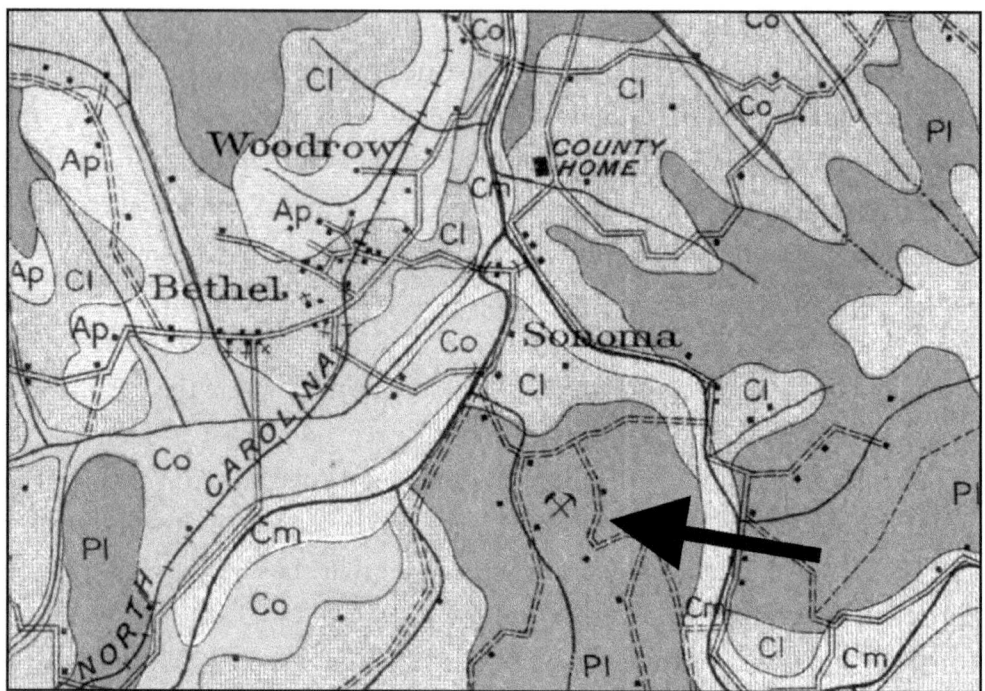

This cropped image from a 1925 Haywood County Soil Map shows the location of the old kaolin mine in Bethel, North Carolina. It was in operation from 1916 until the mid-to-late 1920s.

A wonderful panoramic photograph captured the north cut of the kaolin mine that operated in Bethel from 1916 until the mid-to-late 1920s. Note the rails that were used to transport minecarts filled with the excavated raw kaolin to a water flume, where it was conveyed downhill in the flume to the refining equipment. (from the Plott collection held by the Bethel Rural Community Organization)

The Old Garden Creek School... and the Swinging Bridge

Introduction

Although my memory is fading in these senior years, thoughts of long-ago rides up the "backside" of the Pigeon River from Canton, North Carolina, to the Bethel community are still vivid and real as ever. About once a week my brother and I would hop in the car with our mother and make a four-mile trip along N.C. Hwy 215 to the Hargrove farm. There, we got to visit with Granny, pick and string green beans, hike up the mountainside, swim in the river, search for arrowheads, and even milk the cows.

Often, while riding along the river road, mother would call our attention to a particular spot where a swinging bridge had once spanned the river. She would say something like, "There...right over there is where the swinging bridge was. We used to walk across it on our way to school."

Yet, all I could see were trees and wilderness. There was no bridge or schoolhouse in the view from our automobile. Maybe a degree of wonderment was aroused in me, but that soon passed as we drove by swimming holes, beautiful pastures, corn and tobacco fields, and molasses-making grounds on our way to Granny's house.

Today, as I drive through that same general area where Mom had crossed the river on her way to school, those long-ago boyhood memories are refreshed. After all, it was the spot where a pretty little girl, all of seven to ten-years old at the time, walked across a swinging bridge and up a steep hill to get to her schoolhouse. And that was after hiking almost a mile down the railroad track just to get to the river crossing.

I have learned it was the Garden Creek School that Mother once attended and have finally been satisfied to know the exact locations of the school and the swinging bridge—both of which disappeared many years ago. Readers, especially those who are bothered by a nagging history bug as I am, are invited to read on and discover more about the Bethel community's Garden Creek School and that swinging bridge the young scholars walked across to get there.

Garden Creek School

The Garden Creek schoolhouse was built in 1916 on top of a low hill in Haywood County's Garden Creek community. This rural farming country was occupied by Indians for ten thousand years until white settlers claimed the land as their own following the Revolutionary War.

Running near one side of the school site was the motor road precursor to N.C. Hwy 110 that joined the town of Canton with the rural Bethel community. Just a few hundred yards on the opposite side of the new school structure and at the bottom of the hill flowed the waters of the Pigeon River, meandering out of Bethel toward Canton and beyond.

At that time, the tracks of a pea vine railroad, owned and operated by the Tennessee and North Carolina Railroad Company (T&NCRR), twisted and turned along the far bank of the river. Every day except Sundays, huffing and puffing steam locomotives pulling cars loaded with logs and lumber passed below the school site on the short journey from Sunburst logging village down to the mill town of Canton.

Since there was no bus service at the time, most of the students had to walk to the new Garden Creek School. The hilltop school might have been convenient for students living in the Garden Creek and nearby Henson Cove communities. However, a formidable barrier stood in the way of those schoolboys and girls from the former Piney Grove School in the Stamey Cove community. That barrier happened to be the Pigeon River, and to facilitate the students' passage to the new school, the county had a swinging bridge built over the river. Yes, this was the same swinging bridge my mother talked to us about.

Accounts from former students and teachers describe the new Garden Creek schoolhouse as being a wooden frame building housing two classrooms with a single porch in front. At each end of the porch was a cloakroom where students could store their coats and lunch pails. Since there was no indoor plumbing, a separate well house with a hand pump supplied water to the teachers and thirsty young scholars. Two outdoor toilets (johnnies)—one for the boys and one for the girls—served the students as well as their teachers. A few years after the founding of the school, a third classroom and another teacher were added.

Former Garden Creek teachers and students recalled that each classroom had its own coal-burning stove to provide some level of comfort during the daily winter sessions. Teachers, with a little help from the older students, would gather kindling from the nearby woods and set it ablaze in the stoves to get the coal fires burning.

There were no janitors at the Garden Creek School. Weighty maintenance tasks fell upon the shoulders of the teachers and students to handle. These duties included dealing with the coal ash, sweeping floors, and even oiling the wood floors once a week.

In 1921, the Haywood County Board of Education mandated that Garden Creek, Cruso, and Bethel be consolidated into one high school district. Free transportation to Bethel High School was offered to all Garden Creek and Cruso high school students who had completed the seventh grade. This meant that starting about 1922 the Garden Creek School taught first through seventh grades only.

Another sweeping measure was taken by the county school board in 1933. It was then that the remaining grades at Garden Creek School were consolidated with Bethel Elementary School. So, after approximately 17 years of service to the community and with all students attending the Bethel schools, Garden Creek School ceased scholastic activities forever.

Discovering the Garden Creek School and Swinging Bridge Sites

Over the years, I have become familiar with the Garden Creek community and its old Plott house overlooking beautiful farm fields next to the Pigeon River. These same fields hosted a drive-in theatre many years ago when I was growing up in Canton. Perhaps more meaningful, archaeological digs on these grounds and subsequent research work on the ancient artifacts that were discovered have proven Indigenous people inhabited Garden Creek for thousands of years.

Approximately one-half mile up the river from the Plott house and situated next to Hwy 110 are the Central Pigeon Fire Station facilities. For years, I had been told the Garden Creek School once stood on the high ground above the fire station. However, it seemed that all those knowledgeable people promoting this insightful information had different ideas of where, precisely, on that hillside the schoolhouse was located.

Recently, I decided to do a bit of research of my own and try to pin down the Garden Creek School location once and for all. As it turned out, it did not take long to discover the sites of both the schoolhouse and the swinging bridge that my mother had used to cross the Pigeon River on her way to school.

The investigation turned up two historic maps revealing the locations of both the school and the swinging bridge. A 1925 Haywood County Soil Map (date depicted is 1922) illustrates the "Garden Creek School" in bold text and with a school symbol. The school is located on an unnamed road stemming off the early Hwy 110. Although this map does not show the swinging bridge, it does identify the "Piney Grove Church" and illustrates a railroad running along the far bank of the river.

Another illuminating resource turned out to be a 1935 USGS Canton, North Carolina, Quadrangle Map. That same unnamed road stemming off "State Highway No. 110" is depicted on the map. Although there is no label or symbol for the Garden Creek School (the school had been closed in 1933), a structure is shown on this road exactly where the 1925 Soil Map depicts the school. From the terminus of the short unnamed road, the 1935 map clearly highlights a trail leading down to the Pigeon River where there is a bridge symbol shown. Undoubtedly, this symbol illustrates the swinging bridge used by the young students to cross the river on their way to school.

On the far side of the river from the school, the 1935 USGS map also gives the location of "Piney Grove Ch" (Church), which is still very active to this day. Additionally, it shows a roadway running along the riverbank exactly where the railroad had previously been routed. As it turns out, the railroad track was taken up in, or around, 1933. This was soon after the Champion Fibre Company in Canton impounded the waters of the West Fork of the Pigeon River, creating Lake Logan at the site of the former Sunburst logging village.

It was then a simple matter to link the historic map locations of Garden Creek School, the unnamed road the school was located on—now named Lindsey Drive, and the swinging bridge with the current landscape found on a Google Earth aerial view of the Garden Creek Community. Although this gave me some satisfaction in knowing precisely where the school and bridge once stood, my history bug itch still needed some scratching. Could there be remaining physical traces of the old school and bridge? A search of the grounds seemed to be in order.

Traces of Garden Creek School and the Swinging Bridge

Contact was made with the current owner of the property at the end of Lindsey Drive, where the Garden Creek School was originally located. This gentleman was very welcoming and forthcoming in answering questions about the school and bridge sites. He let it be known that the existing house where he resides sits on the site of the former schoolhouse. Although there seemed to be some uncertainty whether the house had been built around the old school structure, he was sure of one thing. The old well that once provided drinking water for the students and teachers survives to this day, and he showed us where it was located.

Interestingly, this property owner mentioned that many old clay marbles had been discovered on the grounds over the years. One can envision young boys and girls playing with these tiny spherical objects during school breaks, while hollering, laughing, and having a grand time competing with their friends. Fortunately for us, the children left some of these hundred-year-old artifacts behind as a reminder of their Garden Creek School days.

Lastly, the owner mentioned there were signs of the old swinging bridge down at the river. On the near bank—or school side—of the river, a large rock had anchored the bridge, and he believed there was remaining evidence of that anchorage. *Hmm, very interesting,* I thought while at the same time thanking him for his time and the information he had shared. All I could think about was finding that big rock along with evidence of the bridge anchorage.

A well-beaten trail once led down from the hilltop school site to the swinging bridge spanning the river. Remnants of that approximately one-quarter-mile long path still exist, curving with the contours of the hillside and passing through four different property lots, including the one where the school site is located.

Permission was sought and received to walk through private property situated along the Plott Farm Circle Road down to the swinging bridge site. This was a large tract of dense forest and, on my way downhill toward the river, I had to dodge a young king snake. Having done that and garnered enough courage to keep going, it was not long before the noise of rushing water could be heard and shiny glimpses of the river could be seen through thick stands of mountain laurel.

In no time, the huge rock that reportedly anchored the bridge was discovered. It was exactly where the USGS map's bridge symbol indicated. A great deal of searching turned up no evidence of bridge anchorage anywhere on that large rock itself. However, there was something else that caught my attention on the nearby river embankment.

A short distance behind the massive rock outcropping, a steel anchor rod could be seen protruding up through the undergrowth. It was surely embedded deep into the earth in a mass of concrete, but there was only a couple of feet of this anchor rod sticking out of the ground. The eye formed on the end of the steel rod would have undoubtedly served as the attachment point for one of the main suspension cables.

Realizing there would likely have been two suspension cables supporting the bridge, I immediately began searching for a second anchor rod. It did not take long to uncover it hidden away in the thick undergrowth just a few feet away. This anchor rod was bent over against the ground and barely visible, but it was an exact match of the first rod with a similar eye formed at its end. Undoubtedly, it was the anchor for the bridge's second suspension cable.

Conclusion

Soon after that snake encounter and the arduous trek through a beautiful wilderness setting, I realized late spring was not the ideal time to scavenge through rural riverbanks for traces of an old swinging bridge. Also, the dense undergrowth and overgrowth on the far side of the Pigeon River—opposite side from the Garden Creek School—helped convince me to wait until winter to search for the other anchor rods and further evidence of the bridge. Readers can rest assured that a continuation of the search is already on my calendar.

Thankfully, this little exploration of mine has placed on solid ground the former locations of the Garden Creek School and the nearby swinging bridge. My mother, bless her heart, had tried to tell me where the bridge was located, and it took me almost 70 years to discover its exact location.

Note: Much of the information presented in this article about the former Garden Creek School is taken from the book *Haywood County Schoolin': A Rich Heritage*. This spiral-bound paperback book has more than 500 pages and was published by the Haywood County Schools History Book Committee in 1992.

Students are posing in front of the Garden Creek School building in this cropped 1920 panoramic photo. The porch can easily be seen behind them with cloakrooms at each end and the classrooms at the rear. (courtesy of Canton Historical Museum)

Shown here is the author's mother, Jimmie Hargrove, who attended Garden Creek School in the late 1920s and early 1930s. (author's collection)

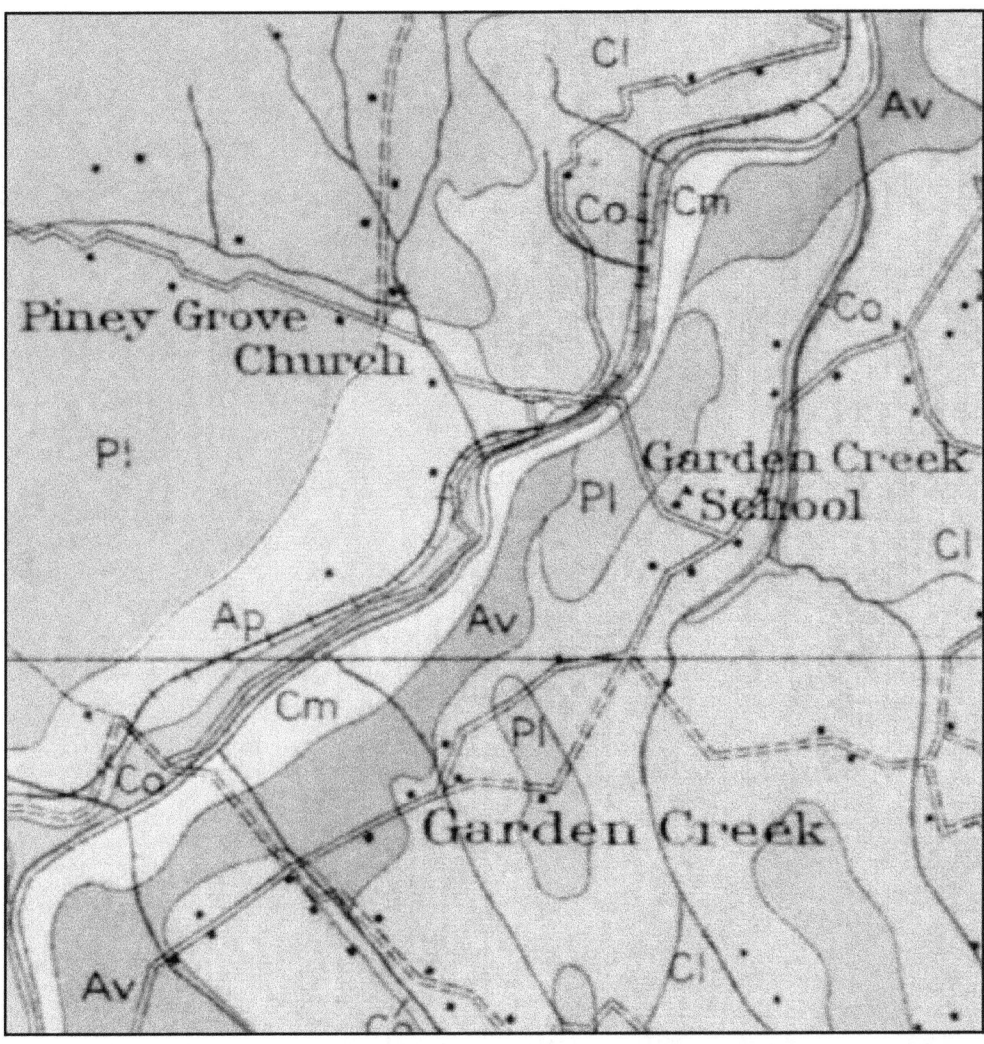

Garden Creek School's location is clearly identified on this screenshot from the 1925 Haywood County Soil Map. Note the railroad track running along the opposite side of the Pigeon River.

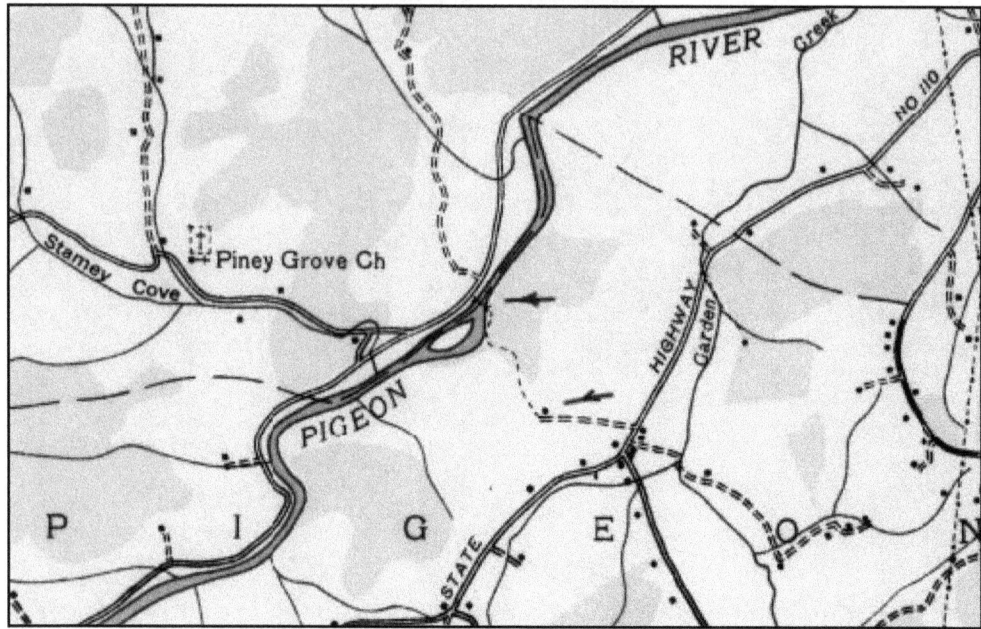

The former Garden Creek School location and swinging bridge spanning the Pigeon River are illustrated on this screenshot from a 1935 USGS Canton Quadrangle Map. Arrows drawn by the author point to these sites. As can be seen, the railroad track alongside the river has been removed and replaced with a roadway.

Two steel anchor rods were found embedded in the ground at the swinging bridge site, on the school-side of the river. This photo shows one of those anchors that supported the bridge. (author's collection)

The swinging bridge ran across the top of this huge rock on the school-side of the river. Just behind the rock, two steel anchor rods were found embedded in the earthen embankment. The bridge's support cables were once attached to these anchors. (author's collection)

Memories of Mountain Thanksgivings

November in the Pigeon Valley of western North Carolina, way back when, was indeed a time for the mountaineer farmers to be thankful. During the spring and summer, hard work along with keen wits and the grace of God were enjoined to fullest advantage to coax grain crops from rich bottomlands and the thin, rocky soils covering the hillsides. By the time November came around, corn and wheat harvests were "laid by" and the vegetables and fruit had already been gathered and rendered into a variety of nutritional provisions. This would ensure the Valley families could survive the long, cold winter ahead.

November was a time when the men of the community would form up wagon trains loaded with surplus produce and livestock and make long droves to distant marketplaces in South Carolina and Georgia. At these foreign trade centers, their farm treasures were sold for scarce currency or bartered for other necessities that could not be grown or easily made at home. The mountaineers would return to their small log cabins and anxious families with spending money jingling in their pockets and valuable provisions of salt, sugar, and even coffee to see them through the coming hard months. Thus, rewarded and with renewed hope and aspirations, the Pigeon Valley farmers could count their blessings and be mighty thankful for their good fortune.

November in the Pigeon Valley also meant that cold weather had arrived and was fixin' to set in. The local farmers prepared themselves because they knew the mountain winters meant…

- the cribs were plumb full of precious maize,
- autumn's brilliant red blazes and orange flames engulfing the trees were sadly extinguished, exposing drab, leafless skeletons standing forlornly and ready for the ravages of yet another winter,

- the golden yellow burley hangs drying from sapling poles inside rustic little barns,
- ragged shocks of corn stalks and fodder stand stacked in the fields, and some of the pumpkins had yet to be hauled to the barn,
- making long droves to faraway marketplaces in South Carolina and Georgia and being away from the family for several weeks at a time,
- there was not much time left to squeeze the last of the cane cuttings and render their greenish yellow juices into a golden molasses syrup,
- corn shuckings with young people laughing and enjoying each other's company and perhaps winning a buss (kiss) from a sweetheart,
- awakening mornings to find a glistening white rime blanket covering the highest mountain knobs and lowest bottoms and everything in between,
- the woods and orchards would be littered with chestnuts spilled from prickly burrs, and if a body didn't hurry with their "tow sacks," the ravenous forest foragers would find them first,
- the grey squirrels were mighty fidgety, having lost their lofty, leafy hiding places, and would be more alert to the perils of flying predators above and sleuthing hunters below,
- hog killing and lye-soap-making time and the hard work that entailed,
- men gathering and going off into the woods to slay the wary ridge runners, whose meat would sustain their families and their lives,
- young'uns pouring bucket after bucket of water into the ash hopper to make lye water for soap making,
- women boiling and cooking a pungent mixture of lye water, fat, pork, and grease to render lye soap,
- the cellar and/or barn smelled of straw-covered apples, buried taters, and cool earth,
- women stooping and stoking and stirring huge boiling kettles of apples, cider, and spices all day long to persuade its conversion into delicious apple butter,
- carrying fresh shucked and shelled corn to the mill to be turned,
- pumpkins overlooked in the field or piled by the barn wearing white frosty caps on a cold morning,

- aromas that make mouths water and bellies growl—the aromas of pumpkin bread, pumpkin butter, and pumpkin pies cooking on the stove and hearth,
- joyful evenings of banter and corn popping with the family before the warm hearth,
- going to school, wearing shoes, learning the ciphers, and being with friends,
- the aroma of wood smoke filling the house and infiltrating the Valley,
- axes flying and cutting firewood and chopping up plenty of kindling for the cook stove,
- hog's meat hanging and smoky fires burning in little smokehouses,
- molasses-pulling affairs for the young folks and romantic yearnings of getting "stuck" to your sweetheart,
- making crackling bread after the first hog killing,
- snow on the mountain peaks and cold gusting winds in the valleys, stirring the leaves and whistling through the chinks in the log houses,
- holiday feasts of pork and roast turkey enjoyed with a mess of leather britches beans, taters, cornbread, apple butter, pumpkin pie, milk, and cider,
- saying grace and giving thanks for all of the above.

November meant all these things and much more to the early settlers of the Pigeon Valley. We can all be thankful for these memories and for the exertions and sacrifices of our Pigeon Valley ancestors before us.

A large family and neighbors are shown in this photo working to process sorghum cane cuttings into golden molasses syrup. A horse attached to the press in the foreground drove the press to squeeze greenish yellow juice from the cane. Men, women, and children are gathered around a steaming vat where molasses is being rendered from the squeezed cane juices. (courtesy of Canton Historical Museum)

During the fall and winter months in the mountains, ragged shocks of corn stalks like this one stood in the fields. Stacking the corn stalks allowed it to dry out so it could be preserved and fed to the livestock. (from Library of Congress)

SUNBURST (OR SPRUCE)

Logging with an oxen train

The Canton-to-Sunburst Pea Vine Railroad

Introduction

Most people living in North Carolina's Haywood County have no knowledge of the "pea vine" railroad that once linked Canton with the logging and farming communities along the headwaters of the Pigeon River. Back in the day, the term "pea vine" was commonly used to describe railways with twisting curves resembling...pea vines. Certainly, the 15-mile, or so, railroad snaking up the backside of the Pigeon River and along the banks of its West Fork tributary complied with the pea vine description.

This old pea vine railroad's route generally followed today's Hwy NC 215, extending from the Southern Railway's tracks in Canton to a bustling logging village located where the pristine waters of Lake Logan are currently impounded. Actually, it reached a few miles beyond the logging village to a place called "Three Forks," where the Left Hand Prong, Middle Prong, and Right Hand Prong streams join to form the West Fork of the Pigeon River. Today, Three Forks is home to Pisgah National Forest's Sunburst Campground, but one hundred years ago it hosted a junction of iron railroad tracks fanning out into the virgin forests brimming with timber treasures.

An article appearing in a local newspaper more than a half-century ago alluded to Haywood County's old pea vine railroad. It was stated that "trains no longer roll on the Pea Vine nor logs fall in Sherwood Forest."[39] For readers intrigued with the notion of a Haywood County pea vine railroad, the following account should prove enlightening. Not only can you learn about the origins and history of the Canton-to-Sunburst railroad, but you will discover the reason that trains no longer roll on that old pea vine.

Now, hop on board and enjoy the ride!

Champion Fibre's Railroad Endeavor

The original Champion Fibre Company pulp mill was constructed in Canton, North Carolina, from 1905 to 1908, with manufacturing operations beginning in 1908. Peter G. Thomson from Cincinnati, Ohio, was the founder of the mill, and he had acquired 40,000 acres of virgin forest lands in the Pigeon River headwaters as a source of wood to support the pulp manufacturing processes. One of his employees, a woodsman named Samuel Montgomery Smith, had convinced Thomson that a flume could be constructed and used to convey pulpwood from the upper reaches of the Pigeon River to Canton, a distance of some 15 miles or more.

The merits of the idea, as Smith saw them, were that all the lumber needed to construct the flume and support the construction of the pulp mill could be sawn at the Pigeon headlands and sluiced down the river to the construction

---

39   *The Mountaineer* newspaper; "No More Trains on the Pea Vine!"; June 18, 1969

site in Canton—at a very low cost. Additionally, after the mill was up and running, the pulpwood could be got out, sawn into the proper size, and conveyed down the flume to the mill, again at a low cost. Smith's flume scheme was surely an enticing idea and one of the reasons the mill was eventually built at Canton.[40]

By the end of June 1906, all rights-of-way along the flume route were finally secured. However, additional surveys of the gradient along the flume line had revealed a significant problem. It was determined that to build the flume to the proper grade, such that pulpwood could be sluiced by water and gravity to Canton, the required elevated flume structures would be prohibitively expensive to build. Moreover, the several rights-of-way that had already been obtained for the flume were not wide enough to allow such substantial lofty structures to be constructed.

It was the summer of 1906 and too late for Peter Thomson to back away from the decision to build his mill at Canton. Great efforts and expenditures were already being made at that place toward constructing the mill. As difficult as it must have been, Thomson had to abandon all further consideration of fluming wood from the Pigeon headwaters. This meant, of course, an alternative method of reliably accessing his 40,000 acres of reserve timberlands would have to be found, and soon.

The head men of the company reckoned the wood would have to be gotten out somehow other than the doomed flume or by horse and wagons over an unreliable road with difficult stream fords. So, it was ultimately decided by Thomson and his associates that the most practical solution for reaching and marketing these valuable timber holdings was to build a standard gauge railroad up the river, extending from Canton all the way to Three Forks. By then, Samuel Smith had already assembled a logging village at this junction of Pigeon River tributaries, and Peter Thomson had promptly named it "Sunburst" for the way the morning sun burst over the eastern ridges.[41]

---

40   Carroll C. Jones, *Thomson's Pulp Mill*; 2018
41   Newspaper clipping in possession of Doug Trimmler (possibly from the *Asheville Citizen-Times*, Asheville, N.C.) reporting on the Champion Y.M.C.A. dedication in about 1920

Champion's attorney George Smathers was directed to handle the legal affairs for establishing a railroad, and in November 1906, he successfully obtained a state charter for the Pigeon River Railway Company. Incorporation papers were immediately filed in the Haywood County courthouse, establishing the railroad as a common carrier—one that carried not only freight but passengers as well.

Peter Thomson's son-in-law, Reuben B. Robertson, recounted later that he and Smathers spent week after long week traveling up and down the Pigeon River Valley, negotiating and haggling with farmers for the rights-of-way to construct a railroad through their properties. During this same time, John N. Shoolbred from Waynesville completed a survey of the route, including a profile of the line to be built.

Rough cost estimates for the railroad were coming in at $8,000 to $9,000 per mile of track.[42] In March 1907, a contract was awarded to the firm of W.J. Oliver Company out of Knoxville, Tennessee for the grading and building of a roadbed from Canton to the Sunburst logging village. Oliver was well-known and had a substantial amount of work in progress. Because this firm was on the verge of dedicating its resources to a much larger contractual undertaking—construction of the Panama Canal—the relatively modest Pigeon River Railway project was sublet to Yandle Brothers, also out of Knoxville.

Plans were immediately set in motion to get the job started. Several camps were established along the Pigeon and West Fork rivers and hundreds of men and mules put to work. By early spring of 1907, clearing and dangerous dynamite-blasting activities had gotten underway on the badly needed railroad.[43] Although things were being pushed ahead as rapidly as possible, it was still very much up in the air whether the railroad would be completed by the end of 1907 and in time to supply pulpwood to the operations at the new Canton mill.

Yandle Brothers' safety record was anything but safe during that initial year of their contract in 1907. About a month after the grading work began, an extraordinary accident occurred along the route. It was reported at the time that a premature dynamite explosion injured eight to ten men, and one was dead.[44]

---

42   *Charlotte Observer*, Charlotte, N.C. (March 15, 1907)
43   *Charlotte Observer*, Charlotte, N.C. (March 15, 1907)
44   *News and Observer*, Raleigh, N.C. (May 22, 1907)

Evidence of still another accident is gleaned from a court settlement where Mr. Dred Blalock was awarded five-hundred dollars, to be paid by Yandle Brothers, on account of the death of Blalock's son, Ben. Apparently, Ben was fatally injured by a Yandle Brothers' blasting operation while working in a field near the railroad grade.[45]

Besides awful accidents such as these, a labor strike, and tax troubles, there was still another significant event that brought Peter Thomson's pulp mill project and the railroad construction to a standstill in the fall of 1907. It was called the "Banker's Panic," which took place over a several-week period beginning in mid-October with the collapse of the New York Stock Exchange.

There were numerous runs on banks and trust companies as the panic spread across the nation, causing many banks and businesses to declare bankruptcy. Unfortunately, Thomson was caught off guard like so many others and found himself in an over-extended financial condition when the panic struck.

On November 7, 1907, about half of the construction workers at the Champion Fibre Company's pulp mill in Canton were discharged because of the money stringencies. It was also about this time that all work on the Pigeon River Railway was shut down as another austerity measure.[46] Yandle Brothers did not go back to work until the latter part of 1908, and the railroad was not completed until 1913.

Canton and "Sunburst" Finally Joined

Peter Thomson's surrogate and son-in-law, Reuben B. Robertson, ran things at the new Canton mill from the days of startup in early 1908. By June of that same year, the Champion Fibre Company was shipping eight to ten railcar-loads of pulp daily to Thomson's coated paper mill in Hamilton, Ohio. The demand for pulpwood and inability to harvest the Pigeon River headlands led Robertson to later write "the supplies of pulpwood purchased from independent timber operators and those obtained from scattered company-owned tracts barely sufficed to keep Champion Fibre ahead of the sheriff."[47]

Inadequate funds continued to hinder progress on the Pigeon River

---

45 *Asheville Citizen-Times*, Asheville, N.C. (June 26, 1907)
46 *If Rails Could Talk: Vol. 2, Sunburst and Champion Fibre*, p. 12
47 Carroll C. Jones, *Thomson's Pulp Mill*; 2018

Railway's line to the logging village located at Sunburst (Three Forks). Without the railroad, Sunburst and the valuable timber in the surrounding Pigeon River headlands remained virtually inaccessible. Consequently, Thomson and Robertson availed themselves of a business opportunity that would allow them to contract for a 20-year supply of pulpwood for the Canton Mill.

In early 1911, they allied Champion Fibre Company with the interests of William Whitmer & Sons. This investment logging concern with headquarters in Pennsylvania controlled the new Champion Lumber Company, owner of several vast boundaries of virgin timber in western North Carolina and a huge band sawmill at Crestmont, located in northern Haywood County. Hard as it must have been for them, Thomson and Robertson decided to exchange their ownership of the Pigeon River Railway's graded but "un-ironed" railroad, the 40,000 acres of timberlands surrounding the Pigeon River headwaters, and Sunburst logging village for the guarantee of a pulpwood supply from Champion Lumber Company.

By 1912, Champion Fibre Company had agreed to purchase from Champion Lumber a minimum of one hundred cords of spruce and hemlock per working day at fixed prices set by contract. Champion Fibre also committed to buy at market price all the chestnut cordwood that Champion Lumber could cut, up to one hundred cords per day.[48][49] Although this contract relieved Peter Thomson of his treasured Pigeon River headlands and the unfinished railroad to Sunburst, it significantly eased Reuben B. Robertson's pulpwood supply problems at his father-in-law's pulp mill. With this agreement in place, Robertson could direct his full energies toward the operation of the Champion Fibre Company.

Wasting little time, Champion Lumber Company hired Col. David L. Boyd of Waynesville to supervise the completion of the standard-gauge railway up the Pigeon River from Canton to Sunburst. On March 13, 1912, Boyd announced that work would begin immediately and with favorable weather the road should be completed and trains running in four months. It was his opinion that the regrading and reshaping of the work already completed by Yandle

---

48 *If Rails Could Talk: Vol. 1, Crestmont and Champion Fibre*, pp. 20-37
49 *Asheville Gazette-News*, Asheville, N.C. (April 1, 1911)

Construction would be the most difficult challenge.[50]

One month later, a newspaper reported that more than two hundred "hands" were employed in the work of grading, laying track, and building bridges on the railroad. The estimated completion date was expected to be in August, or sooner.[51] By mid-summer, the citizens of Bethel held a July 4th banquet to celebrate the completion of the railroad to their rural community. A keen observer of the construction work in the Bethel area noted, "The Colonel (Col. Boyd) certainly knows how to grade railroads…He permits no drunkenness among his hands, but goes right along quietly and does the work."[52]

By August of 1912, Col. Boyd completed the railroad to Penland, a point on the West Fork of the Pigeon River approximately three miles below Sunburst. It was at Penland—named for the family who had previously owned this West Fork property for many years—where Champion Lumber Company was in the process of constructing a huge steam-powered sawmill. In October 1912, reports indicated that more than three hundred men were employed at Penland and work was "progressing finely."[53]

Interestingly, within a year's time, Penland became officially known as "Sunburst," and the original Sunburst—or Three Rivers—was tagged with the name "Spruce." Former Champion Fibre Company employees and others still residing at the original Sunburst village failed to appreciate the new name—not one bit. Evidence of their disgust was reflected in the moniker they used when referring to the new Sunburst. They called it the "Bastard Sunburst."

The new Sunburst's double-band sawmill was up and running by early 1913 and a logging village began to quickly sprout up around it. Village residents received electric lighting for free and were able to enjoy telephone and water systems. As one newspaper reported at the time, it was almost as if a "new town had sprung up in a day."[54]

In January 1913, the Pigeon River Railway Company's entire railroad infrastructure linking Canton and Spruce—either constructed or to be constructed—was

---

50 *Asheville Gazette-News*, Asheville, N.C. (March 13, 1912)
51 *Asheville Gazette-News*, Asheville, N.C. (April 16, 1912)
52 *Waynesville Courier*, Waynesville, N.C. (July 5, 1912)
53 *Waynesville Courier*, Waynesville, N.C. (October 4, 1912)
54 *Waynesville Courier*, Waynesville, N.C. (May 9, 1913)

leased to the Tennessee and North Carolina Railroad Company (T&NCRR). Robert F. Whitmer, who was the president of both these railroad companies, as well as the Champion Lumber Company, approved and signed the 30-year indenture in two places—as the lessor and the lessee.

It happened that there was another pea vine railroad operating under the auspices of the T&NCRR in northern Haywood County, near the Tennessee state line. In 1911, at a place called Crestmont, the Champion Lumber Company had purchased another huge band sawmill. Along with the sawmill, the Whitmers had also acquired vast tracts of timberlands and a railroad linking the Crestmont lumber operation with Newport, Tennessee. This railroad company was the T&NCRR, and at Newport its tracks linked up with the Southern Railway, which offered access to lumber markets outside of the Appalachian Mountains.

At the time, Champion Lumber's new logging venture at Sunburst prompted much speculation and reporting about extending the T&NCRR from Crestmont up the Pigeon River to Canton. Supposedly, the extension would serve a two-fold purpose: pulpwood could be conveyed to Champion Fibre's mill and hardwoods could be shipped to the Whitmers' big band sawmills at both Canton (Sunburst) and Crestmont.[55] Although a difficult route was surveyed and grading begun, this railroad was never completed.

The Tennessee and North Carolina Railroad (T&NCRR)

In early 1913, the T&NCRR commenced freight train service from Sunburst to Canton. There were already hundreds of workers and family members calling Sunburst home. They lived in small residences and boarding houses surrounded by a growing village infrastructure which included a hotel, commissary (or company store), barbershop, post office, jailhouse, church, schoolhouse, and railroad depot.

Importantly, the T&NCRR's tracks also linked Champion Lumber Company's operation at Sunburst with the former logging village that was once named Sunburst—now being called Spruce—just a few miles to the south at Three Forks. Beyond there, Champion Lumber was actively grading and

---
55   *The Asheville Times*, Asheville, N.C. (Feb. 21, 1912)

laying rails deep into the wilderness forests surrounding the Pigeon River headwaters, where logging camps were being established.

Once the timber was cut, loaded on rail cars, and delivered to Champion Lumber's sawmill at Sunburst, it was processed into pulpwood and lumber before being hauled a short 12 miles to Canton over the T&NCRR. Of course, the pulpwood—spruce, hemlock, chestnut, and other hardwoods—was delivered to Champion Fibre Company for conversion into pulp and paper. The sawn lumber product was switched to the Southern Railway's tracks and carried to customers across the east coast of the United States.

A February 1913 edition of one local newspaper reported that passenger service, with regular and first-class accommodations, would soon be available on the Canton to Sunburst railroad route. "In addition to lumber and freight trains which are already on the road, the company (T&NCRR) will install a passenger service at an early date, having ordered several locomotives with which to further equip the rolling stock of the road. A large and convenient passenger station will be constructed at the point where the new road connects with the Southern, here (in Canton), and a station will also be built at Bethel."[56]

One month later, the same news outlet credited Mr. W.J. Parks, who was the superintendent of the Pigeon River Division of the T&NCRR, with an announcement that a regular passenger schedule had started and "large numbers of travelers are carried from this place (Canton) to Sunburst every day."[57] For the better part of 1913, only Champion Lumber Company's trains loaded with logs were running between Spruce and Sunburst. However, by November of that year, the T&NCRR had extended their regular passenger service to Spruce.[58]

By accounts available today, it appears the Pigeon River Division of the T&NCRR was fully functional in 1914, providing both daily freight and passenger service between Canton, Sunburst, and Spruce. The promised "large and convenient" passenger stations—or depots—were constructed at West Canton and at a place called Woodrow, located in the Bethel community.

---

56   *Waynesville Courier*, Waynesville, N.C. (Feb. 7, 1913)
57   *Waynesville Courier*, Waynesville, N.C. (March 28, 1913)
58   *Waynesville Courier*, Waynesville, N.C. (Oct. 24, 1913)

Sidings—or sidetracks—were also installed at Retreat, between Woodrow and Sunburst, and at Burnett Siding which was situated between Sunburst and Spruce.

Generally, the trains of the T&NCRR pea vine ran on a regular schedule from Sunburst to Canton every day except on Sundays. Departure from Sunburst was at 7:15 a.m. with arrival at west Canton at 8:30 a.m. On the return trip, trains left west Canton at 10:35 a.m. and arrived back at Sunburst at 11:50 a.m.

For years to come, steam locomotives heading to Canton and pulling cars loaded with passengers, pulpwood, lumber, livestock, apples, and other local crops and products became a common sight and sound in the Pigeon River bottomlands. The train tracks ran awfully close to many modest homes and farms, and often, lucky children waiting and waving at a passing train were treated to candy tossed out of a window or door by T&NCRR employees.

In the latter years, there was even a "jitney bus" placed in service to comfortably accommodate passengers. The bus, which operated under its own power over the rails, was used to transport as many as 24 people between Sunburst and Canton.[59] Tales were told of young boys and girls flagging down the bus in Bethel and riding it to school or to Canton to catch a popular movie, purchase groceries, and such.

During the life of the pea vine railroad, several events occurred that had significant impacts on the train's schedule, service, and tenure. In early 1914, a fire burned down much of the logging village that remained at Spruce. Started by sparks from a steam locomotive, the fire destroyed two boarding houses, a large commissary store, three residential houses, and the office of the Champion Lumber Company.[60]

Newspaper reports a few months after the fire announced that only "six more days remain for the people of Spruce to vacate their homes, and it is expected the Champion Lumber Company will have that town completely erased from the map within a month." Concern for the people living in

---

59   *The Mountaineer* newspaper; "No More Trains on the Pea Vine!"; June 18, 1969

60   *Western Carolina Democrat*, Hendersonville, N.C. (Jan. 29, 1914)

Spruce was downplayed with an assurance those uprooted laborers and their families "will be furnished homes at Sunburst."[61]

Unfortunately, in 1916, the Champion Lumber Company had to declare bankruptcy, and for the next two years the Sunburst sawmill and logging operations continued under the supervision of receivers. A forced sale in 1918 required Champion Lumber to relinquish all its property, assets, and debts to the newly founded Suncrest Lumber Company. This company's name was derived from the two Champion Lumber sawmills it had purchased at Sunburst and Crestmont.

Just two years later, in 1920, a fire ravaged the sawmill at Sunburst and destroyed almost everything above the mill's concrete foundations. The Suncrest Lumber Company used equipment from its abandoned Crestmont sawmill in northern Haywood County to quickly rebuild the Sunburst mill.

Finally, a vast forest fire swept through the high country of the Pigeon River headwaters in 1925 and burned for three weeks. More than 25,000 acres of precious timber and miles of railroad tracks snaking through the high forests were destroyed. It was a catastrophe the Suncrest Lumber Company could not overcome, and all logging and sawmill operations at Sunburst were shut down.

Several months after this inferno, during the winter of 1925-1926, the sawmill equipment at Sunburst was dismantled and hauled to Waynesville, where it was reassembled and placed in operation at the "sawmill bottom" (near today's Waynesville Plaza). In only a couple of years, the once busy Sunburst village became deserted. Its fate, along with that of the Canton-to-Sunburst pea vine railroad, would eventually be determined by a familiar entity—the Champion Fibre Company.

When the Trains Stopped Rolling on the Pea Vine

In 1927, Champion Fibre Company leased the Canton-to-Sunburst railroad from the Pigeon River Railway Company in anticipation of a critical project Reuben B. Robertson was contemplating. The very next year—three

---

61   *Western Carolina Democrat*, Hendersonville, N.C. (April 14, 1914)

years after the logging and sawmill operation at Sunburst had shut down—the paper company purchased the 125-acre Sunburst village tract from Suncrest Lumber Company. This property surrounding the West Fork of the Pigeon River was still connected to Canton by the railroad—the same one formerly operated by T&NCRR and now leased to Champion Fibre.

For several years, Robertson had been concerned about the water supply from the Pigeon River being sufficient to meet the growing demand at his pulp and paper mill in Canton. With the ownership of the Sunburst property, he figured Champion Fibre could now construct a large water reservoir by impounding the West Fork River. During extended dry spells, additional water in the reservoir could then be released into the Pigeon River tributary to support the paper mill's manufacturing processes.

Undoubtedly, Robertson had anticipated the railroad would be invaluable in supporting the construction of a massive dam across the West Fork of the Pigeon River. Not only would it offer a means to haul workmen, equipment, and materials to the construction site, but it could also be used to carry away the excavated soil and rock.

Dam construction work got underway in late 1931 and, as Robertson had foreseen, Champion's trains running along the pea vine from Canton to Sunburst proved extremely useful. By the end of the summer of 1932, a single arch, 56-feet high concrete dam was completed across the West Fork River. Behind the new structure, approximately six-hundred-million gallons of water were impounded, thus ensuring the paper mill's continuous operation for many years to come. And, as a matter of fact, the mill ran without water shortages until it was finally shut down in 2023.

After completion of the water reservoir—named Lake Logan in honor of Peter G. Thomson's son, who was named Logan—there was no longer a reason for Champion Fibre to maintain and operate a railroad from Canton to the Pigeon River headwaters. The company neither owned large reserves of forest land in the vicinity nor was it engaged in large-scale logging operations where the railroad might prove profitable. By this time, in the 1930s, better motor roads and trucks allowed smaller scale, independent logging operators to transport pulpwood from the nearby forests to the Canton mill.

So it was, after construction of the Lake Logan water reservoir, Champion Fibre Company terminated its railroad lease from the Pigeon River Railway Company. Soon after, in about 1933, the railroad's tracks were removed, and the trains no longer rolled on the old Canton-to-Sunburst pea vine railroad.

Today, it is still possible to drive along the greater part of the former pea vine railroad's route from Canton to Sunburst—Sunburst being the site of Champion Fibre Company's early 1900's logging village and where the Pisgah National Forest's Sunburst Campground is currently located. The current North Carolina Hwy 215 generally follows the old train tracks for much of the 15-mile, or so, trip.

While motoring along this scenic highway through southern Haywood County's beautiful countryside, you will soon understand why this route might be likened to a twisted pea vine.

The original Sunburst logging village is shown here in about 1910, located at Three Forks and astraddle the Right Hand and Middle Prong streams. (courtesy of Canton Historical Museum)

Yandle Brothers' workmen shown in this photo appear to be taking a water break during construction of the Pigeon River Railroad. The sledgehammers and hand drills they were holding probably meant yet another dynamite blast was imminent. The young water boy's bare feet must have been as tough as these men. (courtesy of Gerald Ledford)

The second (or "bastard") Sunburst logging village is pictured here looking downstream, circa early 1920s. Residences, commissary, and a hotel are on the left and the large sawmill and lumber yard can be seen beyond the log pond. (courtesy of Canton Historical Museum)

The T&NCRR's #4 American-style locomotive (4-4-0) with two passenger cars is shown stopped at what appears to be the Woodrow station. (courtesy of Gerald Ledford)

The T&NCRR's #5 Lima locomotive (2-6-2) is shown stopped and waiting on passengers at what appears to be the Sunburst station. (courtesy of Gerald Ledford)

This photo taken in the 1940s shows the once "large and convenient" West Canton passenger station. (courtesy of Gerald Ledford)

The old Sunburst train station is shown here perched at Lake Logan's edge, circa 1939. It was just a few years after the West Fork of the Pigeon River waters were impounded to form the lake. (courtesy of Gerald Ledford)

An Illuminating Panorama of Three Forks (Sunburst)

Introduction

A few months after a devastating Pigeon River flood in 2021, some friends of the Canton Area Historical Museum gathered at the flood-ravaged building to study a couple of photographs that had been donated to the museum. One of these was obviously an early panoramic view of the Sunburst logging village that once thrived where the waters of Lake Logan are now impounded. However, the other photo required a bit more thought and analysis to finally conclude whence it was taken.

Measuring 29-1/2 inches wide by 6 inches tall, this panoramic photo offers a wide sweeping vista with mountains in the background, an expansive tent encampment on one side, railroad infrastructure in the center, and a village of some sort on the opposite side. We friends of the museum quickly worked out that it was not another photo of the Sunburst logging village.

The juncture of three mountain streams, railroad tracks running everywhere, and the small village with a building adorned with an impressive belfry were clues that soon helped bring things into better focus. We concluded it had to be the region known as Three Forks in the late 19th century—where the Middle Prong, Right Hand Prong, and Left Hand Prong tributaries join together to form the West Fork of the Pigeon River. Today, this same Three Forks area is home to Pisgah National Forest's Sunburst Campground.

One hundred years ago, the site of the modern Sunburst campground hosted a junction of iron railroad tracks fanning out into the virgin forests brimming with timber treasures. The panoramic imagery we were so fortunate to find presents an intriguing glimpse into yesteryear, providing much insight into the logging infrastructure that once existed at Three Forks.

This is an early panoramic photo of Three Forks, where the Right Hand, Middle, and Left Hand Prong tributaries join to form the West Fork of the Pigeon River. (courtesy of Canton Historical Museum)

And that is not all. Those who read on will be presented with many other revelations this amazing photograph offers and will surely learn what in the world that old "tent encampment" was all about.

Extracted from the panoramic photo, this zoom view of Spruce (original Sunburst) shows how the village looked after the fire of 1914 burned down several of its buildings. The schoolhouse/church building still stands out very prominently, boasting its wonderful belfry.

Original Sunburst or Spruce *(right-hand side of the panoramic photo)*

As can be seen on the right-hand side of the Three Forks panoramic photo, there is significant evidence of a settlement on the banks of the Middle Prong and Right Hand Prong tributaries of the Pigeon River. Peter Thomson, founder of the Champion Fibre Company, built this little village in the very early 1900s to supply pulpwood to his new pulp mill in Canton, North Carolina. It is reputed that Thomson named the village "Sunburst" for the way the morning sun burst over the eastern ridges.

However, other sources credit the name to Eli Potter who designed several of the large buildings in the village, including a two-story schoolhouse/church with a wonderful belfry. Apparently, the gables of one or more of Potter's structures were sculpted in a striking fashion that resembled a bright sunrise, thus inspiring the name "Sunburst."

The Champion Fibre Company was never able to take advantage of its Sunburst logging village and 40,000 acres of timberlands surrounding the Pigeon River headwaters. Several factors including a "banker's panic," poor roads, and inadequate funds to complete the construction of a railroad to Sunburst caused Champion to take a drastic measure.

In 1911, the Champion Fibre Company agreed to exchange ownership of the Pigeon River Railway with its graded but "un-ironed" railroad, 40,000 acres of timberlands, and the Three Forks logging village known as Sunburst for the guarantee of a pulpwood supply. They reached this agreement with William Whitmer & Sons who controlled the Champion Lumber Company, owner of several vast boundaries of virgin timber in western North Carolina and a huge band sawmill at Crestmont, located in northern Haywood County.

Champion Lumber Company completed construction of the railroad from Canton to Sunburst and a new double-band sawmill at Penland in 1913. Penland, named for the family who had owned the land for years, was located some three miles downstream of Sunburst on the West Fork of the Pigeon River. Interestingly, within a year's time, the new sawmill village at Penland became known as "Sunburst."

The original Sunburst village at Three Forks was tagged with the name "Spruce." Former Champion Fibre Company employees and others still residing at the original Sunburst failed to appreciate the new name. Evidence of their disgust was reflected in the moniker they used when referring to the new Sunburst. They called it "Bastard Sunburst."

Although imperceptible to most eyes examining the panoramic photograph, the former logging village was on its last legs at the time the photo was made. The impressive schoolhouse/church building had served as a venue for Dr. Carl Schenck's Biltmore Forest School from 1910 through 1913. At the end of the last school year in 1913, the Biltmore Forest School closed its doors when Dr. Schenck returned to Germany to fulfill his military obligations.

Less than a year later, in early 1914, a fire burned down much of the village that had remained at Spruce. Started by sparks from a steam locomotive, it destroyed two boarding houses, a large commissary store, three residential houses, and the office of the Champion Lumber Company.[62]

Newspaper reports a few months after the fire announced that only "six more days remain for the people of Spruce to vacate their homes, and it is expected the Champion Lumber Company will have that town completely erased from the map within a month." Concern for the people living in Spruce was downplayed with an assurance those uprooted workmen and their families "will be furnished homes at Sunburst."[63]

---

62 *Western Carolina Democrat*, Hendersonville, N.C. (Jan. 29, 1914)
63 *Western Carolina Democrat*, Hendersonville, N.C. (April 14, 1914)

As will be disclosed later, this panoramic photo was taken a few years after the 1914 fire. Readers will note that several houses remained occupied with laundry drying on outside clotheslines, and Eli Potter's two-story schoolhouse/church building is still standing. It appears that the village of Spruce had survived the fire and the threatened "erasure" by the Champion Lumber Company.

The railroad infrastructure shown in this zoom view from the panoramic photo is located at the juncture of the Middle Prong and Left Hand Prong streams, where they combine to form the West Fork of the Pigeon River. The depot and junction of railroad tracks are on the site of today's Sunburst Campground.

Railroads *(center of the panoramic photo)*

The Pigeon River Railway Company's entire railroad infrastructure linking Canton and Spruce—either constructed or to be constructed—was leased to the Tennessee and North Carolina Railroad Company (T&NCRR) in 1913. Robert F. Whitmer, who was the president of both these railroad companies at the time, signed the 30-year indenture in two places—as the lessor and the lessee.

From the accounts available today, it appears the T&NCRR was fully functional in 1914, providing both daily freight and passenger service between Canton, Sunburst, and Spruce (the original Sunburst). In the center of the panoramic photo several railroad tracks, loaded and unloaded rail cars, logging equipment, the T&NCRR's Spruce depot, storage sheds, and employee houses can be recognized in the precise location of today's Sunburst Campground.

This junction of three rivers and railroad tracks was a hive of activity during those early logging days. The T&NCRR's main line followed the West Fork of the Pigeon River from the Sunburst logging village (three miles downstream and beyond the left side of the panoramic photo) to Spruce's depot shown in this zoom view of the photo. From there the Champion Lumber Company's rails reached into the vast timber forests of the Pigeon River headwaters.

As can be seen, one set of Champion Lumber's logging tracks makes a gentle curve across the mouth of the Middle Prong stream and heads up a gap in the mountains, hugging the Left Hand Prong (or West Fork) of the Pigeon River as it climbs forever toward Beech Gap. Another logging railroad branches from the main line and gradually bends around a low grassy hill into the village of Spruce. From there the railroad splits, with one set of tracks running up the Right Hand Prong (off of this zoom view to the right) and the other tracks following the Middle Prong.

Today, there is little remaining evidence of the village of Spruce. The entire site where houses and the schoolhouse/church building are pictured has been shrouded by the Pisgah National Forest's heavy wilderness growth. Nevertheless, the old railroad grades leading up the Right Hand Prong and Middle Prong streams offer today's adventurers wonderful opportunities to access the beautiful forests where they can trout fish, hunt, hike, explore, and experience nature's beauty at its best.

Before moving on, there is something else that might interest readers. Direct your attention to that low grassy hill behind the railroad infrastructure where the Sunburst Campground is situated today. At the time the photo was taken, the hill was obviously used as pastureland, whereas today it is covered with a dense stand of timber.

On this hilltop, in the right foreground of the photo, you will note some ground disturbance with exposed soil and several small wooden-fence enclosures. This scene just happens to be located at the same spot where an old cemetery is hidden away today, along with a few remaining gravestones dating back to this same period.

The forest has very effectively obscured the cemetery over the past century, yet determined sleuths can still discover the old gravestones that remain in the area depicted in the photograph. It is likely the photo has preserved an early view of some fresh gravesites linked to the influenza epidemic raging through the country at the time the photo was made. The small wooden fence enclosures would have protected the graves from the grazing livestock that kept the hillsides so clean.

Shown in this zoom view from the panoramic photo is the U.S. Army's tent encampment on the West Fork of the Pigeon River.

During World War I, the U.S. Army set up this tent encampment next to the West Fork of the Pigeon River. (courtesy of Canton Historical Museum)

The Tent Encampment *(left side of the panoramic photo)*

Tucked close to the left border of the panoramic photograph, between the railroad tracks of the T&NCRR and the West Fork of the Pigeon River, an encampment of approximately 40 canvas tents can barely be discerned. With little doubt, this camp can be associated with the United States Army's venture to Spruce during World War I.

In early May of 1918, a local newspaper printed the following report to give Haywood County citizens a heads-up about what was happening at Spruce—or Three Forks:

"Five cars loaded with about 200 army engineers arrived at Canton...and were carried to Sunburst (actually Spruce), where they will extend the T&NCRR railroad a few miles into the forests so the Champion Lumber Co. can secure quickly quantities of balsam and spruce timber which is needed by the government to be used in making aeroplanes."[64]

The United States had, at this time, joined the allied forces in Europe who were at war with Germany. We know that World War I ended in late 1918, so it is believed the army troops' mission to build logging railroads at Three Forks lasted only a few months. In consideration of that fact along with the obvious abundance of leaves on the deciduous trees and wildflowers pictured in the lower right corner, this wonderful and informative panoramic photograph was likely taken in the summer of 1918.

At the same time the U.S. Army was encamped at Three Forks, the Champion Lumber Company, which had declared bankruptcy and was forced into receivership two years earlier, sold their Sunburst property to the Suncrest Lumber Company. Suncrest would operate the Sunburst sawmill and log the 40,000 acres of timberland until a vast forest fire swept through the high country of the Pigeon River headwaters in 1925. More than 25,000 acres of precious timber and miles of railroads snaking through the high forests were destroyed by the inferno.

It was a catastrophe the Suncrest Lumber Company could not overcome, and all logging and sawmill operations at Sunburst were shut down. In 1928, Champion Fibre Company purchased a 125-acre tract of land where the Sunburst logging village had been located. The pulp manufacturing company impounded the waters of the West Fork at Sunburst in the early 1930s, forming today's beautiful Lake Logan which served as a water reservoir for the Canton paper mill's operations until the mill's closure in 2023. Suncrest Lumber's 40,000 acres of mountain timberlands at the Pigeon River headwaters were also sold, and this property eventually became national forest land.

---

64 *The Carolina Mountaineer and Waynesville Courier,* Waynesville, N.C. (May 2, 1918).

Conclusion

The author has spent a considerable amount of time in the Three Forks area over the years. Whatever the sport or diversion, whether it be flyfishing the upper reaches of the Middle Prong, hiking up the Right Hand Prong to Double Spring Gap, searching for and finding the sites of logging camps and old funicular railroads, tracing miles of historical railroad grades and discovering century-old artifacts, locating the site of Dr. Carl Schenck's home, and much more, this region has been a source of considerable enjoyment and learning through the years.

Imagine my feelings when presented with this old panoramic photograph of the Three Forks area. Suddenly, uncertainties such as how the railroads were laid out, the location of the T&NCRR depot, and whether Champion Lumber Company actually erased Spruce from the map in 1914 were clarified simply by studying the photo.

Not only that, but this old photo offered a few surprises as well. It reminded us of the U.S. Army's mission at Three Forks during World War I and actually revealed the exact location of their tent encampment. And for those who have trekked up the steep forested hill behind the Sunburst Campground in search of the old cemetery, we could not have been more surprised to see the image of fenced graves on top of that grassy knoll.

It is my hope that the wonderful panoramic photograph of Three Forks will be an inspiration for everyone. Let us guard and use this valuable glimpse back in time to ensure future generations will understand how Three Forks looked in 1918 and the role this area played in consequential industrial, cultural, and even military matters.

Note: For those interested in learning more about the old railroad that once joined Canton with Sunburst and Spruce, the author's story of *The Canton-to-Sunburst Pea Vine Railroad* offers an important history of that winding iron road.

Ghosts of An Old Funicular Railroad

Introduction

Haywood County's Middle Prong Wilderness is a favorite venue for fly-fishing and hiking. Native speckled trout abound in its namesake stream, the Middle Prong of the Pigeon River, whose pristine waters tumble out of the mountains bordering the Blue Ridge Parkway. A primitive hiking trail runs alongside the rumbling watercourse, while other paths wind through the Wilderness Area's dense mountain forests. Interestingly, several miles of these rough trails are routed on top of century-old logging railroad beds.

Believe it or not, there was once a *funicular* railroad operating amidst the Middle Prong's wilderness. It is likely many readers are not familiar with this unique type of rail transportation system—funicular. So, herein lies the story of a funicular railroad and how it was used to harvest timber along the steep slopes above the Middle Prong of the Pigeon River.

All aboard!

A Demand for Timber Products

In the early 20th century, loggers and railroad builders invaded southern Haywood County in quest of the timber growing across the mountainsides. They built twisting ribbons of steel tracks to reach stands of chestnut, oak, poplar, cherry, and hemlock trees covering the lower slopes and dark bands of spruce and fir trees shrouding the mountain crests.

An industrialist named Peter G. Thomson established the Champion Fibre Company operation in Canton, North Carolina, to take advantage of the region's enormous timber resources. By 1908, his mill was converting huge amounts of wood into dried pulp. This pulp was then shipped by train to Hamilton, Ohio, where it was used in another Thomson mill to produce coated-paper products.[65]

To satisfy Champion's demand for pulpwood and the country's immense requirements for timber products, a large lumber company began harvesting the timber treasures on both sides of the Middle Prong stream. In about 1912, they began the difficult job of grading and laying rails up the watercourse to its highest reaches. Special geared steam locomotives were used on these steep, standard-gauge railroad tracks to penetrate the wilderness and haul out rail cars loaded with enormous saw logs and pulpwood.

The lumber company's sawmill was located just a few miles downstream at a place named Sunburst. There, the valuable timber was processed and then shipped by train to nearby Canton. Every stick of pulpwood was consumed by Champion Fibre Company's mammoth pulp factory, and the sawn timber products were transported over the Southern Railway's lines to customers within and outside of the mountains.

Extracting the Timber

On either side of the railroad bed running beside the Middle Prong stream were steep sloping forests rising thousands of feet to the high ridgetops—Fork Ridge on the east and Lickstone Ridge on the west. The loggers employed several methods to access and "get out" the timber at the higher elevations where the railroads could not reach. Sliding, or "ballhooting," the logs down the sheer slopes and hauling them by oxen teams down skid paths were practical ways the timber was moved within range of the railroad's loading equipment.

Another more sophisticated method entailed conveying logs suspended from an aerial cable to the railroad. The heavy cable was stretched from a towering tail tree located on a ridgetop down to the vertical steel spar of a railroad skidder, sometimes as much as a mile apart. Logs were then attached to a "skidder" carriage that traveled back and forth along the aerial line, aided by gravity and pulled by cables connected to a hoisting machine.

---

65 More information regarding Canton's original pulp mill can be found in *Thomson's Pulp Mill: Building the Champion Fibre Company at Canton, North Carolina — 1905 to 1908,* a book by Carroll C. Jones

Yet, there was still another method used in the Middle Prong forest to lower logs down a precipitous mountainside. It involved laying a set of railroad tracks straight up a steep slope for more than half-a-mile to reach the timber. Known as an incline railroad, traces of one of those rare logging infrastructures can still be found to this day.

The Middle Prong's Funicular Railroad

Approximately four miles above its confluence with the West Fork of the Pigeon River, the Middle Prong stream receives the waters of a much smaller tributary, Buckeye Creek. It was just below this convergence where a railroad surveyor by the name of Ted Rorison was faced with a design dilemma. He had to figure out the best way to access the valuable evergreen timber stands on the upper reaches of Fork Ridge.[66]

Rorison planned on having a high rail line to run along the ridge at a contour elevation of roughly 5,400 feet. That was more than a thousand feet above the main line of the railroad running alongside of the Middle Prong stream. Apparently, in consideration of the geography, construction difficulties, and costs, Rorison ruled out joining the high line and the main line with a series of railroad track switchbacks. That was the normal design practice, which enabled geared logging locomotives tugging or pushing trains of rail cars to reach the higher elevations over workable grades of up to seven percent.

Instead, Mr. Rorison chose to build an incline railroad straight up the steep mountainside to connect the main line and the high line. His idea being that the rail-car loads of logs harvested across Fork Ridge's elevated slopes could be lowered down the incline tracks utilizing a steam-powered hoisting system. This construction work could be done quicker and at a fraction of the cost of building a much longer railroad with multiple switchbacks to accommodate the geared locomotives.

The incline railroad was eventually completed in about 1914 to connect the main rail line along the Middle Prong stream to the upper tracks on Fork Ridge. It was approximately 3,000 feet long and climbed 670 vertical

---

66 Larry W. Mull, *Sunburst Story*

feet to a relatively flat knoll just below the 5,000-feet elevation range. The average grade of the incline was around 22 percent, with the steepest section being almost twice that. Clearly, the incline was too steep for the puffing locomotives to use, but it was well within the capabilities of a *funicular* railroad.

Funicular meant a simultaneous and counter-balanced railroad operation that utilized gravity, a heavy steel cable, and the heavy weight of descending loaded cars to help pull the ascending cars up the mountain. This was made possible by a set of "passing tracks" located midway up the incline. The descending and ascending cars simply passed each other at the section of double passing tracks. The ascending car's weight also helped keep the speed of the descending car from going out of control. Since both railcars were attached by the same continuous cable to a steam hoist and brake—or incline machine, its steam engine had to only provide enough force to handle the difference in weight between the ascending and descending cars and the friction forces involved.[67]

Just as soon as the incline tracks were laid, the railroad builders went to work lugging the heavy incline machine to the top of the tracks. Taking a very clever approach to the job, they temporarily mounted the boiler, steam engine, and hoisting equipment onto a logging flat car and rigged the haul cable up the incline and back to the machine. Then, the steam incline machine was fired up and allowed to pull itself up the slope to the top of the tracks, where it was soon placed into operation.

Today, rusting anchor bolts protruding from crumbling concrete and stone walls bear evidence of the substantial foundation that held the incline machine in place. Additionally, the machine was reportedly anchored to "dead man" trees in all directions.[68] Certainly, it had to be adequately secured to resist the extreme forces that were involved in the funicular railroad operation.

Once the incline machine was up and running, the loggers and railroad construction crews began building the necessary infrastructure to support

---

67   William H. Gibbons, *Logging in the Douglas Fir Region*
68   Larry W. Mull, *Sunburst Story*

their logging activities. This included constructing the Fork Ridge high line itself, totaling three and a half miles of trackage when finally completed in 1919.[69] Locomotive engines, rail cars, steel rails, timber ties, log loaders, lumber, and other tools and equipment were hoisted up the incline to support the construction and timber-harvesting work. Of course, a busy logging camp quickly grew up at the top of the incline railroad where yarding tracks, workers' quarters, a food kitchen, coal storage, water tanks, storage sheds, and other support facilities and supplies were located.

The Middle Prong incline railroad operated from about 1914 into the 1920s. In 1925, a ravaging forest fire burned 25,000 acres of timberland at the heads of the East and West Forks of the Pigeon River. Included in this vast scalded territory were the remaining hardwood and evergreen timber stands straddling Fork Ridge's high line railroad. It was indeed a catastrophic inferno, resulting in the closure of the lumber company's sawmill at Sunburst and the shutdown of its woods operations. The band mill and its steam plant were disassembled and relocated to nearby Waynesville, and all the steel trackage was taken up and hauled away, including the tracks of the Middle Prong funicular railroad.

Funicular Railroad Ghosts

More than a hundred years have passed since loggers clear-cut the mountain slopes on both sides of the Middle Prong of the Pigeon River. Those lands are now included in one of our nation's designated wilderness areas, which is named for the beautiful stream that flows through it. Over the past century, the Middle Prong Wilderness Area's forests have grown over the scars left by the logging operations, very effectively concealing evidence of the old incline railroad which once operated there. However, close study of historic photos and maps, along with hiking treks and dedicated searching have revealed the exact location and remains of the funicular operation.

The site can be reached by wilderness hiking trails from both Buckeye Gap and Haywood Gap off the Blue Ridge Parkway. Another trail originating

---

[69] Ronald C. Sullivan and Gerald Ledford, *If Rails Could Talk...Volume 2: Sunburst and Champion Fibre*

from Hwy 215 near the Sunburst Campground meanders up a Forest Service road beside the Middle Prong stream and then along the Haywood Gap Trail to reach the incline location.

At the upper end of the funicular railroad site, which is located on a beautiful, forested knoll, one cannot help but stumble upon the ruins of the old incline machine foundation. It is located near the Buckeye Gap Trail and can easily be seen and recognized as a man-made structure. Several large steel anchor bolts still protrude from the deteriorating concrete and stone walls, which once held the powerful steam engine and hoisting equipment in place. Upon discovering it, the hiking sleuth will realize the top of the incline railroad has been reached.

Those persons genuinely interested in this old funicular railroad may want to explore further. If that is the case, then take the plunge and strike off down the steep incline path toward the waters of the Middle Prong. Undoubtedly, rusting artifacts associated with the railroad operation will be discovered among the dense undergrowth, fallen trees, and lush forest now covering the steep path.

In places, it will take keen observation and an imaginative mind to detect the linear parallel embankments—or cuts—defining the sides of the incline. Both intact and partial steel rollers can be found along the sides of the incline path. These old pieces of equipment were once mounted between the steel tracks so that the haul cable attached to the rail cars could ride over the tops of the rollers, instead of dragging across the wood ties and along the ground. The utility of the rollers can clearly be detected, as some have been cut in two by the haul cable and others have deep wear marks. What better evidence can there be of the heavy weight of the suspended logging cars and the tremendous pressures exerted against the rollers by the haul cable.

There are other artifacts scattered across the site, including parts and pieces of rail cars, a steel rail, sections of steam and water piping, and even a metal bed frame. Surely, more items await discovery by diligent, yet respectful, explorers interested in history and anxious to uncover more ghosts from the Middle Prong's old funicular railroad operation.

Note to Readers: My personal interest in the intriguing story of the Middle Prong Wilderness Area's funicular railroad stems from reading a book by Ronald Sullivan and Gerald Ledford titled *If Rails Could Talk... Logging in the North Carolina Great Balsams: Vol. 2, Sunburst and Champion Fibre*. That excellent read along with an old hand-drawn map by Mack Ledbetter laying out most of the railroads associated with the Sunburst logging activities during the early 20th century inspired me to venture into the dark Middle Prong forest and re-discover the remains of an old funicular railroad.

These men are using teams of oxen to haul large logs down mountain skid paths to reach the logging railroads. (courtesy of Canton Historical Museum)

An early photo of the Middle Prong funicular railroad shows how the tracks were installed straight up the mountain slope. Note the passing tracks that allowed for a counter-balanced operation, with one car ascending the tracks while another descended at the same time. This photo was taken not long after the incline tracks were installed and just as the steam-powered incline machine (at left) was being prepared to hoist itself up the tracks to the top of the incline. (courtesy of Gerald Ledford)

The logging camp (camp #3) at the top of the Middle Prong funicular railroad is shown in this photo. Apparently, the photographer had drawn the attention of the cooks in long white aprons who appear to be posing for the shot. A locomotive and an American loader are idling in the yard along with a few empty skeleton cars. Beyond the trees in the background, the terrain and the incline railroad slope dramatically downward toward the Middle Prong stream. (courtesy of Gerald Ledford)

This is a modern view of the Middle Prong funicular railroad site, looking up the slope from a spot near the Middle Prong stream. As can be seen, the forest has completely grown over the old incline path and the erosive forces of rainwater runoff are gradually carving away at the railroad bed. (author's collection)

Artifacts such as the one in this photo can be found scattered across the funicular railroad site. Railroad historian Gerald Ledford identified this one as being a broken part from a railroad log car that was likely involved in a wreck. (author's collection)

This photo shows one of the many steel rollers that were installed between the tracks of the incline railroad. The haul cable attached to the rail cars rode across the top of these rollers, instead of being drug across the wood ties and along the ground. As can be seen, this roller was practically cut in two by the haul cable. (author's collection)

Next to the Buckeye Gap Trail, hikers can easily spot this crumbling foundation. Large steel bolts protruding from the deteriorating concrete and stone walls once anchored the steam boiler and engine, as well as the hoisting equipment that powered the funicular railroad. (author's collection)

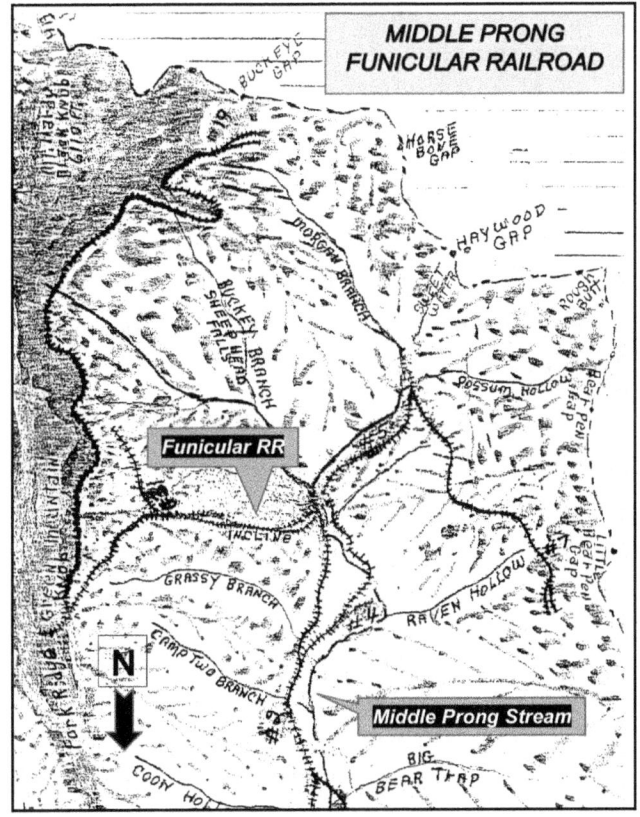

This illustration is a cropped section from Mack Ledbetter's hand-drawn map of the Sunburst logging railroads in the early 20th century. The funicular (incline) railroad is shown connecting the main line alongside the Middle Prong stream and the high line running along Fork Ridge. The shaded area on the left depicts a portion of the great swaths of timberland that were destroyed by the 1925 forest fire.

My Middle Prong Passion

Introduction

I have fly fished the high Middle Prong waters many times over the years. This beautiful boulder-strewn tributary that tumbles out of a western North Carolina mountain wilderness into Haywood County's West Fork of the Pigeon River never disappoints. Even when the wild speckled trout show no interest in my dry fly presentations, I still get a thrill out of climbing and scaling boulders and fishing one plunge pool after another. This day would be no exception.

However, a fisherman must first reach this far-away trout wonderland before wetting his or her fly, and it is quite a challenge to do so—especially for one who is well past his 70th year on this earth. Starting at the Sunburst Campground gate that blocks all vehicles from entering the U.S. Forest Service Road 97, it is a good two-mile hike along the steep gravel road before gaining the Haywood Gap trailhead—or the old logging railroad grade—that leads farther into the forest recesses. Then, it is still another mile, or so, of trudging along the old railroad grade to reach the high Middle Prong waters. From there, I normally fish up the mountain stream for three to five hours before finally crawling out and regaining the trail down the old railroad grade. It will take another hard hour or so of tramping back down the mountain to reach my truck. That is the usual regimen, and truthfully, it is becoming quite a physical challenge for me.

While lacing up the stiff, felt-soled wading boots, I could not help but wonder how many more of these Middle Prong fly-fishing trips might be left in me. *Hopefully a few more*, I thought while shouldering my sling pack, grabbing the fly rod, and beginning the trudge up the gravel road.

Hiking Up the Mountain

A July morning sun paired with the grueling climb up the forest service road had me drenched with sweat in little time. With each deep gasping breath, I could almost taste the strong aromas of the forest: mountain laurels still blooming in places where the sun never shines; a lush green undergrowth emblazoned with myriad flowering plants boasting white, yellow, and even lavender colors; and the sharp smell of moist organic soil blended with occasional whiffs of—uh—horse manure.

That winding route up the mountain is also popular with horseback riders, so smelly piles of dung must be sidestepped every now and then. Speaking of "smelly," I guess it is best to divulge an innate feeling I have been cursed with—I hate snakes! Believe it or not, the earthy horse manure smells remind me of snakes, causing my heart to beat a little quicker. The reason being, I have heard that people can often smell a snake before they see one, and this old myth, whether true or not, has forever been stuck in my head. The faintest pungent whiff along the trail usually sparks my built-in radar to begin scanning about for slithering, crawling creatures. As it would turn out on this hot day, my trusty radar was disengaged when I needed it the most.

But we will get to that later. Thirty minutes of hard uphill hiking behind me, I finally reached a switchback where the forest service road turned away from the old railroad grade and headed off in an opposite direction from the Middle Prong stream. At this point, I plodded off the graveled surface onto the Haywood Gap Trail and continued along the old logging path that disappeared into the dense woods. The steady grade was easy enough, but the trail was grown over, and years of erosion and neglect sometimes made walking difficult. As the lure of catching those pretty speckled trout pulled me deeper and deeper into the dark natural environs, I could not help but marvel at my surroundings.

Here I was, all alone and at one with nature, and no one around to disturb or bother me. Alas, these blissful thoughts soon became tainted with guilt and memories of my wife's wise counsel and admonitions: "You shouldn't go up on the Middle Prong alone, Carroll! What if you get hurt up there all by yourself?"

My dear Maria is right, you know. But my fishing buddy, who lives in Florida, is coming up to join me in September for another excursion up the Middle Prong. So, you could say that this little July outing is simply a scouting trip to check things out. Now, see how easy it is to come up with some ridiculous justification for a fool's solo venture into the wilderness. That is what I would tell her—it was a scouting trip. She'll understand. Well, I knew better than that, but it was a reasonable discussion point and a good enough excuse to keep on going.

At several points along the upward grade, I could see where very old metal drainpipes still carried seeping and running creek water underneath the former railroad bed. More than a century old now, these rusting pipes have miraculously survived and continue to provide an essential utility. Everywhere along the grade I saw evidence of the constructors' labors building a railroad to carry equipment, supplies, and men into the deepest reaches of the Middle Prong wilderness and to haul huge logs out. Trekking through deep cuts where earthen embankments and sheer rock faces remain to this day, I imagined the hardy men wielding hand-digging tools or even hammer-drills and blasting the rock away. Those drilling scars are still visible in the rock if one looks close enough. Also, scarce rotting timbers that once supported endless ribbons of steel can sometimes be discovered in the old railroad bed. It was over these timbers—or railroad ties—and steel rails that steam locomotives and rail cars once ran.

It is so easy for me to get carried back in time with such notions and dreams—but not today. Today, there were more important "fish to fry," so to speak. Actually, there were native speckled trout to catch, so I was eventually able to make the long hike over the historic logging road without undue delay and at last gaze out upon the clear, cold waters of the Middle Prong.

Just downstream, a series of high falls very effectively blocked the movement of brown and rainbow trout into this pristine habitat. From where I stood and all the way up to the highest trickling headwater creeks another species known as native brook trout abounded. It was these "brookies" that I was after, although I prefer to call them speckled trout because of their bright orange or red spots.

Flyfishing for Native Speckled Trout

Right there in front of me was a sizable pool flowing from beneath an impressive cascading waterfall, and I suspected it was teeming with speckled trout. While smearing flotant all over my favorite dry fly—a Female Parachute Adams—I became convinced it was the perfect dry fly pattern to lure those wily trout onto my hook. Not only was it easy for me to see because of the white "parachute," but it is the same mayfly pattern that I had always used successfully during the summertime on the high Middle Prong.

With well-practiced movements of my fly rod, I cast the Adams out toward the middle of the pool and watched it land lightly upon the water's surface. In scant seconds a hungry trout swam up, took a look, and then darted away into the watery abyss. Of all things, *that fish had just shunned my Female Adams*, I thought. Instantly, a sinking feeling came across me. *Maybe the Female Adams is not the perfect fly to use today. That fish would not take it. What if...* BAM!

I got a strike just as I was thinking I might have to resort to another fly pattern. It was an aggressive strike and, thank goodness, I was not completely asleep. Admittedly, my reaction was not as quick as normal, a fraction of a second late, but when I flicked the rod tip up, I could feel it. I felt the fly hook set in the fish's mouth. I had him! In just one minute of fishing, I already had one. *This Middle Prong fishing is great*, I told myself while pulling the slack out of the fly line with my left hand and hoisting the rod high in the air with my right. The trout tugged hard against the taut line, swam one way and another, and dove deep down into the water in mighty efforts to spit out this awful meal. But after 20 or 30 seconds of trying unsuccessfully to rid itself of the tasteless fly, the exhausted fish finally gave up and I reeled it in.

Straining my eyes at the breaking water to see how big it was, I was literally shocked at what I saw. It was not a single speckled trout. Why, of all things, I had caught two of them—two fish on one fly! Cradling them both as carefully as possible, I could see that each one was about six inches long and as richly blushed as speckled trout can be. In fact, their bellies and flanks were so red that it was hard to distinguish the usual reddish spotting. But two fish—*how in the world had I caught two fish on one fly at the same time?* In my many years of dry-fly fishing, this was the first instance of such a thing.

Well, it did not take long to figure out what had happened. Upon examination, I discovered that one trout had been caught legitimately while it tried to gobble down the Female Adams, as evidenced by the hook still firmly set in its mouth. But the same was not so with the other unfortunate fish. It appeared that the leader had somehow gotten entangled in its lip so severely that it could not extricate itself—of all things! Upon being set free, both trout swam off to the nearest, darkest cavity, certainly blessed with a second chance and seized with an aversion for those Female Adams flies.

In the farthest reaches of this same large pool, I caught a couple more about the same size as the first ones before moving upstream to the next rapids and pools. For more than three hours, I excitedly fished one swift run and pool after another, almost always getting a strike and often managing to snare yet another native speckled trout. Climbing over moss-covered rocks and scaling boulder after boulder, fishing pools and rapids while watching my fly chase down one pretty run after another—yes, this was the life. It is what I often dream about at night. It is my Middle Prong passion.

All afternoon long I pursued this passion up the plunging waters of the high Middle Prong, catching so many trout that I tired of the process which entailed first wetting my hand, then grasping and unhooking and releasing the fish, and, lastly, cleaning the fly. It simply amazes me to catch a "spec" in a small pool, then drop my fly in adjacent waters not six feet away and catch another one! There were a couple of times that I held my rod over my head and reached across a high boulder to snag a fish in a pool of water that was nearly level with my eyes. Tired I certainly became, but bored I was not.

In the hottest part of the afternoon, I had fished up to an area where the stream bed stretched out wider, and the ground bordering the water was relatively expansive and flat. In fact, this was once the site of an old logging camp back in the early 1900s. The loggers camped in tents and shacks bordering the railroad track and from here they spread out and methodically stripped the mountainsides of its virgin forest. It is extremely hard for me to fathom the loggers' destruction today, while standing amidst the beauty and grandeur of the present wilderness setting.

Just When I Needed that Radar

The sun was beaming down hot and bright where the forest canopy did not extend over this widest section of the river. I'm not sure if I was fixated on the heat, figuring where to cast my fly next, deciding which rock to step on, or dreaming about steam engines pulling railcars loaded with spruce logs down the river. Whatever I was thinking at that exact moment and place, I should have been paying more attention to something else. I should have been sniffing with my radar fully engaged. For it was exactly at that time, as I was working up the side of the stream and preparing to flip my fly in just the right place, that I heard the most alarming and frightening sound there can ever be—a rattlesnake's rattlers singing to high heaven!

Instantly, I fell or jumped backwards as awkwardly as humanly possible, while at the same time trying not to break my neck or my fly rod. I knew at once what was making those sounds, although it was the first time I had heard a rattlesnake rattling in the wild. My heart must have stopped for a millisecond or two before beginning to pound furiously again and pump blood and adrenalin through my body. *Where—where is it? Is it moving toward me? How many?*

Those were my instinctive thoughts as I tried desperately to regain my balance and began anxiously looking around to find the snake. The thing was singing so loudly I could easily hear it over the constant roar of the water. I knew it had to be close by—somewhere. And then I spotted it, coiled up on a rock in the sun. *Damn*, I thought. *I had nearly walked over the top of it!*

Why is it so black? I wondered why as I backed off, trying to put a good 10 or 15 feet between me and that ugly, mean-looking reptile. I never knew they could be so black. Turns out it was a timber rattler—a big one—and I learned later that some can be black like that. When I moved farther away from the snake, it finally quit rattling, but the darned thing remained coiled and ready to strike, with its large, triangular-shaped head pointing straight at me.

I must have stood in the middle of that stream for a good five to 10 minutes, looking at the rattlesnake and studying it. After all, I had never seen a real rattler in the wild before, especially so close-up and personal. Why, it must have been four to five feet long and as thick as the business end of a baseball bat. Curiously, as we exchanged stares, it occurred to me that the rattler had warned me away; and I was indeed thankful for that. Believe it or not, I almost thanked it out loud, then and there.

Even so, and I hesitate to say this, I wanted to do away with that scary timber rattler. Realizing that they are an endangered species and are protected in our National Wilderness Areas, I would have shot it then and there if a pistol or shotgun had been handy. And that is a pretty strong statement coming from someone who has a healthy respect for wildlife, does not hunt, and never kills the trout he catches. It just goes to show how utterly shaken I was at the time. Eventually, however, I gathered my wits and courage about me and executed a wide portage around the snake to get going upstream. The last I saw of that rattler, it was coiled up on the rock in the same place sunning itself—and still staring straight at me.

The rest of the day was relatively anti-climatic, even though my snake radar was engaged continuously, and my eyes were scouring every sunlit rock along both sides of the Middle Prong. I fished for another hour or more and figure, all total, I must have caught more than 30 speckled trout. The largest one was the length of the cork grip on my fly rod, which is about 10 inches. With the exception of that snake encounter, it had been another wonderful day on the high Middle Prong, just like all the others. Fighting off the weariness, I proceeded to climb out of the water, find the old logging railroad grade, and drag myself back down the mountain to my truck—without incident and before dark.

Conclusion

My old wading boots were soaking wet, but they had borne me up well that day. As I bent over slowly and reached down to unlace them, it suddenly dawned on me how sore and tired I was. Even before I got the heavy things off, I was pondering once again how many more of these fishing trips up the Middle Prong were in me. *There's got to be a few more, surely,* I reasoned, while stowing the gear and trying to ignore my aching feet and back.

However, it did not take long to dispel these notions and physical pains. When I cranked up the truck and began rolling toward a paved road and civilization, I naturally reflected upon the grueling day. A sense of contentment gradually came over me upon relishing the memorable moments spent in pursuit of my Middle Prong passion. And it did not take long to begin anticipating future excursions into the wild Middle Prong. But Maria need not worry herself anymore, because I promise not to go fishing alone again, ever. She can thank that black timber rattler for that.

It is amazing how much enjoyment one can have flyfishing and catching small speckled trout like this one all day long on the upper Middle Prong. Certainly, the author appreciates the wilderness experience. (author's collection)

It is not unusual to find logging and railroad artifacts strewn along the banks of the Middle Prong and alongside the old logging railroad bed running beside the stream. This heavy cast iron relic once adorned a puffing steam locomotive more than a century ago. (author's collection)

Searching for Boomer Inn

Introduction

Readers are likely searching their own minds now for the meaning of the term "boomer inn." Could it be a hotel or boarding house? Maybe the name is associated with the generation of people known as baby boomers following World War II. Then again, it might only be a clever label for the nesting place of the rare, red mountain squirrels known as boomers.

I recently found myself questioning this "boomer inn" handle while studying two 1935 United States Geological Survey (USGS) maps and tracing a "trail" above North Carolina's Sunburst Campground in Haywood County.[70] This is the same region known as Three Forks or Three Rivers more than a century ago, long before the modern Sunburst Campground era. It is the location where the Right Hand Prong, Middle Prong, and Left Hand Prong streams come together to form the West Fork of the Pigeon River. Over the years, Three Forks has hosted an early 1900s logging community with supporting railroad infrastructure, a U.S. Army encampment during World War I, the Civilian Conservation Corps (CCC) in the 1930's, and today's National Forest Sunburst Campground.

A twisting broken line on the 1935 maps depicts the trail's meandering westward route from a CCC camp at Three Forks all the way up to the crest of Lickstone Ridge, at an altitude of 5,600-feet above sea level. The trail climbs along the lower reaches of the Right Hand Prong stream to the point where the waters of a smaller tributary named Boomer Inn Branch empty into it. From there, it generally follows Boomer Inn Branch up the mountain to Double Spring Gap at the top of Lickstone Ridge.

Interestingly, less than a mile below Double Spring Gap, the early map indicates a solitary structure beside the trail with the label "Boomer Inn." To a

---

70   1935 USGS, Waynesville, N.C. Quadrant and 1935 USGS, Sam Knob, N.C. Quadrant

keen reader of maps, this structure located at such a high elevation in the middle of an unpopulated wilderness area and with such an unusual place name begs the question, *what is this Boomer Inn?*

That is what the search for Boomer Inn is all about. Those of you whose interest might be aroused are invited to read further into the matter and learn more about this Boomer Inn mystery.

Biltmore Forest School

Most western North Carolinians have heard of George Vanderbilt and his Biltmore Estate in Asheville, but they may not be familiar with Carl A. Schenck. A German by birth and training, Schenck earned a Ph.D. degree in forestry sciences in early 1895. That same year, he was hired to take on the forestry management responsibilities for Vanderbilt's Biltmore and Pisgah Forests, covering more than 100,000 acres.

Three years later, in 1898, Dr. Schenck opened a school of forestry named the Biltmore Forest School. It was the first of its kind in the United States, with daily morning lectures and afternoon horseback trips into the forests to instruct students in the basics of forestry sciences.

Unfortunately, Dr. Schenck's services at Biltmore were abruptly terminated by Vanderbilt in 1909; and he, along with his wife and forestry school, were forced to move off the Biltmore property. Reuben B. Robertson, who was the manager of Champion Fibre Company's new pulp mill at Canton, soon became aware that Dr. Schenck had no place to take his Biltmore Forest School students.

Consequently, Robertson invited Dr. Scheck to bring his forestry school over to Champion's new logging village named Sunburst located in Haywood County. The village was woefully underutilized at the time, pending the start of logging operations in the company's vast forest lands surrounding Sunburst on the headwaters of the Pigeon River. Financial issues had thus far delayed completion of Champion's Pigeon River Railway linking Canton to Sunburst, leaving no cost-effective means to transport harvested timber to the pulp mill in Canton.

A grateful Dr. Schenck gladly took Robertson up on the offer, and for a few months of each year, from 1910 through 1913, Sunburst's new schoolhouse/church building boasting a wonderful belfry hosted the Biltmore Forest School. Dr. Schenck and his wife were provided with a comfortable home to live in, and his students were lodged in available houses and tents.

As it happened at the time, on the far side of Lickstone Ridge, a few miles west of Sunburst and beyond Double Spring Gap, Champion had recently purchased the Quinlan-Monroe Lumber Company. Included in the acquisition were a circular sawmill and extensive forests on the headwaters of Allen's Creek, embracing several large bodies of spruce timber.

This situation offered a unique opportunity for the Biltmore Forest School students to travel over the mountain and study Champion's methods for accessing and removing the spruce timber from mile-high forests. These logging efforts would eventually include the construction of railroads, log chutes and flumes, splash dams, and even a Roebling Engineering Company incline railway system.

The Boomer Inn

Dr. Schenck and his students routinely traveled by foot and on horseback from Sunburst to the former Quinlan-Monroe properties beyond Double Spring Gap, where Champion Fibre Company was logging. There, they were able to observe and participate in the various forestry operations employed in cutting, removing, and processing spruce timber.

It was a long strenuous journey to climb the steep mountain slopes to Double Spring Gap. Old and even recent USGS maps illustrate the zigzagging trail route Dr. Schenck and his students likely used; one that is several miles long and gains more than two thousand feet in elevation. Obviously, the zigzagging course up the precipitous mountain slopes was necessary to maintain a grade that man and horse could reasonably negotiate.

The trip from Sunburst across Double Spring Gap to reach Champion's logging activities would have taken at least two hours. It is reasonable to surmise that the students had a camp somewhere along the way for respite and overnight lodging. This would have benefitted those travelers who were either late leaving or returning to Sunburst, or who were needing rest or shelter from inclement weather. It would also have provided a haven for the forestry students engaged in multiple-day projects at the logging sites across the ridge.

Fortunately, there is an existing photograph of the campsite used by Dr. Schenck and his students. It shows the professor posing with five of his future foresters in front of a very rustic log cabin. Of note, the cabin's foundation logs—or sill logs—rested directly on the ground. Also, the materials used for chinking—or filling—the spaces between the cabin logs were slender poles and what appears to be a mixture of mud and moss. The main entry door was made from two vertical wood planks with hinges that look to be fashioned from chunks of leather.

Located near the log cabin was an even more rustic log pole structure with what looks like a sheet of canvas fabric used for the roofing. A surviving photo reveals that this rough assembly of sawn trees served as a stable and was large enough to have sheltered several horses along with hay and other feeds.

Could these hastily constructed structures be the Boomer Inn that is represented on the 1935 USGS Waynesville Quadrant map? That would be the same Boomer Inn shown situated near Boomer Inn Branch on the trail to Double Spring Gap.

It certainly seemed to be a good possibility—good enough to inspire the notion of attempting to locate the actual Boomer Inn site in the field. An inspection of the physical site shown on the map would at least determine if the terrain offered a suitable venue for the log cabin and stable. Although unlikely, there was even a remote possibility that surviving remains or other evidence of the structures might be discovered.

Hence, a present-day search for Boomer Inn seemed to be in order.

Searching for the Boomer Inn

It was a wonderful day in late October that found me and my fly-fishing buddy roaming through the forest wilderness, far above Haywood County's Sunburst Campground. As the sunlight streamed through the remaining leaves on the trees, the red, orange, and yellow fall colors shined brilliantly. Temperatures ranging from the upper 30s in the morning to the 50s in the afternoon made conditions ideal for hiking the old trails, railroad grades, and logging roads in search of the Boomer Inn.

As it happened, bear-hunting season was underway in the Pisgah Forest. When we arrived at Sunburst Campground on N.C. Hwy 215, the gate across US Forest Service Road 97 (FR97) was unlocked and the road was open to vehicular traffic. With raised spirits, we began motoring alongside the beautiful mountain stream known as the Middle Prong of the Pigeon River. After adventuring more than a mile up the forest service road, we encountered two consecutive and very tight switchbacks in the road. These are the same switchbacks that steam locomotives pulling logging cars utilized in the early 1900s on this railroad pathway into the Middle Prong wilderness.

The forest service road veers away from the Middle Prong stream after the switchbacks and twists its way around the mountain slopes until reaching a bridge crossing of the Right Hand Prong stream. We crossed this bridge and not long afterward drove through a fording spot on Boomer Inn Branch, eventually reaching the unmarked hiking trail 97D on the left side of the road. At last, after a five-mile or so drive, we parked the truck beside the road and got started up trail 97D toward Double Spring Gap.

Boomer Inn searchers be forewarned that for most of the year—January through September—FR97 is closed to motor vehicles. In that case, you will have to take a brisk one-hour hike up the Right Hand Prong stream along trail 97B until it eventually intersects with FR97. Just across this gravel roadway is the 97D trailhead that will allow you to continue the search for Boomer Inn.

The hiking trail 97D is unmarked in the field but clearly shown on the Sam Knob (2019) USGS map. Also, a continuation of the trail to Double Spring Gap is plainly illustrated on the Waynesville (2019) USGS map, although the mapmakers failed to label it. Searchers are advised to follow their progress on these maps using a tracking device such as a cellular phone downloaded with the Avenza Maps app.

In less than a quarter of a mile after starting the trek along trail 97D, we encountered a fork in the old logging grade. The lower trail is the one indicated on the map and, likely, the one used by Dr. Schenck and his forestry students. However, both trails eventually merge again so you cannot go wrong whichever one you take.

Searchers should be aware that trail 97D is not a maintained trail, and there will be numerous deadfalls to wade through, climb over, or go around. Please be careful and protect yourself from the stiff limbs and brush that you will sometimes need to bust your way through.

Although it was obvious much of the trail was graded and used by railroad and truck logging crews in the past, there were other sections that were probably used only by Schenck, his students, sporadic hiking and hunting enthusiasts, and the wildlife. Due to erosion and tree falls over the years, these can sometimes be hard to discern and follow. So, searchers, take your time and, if you're using a tracking device, check your location often to make sure you are still on or close to trail 97D.

The first half mile or so of the trail gradually leads in a westerly direction and climbs approximately 400-feet in elevation before crossing an unnamed creek. After the creek crossing, the trail begins a zigzagging path up the steep mountain slope between the unnamed stream bed and Boomer Inn Branch to the west. We crossed the unnamed creek and began plodding uphill while negotiating five switchbacks and gaining approximately 640-feet in elevation. Eventually, we found ourselves in the vicinity of the suspected Boomer Inn site.

The old 1935 Waynesville USGS map indicates the Boomer Inn structure was located near a section of the trail having a shape much like a bird's head—at least it resembles a bird's head to me. In fact, the modern Waynesville USGS map (2019) illustrates the trail with this same bird's head shape, and the beak is situated at the 5,000-feet elevation contour. My friend and I chose the tip of the beak as the point to begin searching for a site where Dr. Schenck, his students, and their horses could have sheltered overnight—the site of the Boomer Inn.

Conclusion

Being over 70 years old now, the author does not usually make strenuous and difficult excursions into the wilderness alone. So it was that I had recruited my fly-fishing buddy to be my Boomer Inn search companion on that fine day. As soon as he and I reached the 5,000-feet elevation and the tip of the bird's beak, we spread out and began looking for expansive and reasonably flat areas that could possibly have hosted a small log cabin and horse stable.

The actual field conditions we encountered were exactly as shown on the topo map. Amongst the scattered spruce and deciduous trees, there was only one expansive, relatively flat area that stood out to us. It was located between a towering domed hill on the upper side and a steep mountain slope below. We envisioned various ways the log and pole structures might have been arranged on this site, and how easily it could have been accessed from the trail. Although other fairly level but smaller areas were found, none would have been as accessible or suitable for accommodating the forestry students' encampment.

As might be expected, we looked around for remains or evidence of the old Boomer Inn structures but failed to find anything. Mother Nature and more than a century of decay had eliminated the wooden structural elements. Of course, there is the possibility small artifacts still exist, hidden somewhere in the undergrowth or buried in the ground. Since neither of us are archaeologists, we decided to forego excavations that might reveal a rusty nail or even a coin or lost folding knife left behind by one of the students. One day, maybe someone will have the motivation and gumption to search for and uncover treasures such as these.

The fact that my friend and I saw no rotting cabin logs or pieces of decaying canvas roofing lying around on the ground changes nothing in our minds. We believe the site where Boomer Inn was likely located has been discovered. For those interested in plotting this Boomer Inn location on a map (for instance Google Maps) or needing additional guidance, we offer the following geographical coordinates to pinpoint the site: N35.376569 degrees and W82.967501 degrees.

By-the-way, I suspect the name "Boomer Inn" was not derived from the small red mountain squirrels—or boomers—that dwelled in evergreen trees at the higher elevations. There is a good possibility the inn took its name from one of the definitions the word "boomer" had at the time: "an itinerant or migratory worker" or "a transient worker."[71]

---

71   See www.thefreedictionary.com and www.merriam-webster.com for "boomer" definition.

Considering their many back-and-forth trips between the school at Sunburst and the logging operations on the far side of Double Spring Gap, the Biltmore Forest School students would surely have thought themselves to be boomers. They would have been proud of their migratory endeavors to learn more about forestry science—proud enough to give their rustic quarters at Double Spring Gap the name "Boomer Inn."

Note to Boomer Inn searchers: Please be aware that if you are undertaking a similar quest to find the Boomer Inn site, this hike is not an easy one. That is especially true if you are beginning the trek from the Sunburst Campground. The hike is strenuous and tiring, and you will have to scramble often and carefully to get around many deadfalls on the trail and stay on course. Yet, it can be rewarding as well. In addition to the Boomer Inn site, we discovered the possible site and remains of an old logging splash dam and a few significant steam locomotive artifacts. Be careful and good luck to you!

An early view of the original Sunburst village shows the impressive schoolhouse/church building on the right. This is where the Biltmore Forest School held classes for a few months each year from 1910 through 1913. (courtesy of Canton Historical Museum)

SUNBURST (OR SPRUCE) | 137

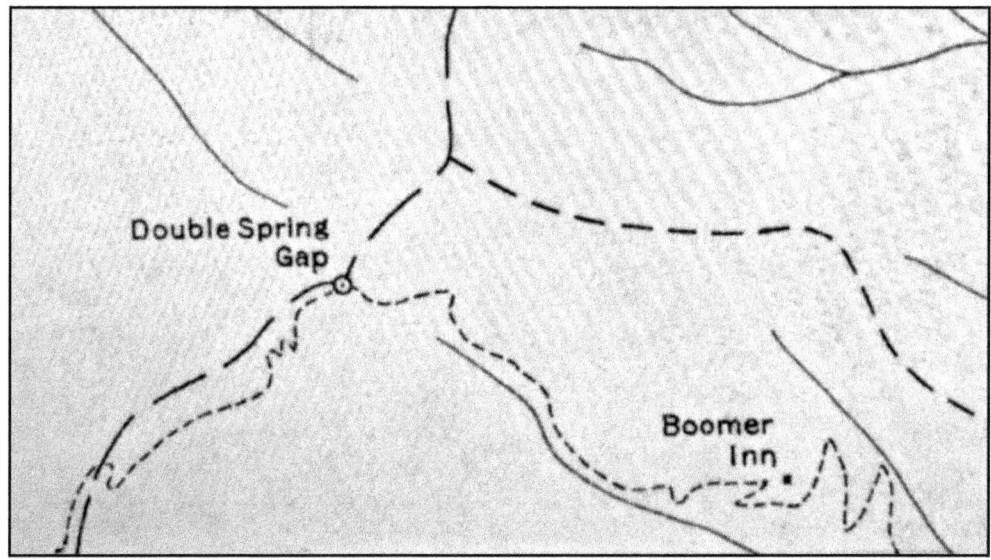

The 1935 USGS map of the Waynesville, N.C., quadrant offers this view of the upper section of the trail connecting the original Sunburst logging village to Double Spring Gap. The "Boomer Inn" is clearly indicated. The lower section of the trail is illustrated on the 1935 USGS map, Sam Knob, N.C., quadrant.

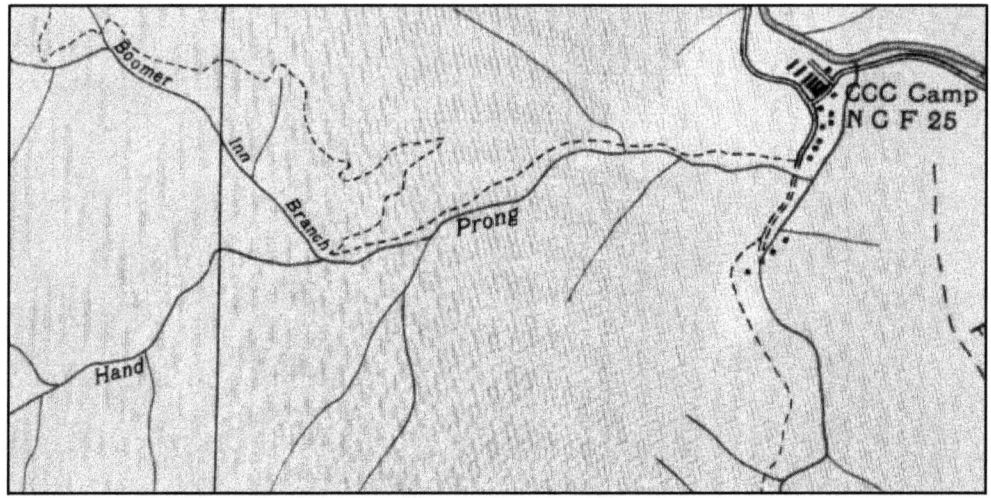

The 1935 USGS map, Sam Knob, N.C., quadrant illustrates the lower section of the trail that connected the original Sunburst logging village to Double Spring Gap. The trail follows the Right Hand Prong stream and then Boomer Inn Branch to where it joins the upper section of the trail, illustrated on the 1935 USGS map of the Waynesville, N.C., quadrant.

Dr. Carl Schenck is shown in this old photo (front row, right) posing with his students at the Boomer Inn cabin. Note the stable where their horses were sheltered in the left background. (courtesy of Canton Historical Museum)

The Boomer Inn's rustic stable was located close to the students' log cabin and is shown here with horses sheltering under the canvas roofing. (courtesy of Canton Historical Museum)

Biltmore Forest School students are shown huddling in this photo to study the Roebling Engineering incline railway installation at Champion Fibre Company's logging operations near Double Spring Gap (circa 1912). (courtesy of Canton Historical Museum)

Busy Biltmore Forest School students in this photo are inspecting and learning how splash dams are constructed. This one near Double Spring Gap looks to be almost complete (circa 1910–1913). (courtesy of Canton Historical Museum)

A "Pioneer Site" on the West Fork of the Pigeon River

Introduction

Recently, I received an e-mail from Carol Litchfield, who is the current President of the Bethel Rural Community Organization and a prominent member of the Haywood County Historical & Genealogical Society. Carol explained how she had been contacted by a person who wrote her the following message: "I recently found an old pioneer site up on a mountain in the Middle Prong and am wondering where I would find any information on whose property it may have been or their story." Upon further questioning by Carol, this person had sent a photograph/map showing the location of the site encircled by a yellow pen marking.

The person who contacted Carol had discovered stonework forming "a huge square wall larger than a football field" with a smaller stone foundation located inside the wall. She described the area as being mostly "flat inside and surrounded by creeks" and there were a "few stone mounds outside of the walled area." Also, "there were a few openings in the wall and an old forest road led up to it with trees growing on the road."

Carol wanted to know if I knew anything about this pioneer site, to which I had to reply no.

SUNBURST (OR SPRUCE) | 141

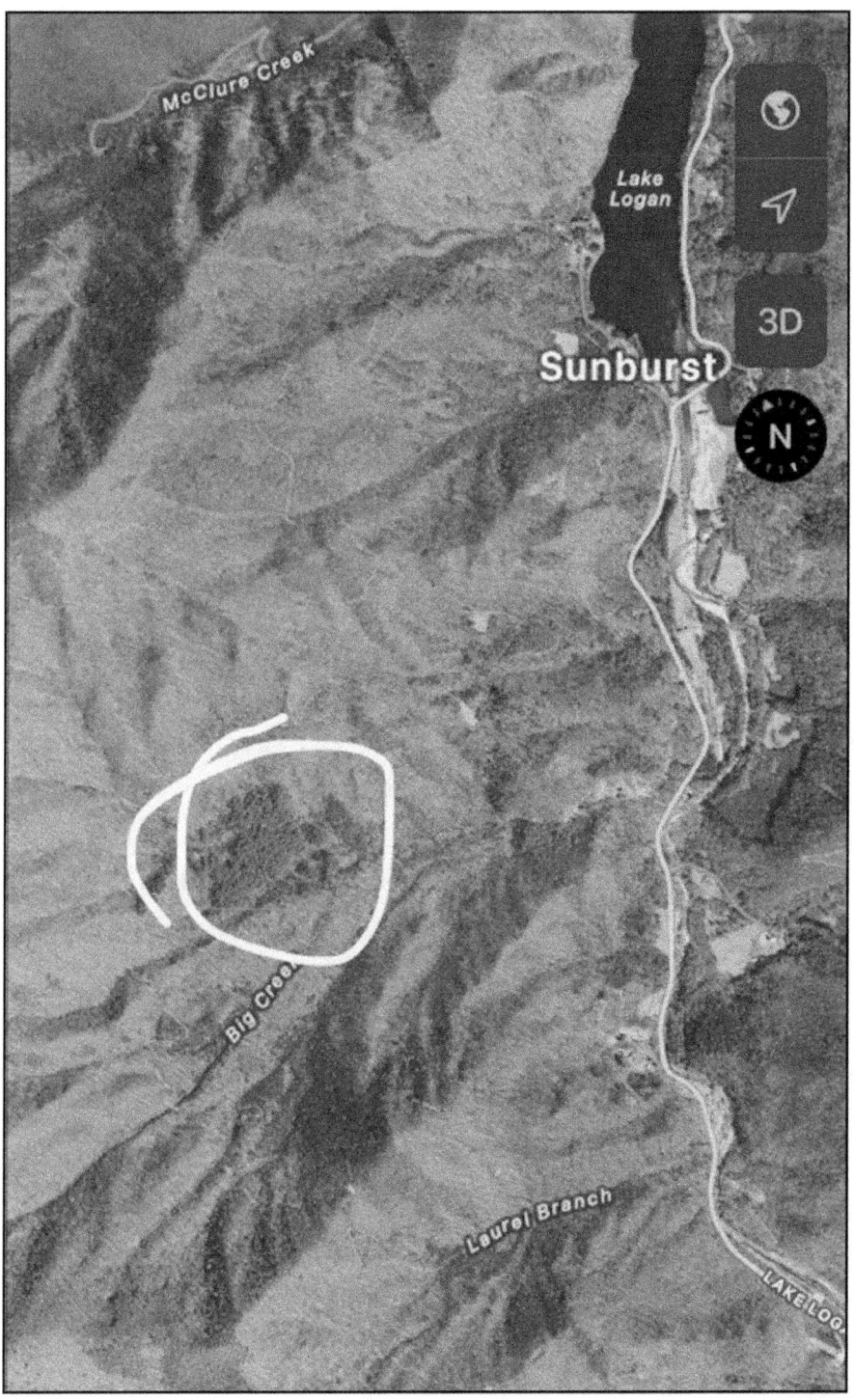

The "pioneer site" located just south of Lake Logan (inside "yellow" circle)

"~~Tiny~~" or "Tine" Inman

Upon examination of the aerial photograph/map that Carol had received, it was apparent that the old stone wall site encircled by a yellow marking was not in the Middle Prong region. It was revealed to be a short distance south of Lake Logan and located along a mountain stream and its tributaries.

Digging into my archives, I found a historic map of Sherwood Forest Inc., Tract no. 70, that was linked to the Pisgah National Forest in Haywood County. This map was dated 1934 and it presented geographic as well as other details such as private properties, motor roads, and railroads. Interestingly, on the 1934 map a large private property tract labelled "Tiny Inman" is shown just to the south of Lake Logan, which had been impounded the year before. This private tract is located where the pioneer site had been marked with a yellow circle on the modern aerial photograph/map given to Carol.

Further investigation by one of Haywood County's finest history sleuths and writers—Evelyn Coltman—has determined that the name associated with the private property is actually "Tine" Inman, not "Tiny." Tine's husband, Ruben Stringfield Inman died in 1925 and the Inman property would have been identified by Tine's name. Thus, her name, albeit misspelled, was associated with the West Fork of the Pigeon River property depicted on the 1934 map.

Ruben Inman's grandparents had moved to the West Fork River area from Newberry, South Carolina around 1825. In 1888, when Ruben was 20-years old, he married Hazeltine L. "Tine" Rhodes who was only 15 at the time. Upon Ruben's death, the couple had engendered nine children of their own.

Intriguingly, Ruben Inman had seen fit to take on a mistress while still being married to Tine. This woman, Lillie Inman who was apparently a relative, was provided a cabin on the property, where she lived and raised seven children born to her and Ruben over the years. Allegedly, the two families lived in accord with each other until Ruben's death, at which time Tine usurped control and forced the extramarital partner and her children off the property.[72] Upon Tine's passing

---

[72] The Inman information is taken from Evelyn M. Coltman's book titled *Legends, Tales & History of Cold Mountain, A Pigeon Valley Heritage Collection—Book 3*; copyright 2007.

in 1941, the property that she, Ruben, Lillie, and 16 children had farmed and shared over the years eventually fell under the ownership and control of the State of North Carolina.

It seems there still exists raw evidence of the old Inman pioneer site with standing stone walls that can be found today. The mere thought that these century-plus old ruins are still out there in the wild forest was too much for this old history buff to contemplate. I had to see them for myself.

So, as soon as the weather was fit—dry and cold enough to keep the snakes underground, my friend and I drove up Lake Logan Road (or Hwy 215) and exited onto an old forest road into North Carolina state property. After a short half-mile drive, we parked at a gate blocking motor traffic and began the trek into the wilderness to find that pioneer site with its huge stone wall.

Ruben Stringfield Inman (1868–1925)

The "Pioneer Site"

The aerial photograph/map that Carol Litchfield sent me clearly illustrated where the old pioneer site was located. A yellow marking encircled the spot and was only a short distance south of Lake Logan and located on a mountainside drained by several streams. The old forest road we were walking up was no longer used by vehicular traffic. That explained the growth of trees and thickets of laurel bushes and briars that had to be dodged or busted through. The going was tough, but we did not have far to go.

In less than an hour, I heard my friend holler out, "There it is!" Looking in the direction he was pointing, I could see a rock wall construction about 20 yards in front of us. As I scanned along the length of the wall, trying to grasp its size, it disappeared into the forest growth—in both directions. Immediately, I thought about the description we were given of the stone wall's size and wondered whether it was actually larger than a football field. No, it couldn't be... could it?

A couple of hours later, after walking along the entire length of the huge wall and studying its construction and condition, a much better idea of its size and shape was reached. The stone wall construction once surrounded a large trapezoidal-shaped area at an elevation of approximately 3,500 feet above sea level. This enclosure was located between two small creeks on a relatively level area of the mountainside.

The wall at the highest point of the enclosed area has essentially disappeared, but at one time it was approximately 500-feet long. At the lowest point, another wall still stretches to about 200 feet in length. The two existing side walls that once joined the upper and lower walls are each approximately 500-feet long. So, given that knowledge, the answer to the earlier doubt I had in mind is *yes*—the stone wall enclosed an area larger than a football field.[73]

The height of the rock wall was in places head-high or higher and in other places slightly less than head-high. Of structural significance was the fact that the wall was between four to five-feet wide—or thick—in the areas that were measured. Also, it appeared that in many places the larger and heavier rocks were placed along the ground and the wall's lowest levels for structural as well as practical reasons. Those big stones were simply too heavy to be hefted very high off the ground.

There seems to be about 50 to 75 percent of the two long sidewalls and the shorter lower wall mostly intact, albeit with a few broken-up or lost sections. Unfortunately, the section of wall that once ran along the upper side of the enclosed area appears to have been destroyed by the construction of an old forest road many years ago. Still, it is amazing that such large sections of the

---

[73] These wall length numbers are rough estimates taken from my tracking information on a USGS quadrangle topo map of Waynesville, N.C. (2019).

hundred-plus-year-old stone walls still exist.

Try to imagine how a mountaineer family in the mid-to-late 1800s or early 1900s might have constructed such a stone structure. When the four walls were completed and in use, the enclosure totaled about 1,700 feet in length and the walls were up to six-feet high and five-feet thick. That would total about 50,000 cubic feet of stonework which likely took years to construct.

In those early days, the mountain farmers would not have possessed gas-powered equipment to build large stone walls such as this. So, every stone would probably have been hauled by horse-drawn wagons or sleds and lifted and laid in place by hand. This hard work, which was likely started by Ruben's parents—Rev. James Anderson and Mary Kirby Inman—would have been completed and maintained by Ruben, his wife and mistress, and the eldest children.

Apparently, the stone wall was used to keep the livestock and wildlife out of the Inman's cultivating fields. As I noticed while studying the wall, a few planned openings could be seen, where the stone construction had allowed for gates to be installed to access the fields of crops. Interestingly, I also spotted some antique wire fencing and rotting fence posts below the lower wall. The age of the wire fencing and whatever reason it might have been installed can only be guessed at.

The stone wall at the Inman pioneer site

A constructed opening in the stone wall at the Inman pioneer site

The stone wall at the Inman pioneer site

Conclusion

Upon retiring from the paper industry some 20 years ago, I became a history enthusiast, mostly researching and writing about Haywood County history. Oh—yes, there was that fiction trilogy I authored, but those stories were based on local history as well. The subject of several of my articles, and even a book, is the founding of the Champion Fibre Company in Canton, North Carolina in the early 1900s.[74]

Of course, those Champion stories included the Canton mill's original sawmill/logging operation near the confluence of the West Fork and Middle Prong rivers. The stories also involved a larger sawmill/logging village that was developed a few years later on the West Fork—where Lake Logan is now located. This larger logging operation took the name of the smaller village just a short distance upstream—Sunburst.

Considering all the research I have done on that West Fork of the Pigeon River area and my many fly-fishing ventures on the West Fork's tributary Middle Prong River, I never realized there were pioneers who settled in that region as early as the mid-1800s—or even earlier. It was my misguided belief that settlement activity on the upper West Fork began around the beginning of the 20th century, when the Canton mill's thirst for pulpwood had to be quenched.

Come to find out, upon reading Evelyn Coltman's *Legends, Tales & History of Cold Mountain, A Pigeon Valley Heritage Collection–Book 3*, settlers such as Ruben Stringfield Inman's grandparents, Joshua and Mary Polly Smith Inman, arrived in the West Fork River wilderness region by the mid-1800s. As you have learned, Ruben's life on the West Fork generated many offspring and surely numerous descendants that populate Haywood County today.

And that's not all Ruben left behind. He and his families constructed an archaeological wonder that we can still see and appreciate to this day. The remains of a magnificent stone wall, built to protect the farm crops, can be found on the old Inman pioneer site near Lake Logan to this day. There is no telling what else might be up there.

---

74   See the author's book, *Thomson's Pulp Mill: Building the Champion Fibre Company—1905 to 1908*, published 2018.

The author stands next to Ruben and Tine Inman's "head-high" stone wall.

Remembering Lake Logan

Introduction

One of the most beautiful settings in western North Carolina is Lake Logan, a sizable body of water captured between steep-forested mountainsides in southern Haywood County. Champion Fibre Company constructed this reservoir in 1932 on the West Fork of the Pigeon River—a tributary of the Pigeon River. Their primary purpose for doing this was to supplement the flow of water when needed to the pulp and paper mill in Canton, especially during dry periods of low rainfall.

After Champion founder Peter G. Thomson's original pulp mill began operation in 1908, the manufacturing demands for water steadily increased. Over the years, additional pulp and paper processing equipment was installed which not only ramped up production but consumed more water as well. By the late 1920s, the situation had progressed to a point whereby whims of nature reducing the amount of water flowing in the Pigeon River threatened the mill's production—and even its survival.

Champion Fibre Company President Reuben B. Robertson, who was Peter Thomson's son-in-law, became keenly aware of the difficulties posed by this capricious situation. Accordingly, between 1928 and 1932, he took the necessary steps to develop the water reserve known today as Lake Logan.

The lake property is currently owned by the Episcopal Diocese of Western North Carolina. Although the paper mill enterprise at Canton no longer owns the Lake Logan property and has recently shut down all manufacturing operations, it still holds the rights to draw water from the lake just as Reuben B. Robertson had intended.

The Rise and Fall of Sunburst Village

Peter G. Thomson's Champion Fibre Company began producing pulp at the Canton mill in early 1908. By June of that year, the mill was shipping eight to 10 rail-car loads of pulp daily to Thomson's coated paper mill in Hamilton, Ohio. Reuben B. Robertson later remembered that the supplies of pulpwood purchased from independent timber operators and those obtained from scattered company-owned tracts barely sufficed to keep Champion Fibre "ahead of the sheriff" during those early days.

Consequently, Thomson and Robertson availed themselves of a business opportunity that would include contracting for a 20-year supply of pulpwood for the Canton mill. In early 1911, they allied Champion Fibre Company with the interests of William Whitmer & Sons. This northern investment concern controlled the new Champion Lumber Company that owned several vast boundaries of virgin timber in western North Carolina.

On the site where Lake Logan would eventually be impounded, Champion Lumber Company and later the Suncrest Lumber Company operated a large band-saw mill from 1913 until 1925. The village that quickly arose and surrounded the sawmill was named Sunburst, taking the name of Champion Fibre's original smaller sawmill village located a few miles upstream.

Hundreds of workers called Sunburst home, living in small residences and boarding houses. The village had a hotel, commissary (or company store), barbershop, jailhouse, church, school, and other such infrastructure that afforded a measure of comfort and civilization for the hardworking men and their families living in the mountain wilderness. And, in a short period of time, electrical and telephone services were enjoyed by the citizens of Sunburst.

Railroad tracks linked Sunburst with the many logging camps spread throughout the headwaters of the Pigeon River. Once the timber was processed into pulpwood and lumber at Sunburst, it was hauled a short 12 miles to Canton over the Tennessee & North Carolina Railroad (T&NCRR).

Of course, the pulpwood—spruce, hemlock, chestnut, and other hardwoods—was delivered to Champion Fibre for conversion into pulp and paper. The sawn lumber product was switched onto the Southern Railroad's tracks and shipped to customers across the east coast of the United States.

Unfortunately, a fire ravaged the Sunburst sawmill in 1920, essentially destroying everything above the mill's concrete foundations. Equipment from Suncrest Lumber's abandoned Crestmont sawmill in northern Haywood County was used to rebuild Sunburst, and it was not long before the band saws were humming again.

However, just five years later, a vast forest fire swept through the high country of the Pigeon headwaters and burned for three weeks. More than 25,000 acres of precious timber and many miles of railroad tracks were destroyed—effectively ending Suncrest Lumber Company's operations at Sunburst.

During the winter of 1925-1926, the heavily used sawmill equipment at Sunburst was dismantled and hauled to Waynesville, where it was again reassembled and placed into operation at the "sawmill bottom" (near today's Waynesville Plaza).

Over the next couple of years, the once active Sunburst village became deserted. Yet, the T&NCRR remained in service, supporting a daily bus service for those people living between Canton and Sunburst.

The Sunburst timberlands owned by Suncrest Lumber—approximately 36,000 acres—were sold to Sherwood Forest, Inc. in 1926. However, the sale did not include the property on which the abandoned Sunburst sawmill village sat.

By then, Champion Fibre Company's Reuben B. Robertson was already concerned about his pulp and paper mill's water supply problem. Undoubtedly, he had been studying and trying to decide where to build a water reservoir and had his eye on that remaining Suncrest Lumber tract.

The property not only included 125 acres of land surrounding the West Fork of the Pigeon River, but it was also still connected to Canton by a railroad. Robertson surely realized the railroad would be invaluable for a major dam project, offering a means to haul workmen, equipment, and materials to the construction site. It could also be useful in hauling away the excavated soil and rock.

In 1928, three years after the logging and sawmill operation at Sunburst shut down, Reuben B. Robertson purchased the 125-acre Sunburst tract from Suncrest Lumber Company.

Impounding the West Fork of the Pigeon River

The quest for more water and additional timber mounted as Champion Fibre added new machinery and increased production at the Canton mill. Spruce, especially, was a desired species of wood, and Champion gradually assembled a spectacular boundary of timberlands straddling the North Carolina and Tennessee border to insure a supply of spruce, as well as several other varieties of pulpwood.

By 1927, the paper company had built an extensive infrastructure in these same timberlands to harvest the wood. This included a large sawmill operation at Smokemont, located in Swain County, and many miles of railroad tracks snaking through the forests. But Champion was not the only party holding a keen interest in those wild lands.

Large groups of enthusiastic nature lovers in Asheville and Knoxville thought these same timberlands were better suited for park land. Spurred on by the activists, legislators in both North Carolina and Tennessee enacted condemnation proceedings to acquire Champion's 110,000 acres of timberlands.

In 1931, after years of bitter feuding and legal proceedings, the U.S. Government finally took this land, which would eventually become the Great Smoky Mountains National Park. As compensation for its precious timberlands, Champion was awarded three-million dollars.

That same year, the Champion Fibre Company initiated a huge development project at the Canton mill to increase its paper production. The project entailed extensions and new equipment being added to the Beater and Finishing rooms, as well as construction of a completely new machine room for installation of the world's largest "book" paper machine.

The capital required for such a mill expansion was huge, and funding would certainly have been supported by the three-million-dollar settlement with the U.S. Government. Importantly, such a large addition to the mill's manufacturing facilities would require additional water for the new processes. The water reservoir that Reuben B. Robertson had envisioned at the site of the abandoned Sunburst sawmill village suddenly became crucial in keeping the mill running at full capacity during the extended dry spells.

The Sunburst property had lain idle ever since the sawmill equipment was removed and relocated to Waynesville in 1926. After purchasing the site in 1928, Champion occasionally sent crews there to work on cleaning up the littered property, including the remaining heaps of concrete from the building and machinery foundations.

In 1931, with the imminent start-up of the new 242-inch-wide book mill machine—the largest in the world—and using funds from the U.S. Government settlement, Rueben B. Robertson set things in motion to construct the new water reservoir. According to company engineer B.S. Colburn, Jr., preliminary work was initiated by Charles E. Waddell & Co., Engineers out of Asheville in August and September of 1931.

Colburn reported in Champion's monthly news publication *The Log* that in August and September, Waddell Engineers made surveys of five possible locations for a water impoundment and several others were inspected. "The location at Sunburst was found to be the best, and work was started immediately on the final survey of the dam site and reservoir basin."

A design was chosen for a single arch, concrete dam rising approximately 56 feet in height and extending across the lower end of the Sunburst valley, through which the West Fork of the Pigeon River flowed. Almost immediately, Champion Fibre Company's employees began excavating on each end of the dam where the massive structure would anchor against the mountainsides.

Interestingly, a hydraulic pump was used to remove soil over the underlying rock by blasting it away with water under high pressure. Once the bare rock was exposed and cleaned, the rock face was drilled in six separate locations with a diamond-core drill to determine the soundness of the rock abutments.

In late 1931, Champion contracted with Smith, Leach and Co., a branch of the W.W. Boxley and Co. of Roanoke, Virginia, to construct the dam. The contractor quickly mobilized and took over the excavation work from Champion Fibre Company's crews. By the first week in February 1932, approximately two thousand yards of earth and stone had been removed.

One might expect that the concrete pours would begin as soon as the foundation rock was exposed and cleaned. However, there was another step taken before that happened. The contractor was required to seal all the cracks and openings in the rock below the foundations.

To accomplish this feat, holes were drilled into the rock 15 feet deep. Then, cement was pumped into these holes under a pressure twice that of the water after the lake was filled. Only then, when the cracks and other openings in the rock were tightly sealed, could the concrete foundation pours begin.

Erection of forms and pouring concrete for the new dam began in early February 1932, and the work was completed in the summer of that same year. Soon after that, approximately six hundred million gallons of water were impounded behind the new concrete dam, creating an 87-acre water reservoir for Champion Fibre Company.

The "Sit 'N Whittle" Heritage

An old Champion publication of *The Log* offers a tantalizing snippet about the naming of the newly impounded lake. Before construction of the dam was completed, it is revealed the new lake was christened "Smith Lake." This was in accordance with an ancient custom in western North Carolina to give Indian names to artificial lakes, as stated in *The Log*.

The inspiration for the name was the great Cherokee Indian Chief Charlie Smith, "whose spirit still roams through the wilds of North Carolina." Apparently, the inspiration was short-lived because in less than a year everyone was calling the new impoundment "Lake Logan," in honor of Logan Thomson who was Champion founder Peter G. Thomson's son. That name has obviously stuck and is the one still associated with the pristine lake puddled on the headwaters of the Pigeon River.

Shortly after Lake Logan was impounded, Reuben B. Robertson began assembling a little village of log structures on the lake's shoreline, reforesting the surrounding mountainsides, and stocking the lake and streams with bounties of trout. Several old log cabins were relocated from surrounding counties and the newly established Great Smoky Mountains National Park. Robertson's own private cabin became known as Sit 'N Whittle, and it along with the entire compound of lodges and lake properties soon became a place of unparalleled beauty and the nucleus for Champion's company retreat.

Employee gatherings of all sorts were held at Lake Logan, including management and foremen's meetings, graduation ceremonies for vocational trainees and apprentices, assemblies to honor Champion employees, gatherings of old timers, and on and on. In the early years, these groups typically rallied in the parking area behind the Champion YMCA in Canton and were transported to and from Lake Logan in company buses.

Local civic clubs, women's associations, hunting and fishing clubs, and various other organizations were also able to enjoy the Lake Logan facilities, where nature's beauty and comfort were always on display. In 1933, for example, the lake property was leased for a five-year period to the Lake Logan Hunting and Fishing Club, a new organization of Haywood County sportsmen which included Reuben B. Robertson's son, Reuben B. Robertson, Jr. Club members gained fishing and boating rights at Lake Logan where fish were reported to be "unusually abundant."

Over the years, Lake Logan became one of the premier destination resorts in western North Carolina. To accommodate the growing number of guests, Champion built many additional facilities around the lake. A paved airstrip added in the mid-1950s made it possible for guests, company officials, and customers to fly into Lake Logan on Champion's private airplanes. There were many notable public figures entertained at Lake Logan over the years, including the Reverend Billy Graham, Hubert Humphrey, Richard Nixon, George Bush, and Carl Schenck to name just a few.

In the 1960s, however, significant changes within Champion Paper and Fibre Company's organizational structure began to take place. It has been suggested that these changes initiated a movement away from the paternalistic management environment which had existed at the Canton paper mill since its early origins.

Reuben B. Robertson, Jr., President of Champion Paper and Fibre Company, was killed in an automobile accident in 1960. Soon after that tragic event, his father Reuben B. Robertson, Sr. asked to be relieved of the company chairmanship responsibility. Then, in 1966, the local Champion workers voted to unionize for the first time in the company's history.

Each of these events, and others, not only impacted the company's management structure and the employee relations at the Canton industrial facility, but the climate at nearby Lake Logan also began to transform and chill. Upon the passing of Reuben B. Robertson, Sr. in 1972, his beloved retreat gradually lost its appeal as a place of relaxation and comfort. The notion of sitting in a rocking chair and whittling away with members of the Robertson family was gone. Instead, for the next two decades, Lake Logan simply continued to be a handy venue for Champion to host employee meetings and entertain customers.[75]

A New Era Begins

Drastic ownership transfers impacted Lake Logan beginning in the late 1990s. It was then that Champion International sold its Canton and Waynesville paper-making facilities along with the Lake Logan property to the mill employees. In the year 2000, Lake Logan was divested to the Episcopal Diocese of Western North Carolina for its present use as a conference center, while the surrounding timberland was acquired by the North Carolina Land Conservancy and transferred to State and Federal ownership.[76]

Beginning in 2001, the Episcopal Diocese of Western North Carolina began developing the Lake Logan property into a Camp and Conference Center designed to accommodate a wide variety of groups. At that time, construction of the Bishop Robert Johnson Dining Hall began, as well as the refurbishment of the Lodge and several historic cabins.

Lake Logan Episcopal Center opened its doors in the summer of 2002, welcoming Camp Henry to its new home. Since then, Camp Henry has taken place at Lake Logan annually and has carried on the legacy of faith, friendship, community, and environmental stewardship.

Grandparents and parents who attended Camp Henry are now seeing the same joy, transformation, and growth that they experienced in their youth on the faces of today's campers. In 2016, the name was changed to Lake Logan

---

[75] Much of the information in this article was taken from contemporary newspaper articles, various editions of Champion's *The Log* publication, and the book series *If Rails Could Talk* by Ronald C. Sullivan and Gerald Ledford.
[76] https://www.lakelogan.org/about/history

Conference Center and Camp Henry, Inc.[77] Today, the property hosts thousands of people each year for retreats, recreation, reunions, outdoor education, artist gatherings, sporting and music events, and—of course—summer camp.

The Author's Personal Connection with the Lake Logan Story

In the mid-1970s and fresh out of college, I began my own professional career with Champion at the Canton mill. One of the first engineering assignments that came my way was to survey the depths of the water at Lake Logan. More water storage was apparently required, and it had been determined the lake was practically filled up with sediment.

A co-worker and I measured the depth of the lake at many points and plotted the data on a map. Using this information, the amount of sediment that could be removed from the lake bottom was determined and a project developed to dredge the lake. Upon approval of project funding, Lake Logan was drained and a local contractor hired to excavate and haul the material away.

Surprisingly, and intriguingly for this history enthusiast, several old concrete foundations were uncovered at the upper end of the lake. It turned out these were the remains of the original sawmill that had been located there. The Champion crews tasked with cleaning-up and removing what was left of the old Sunburst village and sawmill in the late 1920s had left these huge concrete artifacts in place. And that is exactly what I instructed our modern-day excavation contractor to do—leave the old concrete foundations alone! We left them for the next generation of young engineers or archaeologists to discover.

Another project awarded to me in those early days when my engineering experience was extremely raw was to install flashboards along the top of Lake Logan's dam. It was yet another measure to increase the volume of water impounded behind the dam by increasing its height.

We simply installed short pipe columns along the concrete dam's crest and attached sturdy wooden boards—called flashboards—to them. The dam height was raised a couple of feet or so with the wall of flashboards, thus increasing the volume of water impounded behind it by millions of gallons.

---

77   https://www.lakelogan.org/about/history

A decade or so after these early Champion ventures of mine at Lake Logan, another project at the Canton mill came along that was indirectly related to the Lake Logan water reservoir. This one was a little larger in scope and held a much higher level of importance.

Previous assignments in Brazil and Pensacola, Florida building new paper mill facilities had seasoned me for this much larger challenge. I was asked to lead Champion's Canton Modernization Project, a three-hundred-million-dollar engineering and construction endeavor having the manifest goal of bringing the Canton paper mill into compliance with the latest air and water discharge permit requirements.

One of the most challenging requirements was to reduce the daily amount of water usage from more than 50-million gallons per day to approximately 30-million gallons per day. Engineers analyzed every use of water in the mill, leading to the installation of new equipment and many modifications to the pulping and paper-making processes to achieve the required reductions.

The fact that the mill succeeded in achieving this water reduction goal, along with meeting the other water and air permit requirements, is something this local Canton boy will never forget.

One of the most beautiful places in western North Carolina is Lake Logan, located approximately 12 miles south of Canton on Hwy 215. (courtesy of Lake Logan Executive Director)

Between 1913 and 1925, the logging village named Sunburst thrived on the site where Lake Logan was later impounded. This photo offers a view of the village looking north (downstream), with the sawmill and stacks of lumber off in the distance and the log pond and employee residences in the foreground. (courtesy of Canton Historical Museum)

This photo of the Lake Logan dam construction is looking upstream and was taken in late 1931 or early 1932, just as the excavation work was getting underway. (courtesy of Canton Historical Museum)

This photo of the Lake Logan dam construction is looking upstream and was published in the May 1932 edition of Champion's The Log *magazine. It reveals how the construction progressed significantly in just a few months. (courtesy of Canton Historical Museum)*

The July 1933 edition of Champion's The Log *magazine presented this photo of the new Lake Logan dam and water reserve. (courtesy of Canton Historical Museum)*

SUNBURST (OR SPRUCE) | 161

Lake Logan filled up with sediment after little more than two decades of impoundment. This 1955 photo shows the drained lake with excavation and sediment removal work underway. Twenty years later, Lake Logan was dredged again, and the author participated in that project. (courtesy of Canton Historical Museum)

When Lake Logan was drained for sediment removal in 1955, many concrete foundations remaining from the original Sunburst sawmill were exposed, as can be seen in this photo. (courtesy of Canton Historical Museum)

Reuben B. Robertson had several old log structures relocated and assembled on the Lake Logan property after the lake was impounded in 1932. He was especially proud of the one shown here, which became his and his wife Hope's own quarters. They named the lodge Sit 'N Whittle. (courtesy of Canton Historical Museum)

With two large fireplaces, comfortable seating, lovely covered porches for gathering, and delicious meals, Lake Logan's Bishop Johnson Dining Hall (completed in 2003) is a place where guests want to visit and none want to leave. (courtesy of Lake Logan Executive Director)

GEORGE W. VANDERBILT'S BUCK SPRING LODGE — AND THE RAM-JET PUMP

Introduction

A drive along the Blue Ridge Parkway in western North Carolina can offer more than a scenic passage through the mountains with breathtaking views of wilderness forests. For example, motorists who stop at the milepost 407.6 overlook can also experience a magical passage back in time. This was the very spot where a wealthy New Yorker named George Washington Vanderbilt II built a rustic hunting lodge. It was a favorite retreat for the founder of Asheville's Biltmore House and a place where he, his family, and their guests could enjoy close encounters with nature within his Pisgah Forest land holdings.

Vanderbilt called his complex of log buildings "Buck Spring Lodge." As you will discover in this article, the lodge is now gone forever, but tantalizing traces of it can still be found. Today, visitors to the Buck Spring Gap Overlook can experience the same vistas surrounding Mount Pisgah that enchanted Mr. Vanderbilt and his family and friends. These views include the distant monolith Looking Glass Rock and the fabulous flower kingdom known as the Pink Beds. And for history sleuths, intriguing remnants of cut stone stair steps, building foundations, retaining walls, and even an old log structure survive to remind us of the Vanderbilt connection.

Origins of Buck Spring Lodge

Construction of George Vanderbilt's grand French-chateau-style mansion in Asheville, North Carolia was ongoing from 1889 to 1896. During this time, before the advent of motor cars in the mountains, the New York City native Vanderbilt frequently rode on horseback or in carriages along crude roads and trails penetrating his vast Biltmore estate. This included more than a hundred thousand forested acres known then as the Pisgah Forest.

A contemporary newspaper reported that on one of these excursions Mr. Vanderbilt had been high up in the Pisgah mountains when a violent thunderstorm suddenly caught up with him. His description of the fearful encounter leaves no doubt of the deep impression that was made: "The fierce lightning, accompanied by successive explosions of Heaven's artillery, was like the din of a thousand battles raging simultaneously." After taking refuge under a great cliff until the fury had subsided, Vanderbilt pressed on until he and his party had passed "through and above the storm. Standing on a little plateau where the lodge has since been built, we saw the occasional lightning flash and heard the thunder of the subsiding storm in the valley below."[78]

This was the same plateau under the pinnacle of Mount Pisgah where it was said Vanderbilt would sit for hours "on a ledge of rock," his feet dangling over a 1,700-feet-high precipice as he gazed upon the expansive French Broad River drainage tracts of his Pisgah Forest domain. It was this plateau with its rock ledge that was chosen as the site for a hunting lodge, one that the owner would insure "nothing shall be lacking that may conduce to comfort and pleasure."[79]

These conditions were surely demanded of Vanderbilt's architect, Richard Howland Hunt, the son of Richard Morris Hunt who had designed the main Châteauesque mansion named Biltmore. Hunt's specifications called for a rustic main lodge, guest cottage, and dining hall/kitchen, all fashioned out of huge chestnut logs in the Adirondack style. The manager of the Biltmore estate's forests at the time, Dr. Carl A. Schenck, remembered that the project required approximately a thousand logs, 40 feet in length and straight. Since logs of this species and size did not grow at the tops of mile-high mountains, Schenck, who was the founder of America's first school of forestry, endeavored to build a transport road to the lodge site.

Students of the forestry school, or so-called "forestry apprentices," were put to work building a wagon and sled road from Haywood County's rural settlement of Cruso, located in the Pigeon River Valley southwest of Pisgah

---

78 *The Charlotte News*; Nov. 21, 1903; pg. 10.
79 (ibid)

Mountain, to the lodge site. As incredible as it seems, an account given by Schenck states that his students built the four-mile-long road, with a grade not exceeding six percent, in just a few weeks.[80]

Contracts were let to farmers and loggers in the Cruso area to supply the thousand logs needed to construct Vanderbilt's lodge. Apparently, it was impossible to obtain all the chestnut logs required that met Hunt's specifications. So, the architect consented to use logs of other species, provided they were of the proper dimensions.[81] Thus, mainly poplar and chestnut logs harvested from the forests of the Pigeon River Valley were transported by wagons and sleds pulled by horses and oxen over the newly built road to the construction site.[82]

Materials of another sort were also required to construct the foundations, fireplaces, chimneys, and retaining walls. Huge granite stones had to be hauled to the site over the forestry students' road and other primitive sled paths. One contemporary source stated that "twenty-hundred tons of native granite boulders" were used, and "the major part of them put in place with such care that even the natural moss on the outer surfaces remains undisturbed."[83]

Buck Spring Lodge, its name borrowed from a nearby gushing mountain spring, was constructed in 1896. It is believed that the original lodge complex was comprised of only three log structures designed by Hunt, all connected by covered porches and walkways. Later renovations and expansions in 1903 and 1910 increased the footprint of the lodge. A tattered drawing discovered in the National Park Service's digital archives reveals there were more buildings added over the years. This planning document from the early 1960s shows at least five structures associated with the lodge, not including the garage, caretaker's house, sheds, and a small log springhouse.

---

80 Schenck, Carl Alvin; *Birth of Forestry in America: Biltmore Forest School 1898-1913*; published by Forest History Society and Appalachian Consortium; 1974.
81 (ibid)
82 *Pigeon Valley;* edited by Cheryl Haney, Janice Freeman, and Alice Fisher; 1992; story of Buck Spring Lodge by Seth Burnette.
83 *The Charlotte News*; Nov. 21, 1903; pg. 10.

Buck Spring Lodge Described

The main lodge building was constructed on the highest point of the site, with a large porch extending over a rock ledge. It was described as "a masterpiece of quaintness, all of logs and stone. Its front balcony projects over a sheer 1,000-feet-deep chasm. From this most picturesque standpoint, Mr. Vanderbilt's guests shoot at clay pigeons or glass balls."[84] This balcony—or porch—would have offered the same breath-taking views that Vanderbilt had experienced on early exploratory trips while sitting and dangling his legs over the prodigious chasm's sheer wall.

The rustic log structure had a 30-feet square sitting room surrounded by the Vanderbilts' bedrooms and two other chambers. Overhead were galleries that looked down upon the open space, accessed on one side by a rustic winding stairway and the other by a perpendicular "Jacob's ladder."[85] At one end of the sitting room was a yawning stone fireplace and hearth, with an opening measuring nine-feet-wide by six-feet-high. A pair of andirons representing couchant bucks with spreading antlers could cradle eight-feet-long logs to burn. The fireplace was outfitted with a large cooking crane, wrought-iron pot hooks, a rack, pots and kettles, and, naturally, a fire poker.

Beautiful animal pelts collected by Mr. Vanderbilt decorated every wall of the room, including those of bears, deer, catamounts, foxes, skunks, squirrels, birds, and reptiles. Interestingly, this collection also included the hide of a large polar bear. Scattered throughout were "every conceivable design of curious rustic tables, chairs, settees, lounges, and a big block on which to crack walnuts."[86] [87]

The guest cottage was located adjacent and below the main building on a sloping hillside and joined by a covered breezeway. Just below it and connected to the guest quarters by another covered breezeway was the dining and kitchen facility. Reportedly, the dining room was 25 by 35 feet in size with a

---

84 *The Asheville Citizen-Times*; July 23, 1900; pg. 3.
85 (ibid); pg. 10.
86 *The Charlotte News*; Nov. 21, 1903; pg. 10.
87 *Pigeon Valley;* edited by Cheryl Haney, Janice Freeman, and Alice Fisher; 1992; story of Buck Spring Lodge by Seth Burnette.

12-feet-wide stone fireplace. On the building's south side were three French doors that led outdoors to an expansive covered porch. Although there were no pictures decorating the interior walls, "three hundred" tanned skins of wild animals and stuffed birds were lavishly displayed, including "immense eagles perched on the beams."[88] [89]

At the lowest point of the lodge complex were the stables and barn. These facilities were necessary, of course, because in the early years the Vanderbilts and their guests traveled from Asheville to Buck Spring Lodge on horseback and in carriages. In 1910, a motor road was at last completed from Asheville to the lodge, and the 20-mile trip could be made by automobile. Renovations were eventually made to convert the stable area into a large courtyard and garage facility.

By 1903, the lodge had a "perfect system of plumbing supplies including baths of several kinds, and complete toilet arrangements installed. For drinking, the sweetest mountain spring water is...forced up an elevation of two hundred and eighty-six feet by a small hydraulic ram." This ingenious pump was driven by a head of water and did not require electricity—a practical device in the years before Buck Spring Lodge had its own electricity plant.[90]

Relegated into the Limbo of Memory

Soon after George Vanderbilt's death in 1914, his wife Edith sold almost 87,000 acres of the Pisgah Forest lands to the National Forest Commission for five dollars an acre. This transaction excluded the Biltmore mansion with 11,000 surrounding acres, as well as Buck Spring Lodge with 471 contiguous acres. Edith avowed it was her husband's wish to turn the property over to the nation. A member of the Forest Commission stated that the "Pisgah Forest is the most attractive forest in the country...The turning of this large tract into a game preserve is bound to bring thousands of visitors to western North Carolina annually."[91]

88	*The Charlotte News*; Nov. 21, 1903; pg. 10.
89	*The Asheville Citizen-Times*; July 23, 1900; pg. 3.
90	*The Charlotte News*; Nov. 21, 1903; pg. 10.
91	*The Statesville Sentinel*; May 28, 1914; pg. 5.

For the next half century, the Vanderbilt family along with friends and guests retreated to Buck Spring Lodge to enjoy the amenities of nature that George W. had recognized and appreciated from the beginning. However, in 1959, the Biltmore Estate elected to sell the lodge along with its surrounding forestland to the State of North Carolina. The State, in turn, granted a 7,000-feet right-of-way through this property to the National Park Service, specifically for the routing of the Blue Ridge Parkway.[92]

During the initial planning stages for the section of scenic parkway routed through the Mount Pisgah highlands, Buck Spring Lodge was considered as a venue for a visitors' center. Parkway officials recognized George Vanderbilt's involvement with Dr. Carl A. Schenck in founding America's first school of forestry. One official stated, "As part of our Parkway interpretive program, tentative plans are to make this (Buck Spring Lodge) the center for telling the story of the American forest and forestry movement." He went on to add a qualifying statement: "However, no decision will be made until we have investigated its suitability as a visitors' center site."[93]

A year later, in late 1961, ads began running in local newspapers for the sale of salvaged building materials from Buck Spring Lodge. One of these read as follows:

> CHESTNUT PANELING, *beams, house logs, all sizes, lengths, immediately available from Vanderbilt Lodge atop Pisgah Mountain, deliveries anywhere, all kinds of building materials everything must remove at once, very reasonable distressed prices, apply premises anytime…"Salvage Associates."*[94]

Seemingly, the wreckers literally moved in shortly after the Parkway officials ruled out the use of Buck Spring Lodge as an interpretive visitors' center. For reasons unknown, that idea did not pan out, and one can only conclude the project was simply too expensive. Noted historian and columnist John Parris wrote at the time, "Progress sometimes does sad things to historic landmarks. The National Park Service has relegated it (Buck Spring Lodge) into the limbo of memory."[95]

---

92 *The Asheville Citizen-Times*; Aug 21, 1959; pg. 1.
93 (ibid); Sept. 15, 1959; pg. 11.
94 (ibid); Sept. 24, 1961; pg. 37.
95 (ibid); Aug. 27, 1962; pp. 1, 3.

Experiencing Buck Spring Lodge Today

All one must do to revive memories of Buck Spring Lodge is visit the site where it once stood. The Buck Spring Gap Overlook is located on the Blue Ridge Parkway at milepost 407.6. A sign at the road reads "Mount Pisgah Parking Area," so pull off at this overlook and park in the first of two parking areas.

Now, all you need to do is simply walk less than 200 yards to the high ground where George Vanderbilt sat on a ledge and dangled his legs over the lofty abyss. Conveniently, the Mountains-to-Sea hiking trail, which passes through the paved parking area, leads southward directly to the old lodge site.

The first thing you will notice are the broad, cut-stone steps that lead off the pavement and up the gently sloping hill to the lodge site. These 17 granite steps are remindful of the fine stonework used throughout the Biltmore estate. A 1935 photograph made by Parkway architect Edward H. Abbuehl shows these same stone steps leading up to the lodge buildings from a motor road junction near the caretaker's house.

Undoubtedly, one of the roads pictured at the juncture was that original track built by Dr. Carl Schenck's forestry school students leading down into Haywood County's Pigeon River drainage. The other would be the first motor road completed in 1910, connecting Asheville with the Buck Spring Lodge through the Stony Fork settlement.

The short hike up to the overlook passes a leveled grassy area where once a lodge building was located. It was not an original lodge structure, but an addition constructed later and possibly used as a Honeymoon cabin or a schoolhouse for George and Edith Vanderbilt's daughter, Cornelia. Just a short distance beyond this, you will arrive at the high point of the Buck Spring Lodge site where the main building stood for 65 years. In addition to the delightful view of Pisgah Forest, you will know this is the right spot because of the resting benches and an historical interpretive panel conveniently placed there for visitors.

As previously described, the main lodge structure with an expansive viewing porch was founded here on the very top of the ridge. Below it, log buildings housing the guest quarters and the dining/kitchen accommodations were arranged in a cascading fashion on the sloping hillside. A worn path leads all the way down the inclined lodge site, where these buildings were located, to another smaller flight of steps that still survive. Upon descending these stone steps, one will arrive at a beautiful and extensive clearing that served as a garage courtyard at Buck Spring Lodge. Prior to the completion of Vanderbilt's motor road in 1910, this same location was home to the stable grounds where the horses and carriages were sheltered.

Retaining walls made of mountain rock were used to construct the lengthy terrace. Today, these can still be seen, one holding back the steep slope on the upper side and another containing the fill material on the lower side. Thanks to the Carolina Mountain Club's clean-up efforts, the old courtyard has been converted into a beautiful grassy area with shade trees. It is an ideal venue for picnics on the ground in dappled sunlight or just wandering about and dreaming of days gone by at Buck Spring Lodge.

A short stroll along the terraced courtyard leads directly back to the parking area. However, visitors are encouraged not to return to their vehicles without one more exploratory venture. There is a beaten trail leading south from the garage courtyard (direction opposite from the parking lot) down to another remnant from the Buck Spring Lodge—a rustic outbuilding that somehow escaped the Park Service wreckers in the early 1960s.

It only takes a minute or so to walk down the trail and discover an old springhouse that is still standing. The cool spring water captured inside this 10-by-10-feet square log building provided a vital service to the Vanderbilts and their guests back in the day. In addition to being a source of fresh water, it was a place where food items such as meat, fruit, dairy products, and canned goods were stored. The cool spring water environment very effectively prevented food spoilage during the warm-weather months.

Restoration work has obviously preserved this old springhouse, but the logs, joinery, split-shingle roof, and rock foundation still look as strong and authentic as ever. After you have studied and enjoyed the springhouse, retrace your steps back to the terraced courtyard and then on to the parking area. With a new-found appreciation of Buck Spring Lodge, you can now resume your ride along the magnificent Blue Ridge Parkway. On the other hand, if still filled with vim and vigor, you might want to stroll over to the adjacent Mount Pisgah trailhead and surmount that towering peak.

A Cruso Native's Memories

David Henson from Haywood County's Cruso Community recently shared with me a few personal memories of the Buck Spring Lodge. As it happens, his Aunt Clyde and Uncle Paul Stiles were caretakers at the lodge in the 1950s. Their place of residence was called the "Caretaker's House," which once stood where today's paved parking area for the Parkway's Buck Spring Gap Overlook is located—at milepost 407.6.

David remembered spending "many a night" in the old log house when he was a teenager. The front part consisted of "a kitchen and living room together." Bedrooms were on the back side and there was "a good basement underneath it." When David stayed with his aunt and uncle, he helped them with the routine maintenance chores around Buck Spring Lodge.

The Stiles had the responsibility of maintaining and watching over the lodge facilities and grounds, mostly while the Cecil family, who were descendants of George Vanderbilt, were away. They cleaned up inside, as necessary, when the buildings were unoccupied, "raked leaves away from the log houses," and had little mowing to do since the grass was mostly "wild." David recalled helping his Uncle Paul build a "wove wire fence" along the high ridge line "to keep the kids from falling off there."

He, also, recollected that the lodge "had fireplaces all over it because that's the only way they had any heat." In particular, he remembers the huge fireplace in the main lodge building that sat on the highest point of the property, overlooking Pisgah Forest's French Broad River drainage basin. "The fireplace's fire dogs (andirons) had deer heads on them," he said, "and they could hold huge burning logs up to eight feet long."

The conversation evoked memories David had of a water tank located high up near the ceiling of this log structure. It was the lodge's source of water and was accessed by a towering Jacob's Ladder. Interestingly, the reservoir tank was filled with water by a ram-jet pump which was located on a small creek half a mile away and almost 300 feet below the lodge (more about the pump later). From the lofty reservoir, water flowed by gravity through pipes to the various bathrooms, kitchen, and other outlets associated with the Vanderbilt retreat.

If you remember, the Buck Spring Lodge originally included three log structures. The main building was founded at the top of the ridge, with its extensive porch barely clinging to the edge of a great chasm and offering breathtaking views of the Pisgah National Forest below. Arranged in a cascading fashion further down the slope were the guest quarters—or "midway" house, as David described it—and then the dining room/kitchen. All three structures were joined by covered walkways.

In addition to the original three main log structures connected by covered walkways, David recalls more buildings added in later years. The Honeymoon Cottage was located on the north side of the lodge complex and the Schoolhouse was situated in a field just to the south of the three main buildings. As we walked around the site, he pointed out a cleared area where the Honeymoon Cottage had stood. It was between the beautiful stone steps that lead up from the parking area and the high point of the ridge, where a historical marker stands today.

After a futile search through a wooded area for evidence of the Schoolhouse, David led me down to the Garage Courtyard, below where the lodge structures had been located. Upon arrival into this scenic plateaued area with stone retaining walls on the upper and lower sides, a flood of memories rushed into David's head. There had been a large shop building, vehicle shelters, and even a Ranger's quarters lined up along the lower side of the courtyard, all accessed by a gated driveway that led out to the motor roads and Caretaker's House.

David allowed that one of these roads was the old Vanderbilt Road, and it ran over to a nearby hilltop where the Cecil's fenced garden plot had been located, as well as a tennis court. This was the road originally built by Dr. Carl A. Schenck's school of forestry students in about 1896 and used to haul huge chestnut and poplar logs from the Cruso community of Haywood County to the lodge construction site. Today, the garden and recreational spot that David remembers is the venue for the beautiful Mt. Pisgah Picnic Area.

As we stood at the entrance to the picnic area, he explained how the current

Park Service Road descending around the hillside and down to a modern waste treatment facility is located on top of the old Vanderbilt Road. Then, as I was pondering the significance of that first skid-path/wagon road to Buck Spring Lodge, he pointed down into a heavily forested area and off-handedly offered this intriguing comment: "That old ram-jet pump was located down there somewhere."

Struggling to comprehend the meaning of his words and hide my excitement, all I could say was, "So, that's where the old ram-jet pump was."

The Ram-Jet Pump

Further research on the Buck Spring Lodge uncovered the following interesting tidbit from a 1903 *Charlotte News* report describing the lodge's water supply: "For drinking, the sweetest mountain spring water is piped 3,500 feet and forced up an elevation of 286 feet by a small hydraulic ram."[96]

It had not occurred to me that the convenience of water in such a remote and elevated spot might be the most valuable and/or scarcest necessity for habitation. Certainly, drilling thousands of feet into the ground—or rock—to tap a water supply was not feasible at that very isolated spot. The springs and creeks were located hundreds of feet below the high ridgetops such as the one where Buck Spring Lodge was located.

It was likely George Vanderbilt's architect, Richard Howland Hunt, who came up with the solution for the water supply problem. He chose to use a hydraulic ram-jet pump to force water from a small tributary branch of Pisgah Creek up the mountain to the lodge, which was located a half mile away and 286 feet higher than the pump. The water was pumped into the same reservoir tank that David Henson remembers seeing up in the rafters of the main Buck Spring Lodge building.

What made this solution not only elegant but practical was the fact that the hydraulic ram-jet pump did not require electricity or steam to power it. Instead, this type of pump utilizes the momentum—or pressure—of a slight fall of water to force a portion of the water to an elevation many times higher than the fall

---

96   *Vanderbilt Estate; The Charlotte News* (Charlotte, N.C.); Nov. 21, 1903; pg. 10.

used to operate the pump.

One contemporary manufacturer's catalog stated, "The advantages of the Hydraulic Ram are that its operation involves no labor or expense, and when once started it will continue to pump day and night without attention, as long as the supply of water is sufficient. The simplicity, effectiveness, and durability of this machine make it one of the most useful as well as the most economical of the equipment available for forcing water to distant and elevated points."[97]

So it was that this retired engineer/author (me) discovered the unique capabilities of a hydraulic ram-jet pump—one that did not require electrical power to operate but, instead, was driven by the constant pressure of water delivered to it by gravity. This ram-jet pump was used successfully for more than half a century to supply water to the Buck Spring Lodge, up until the Parkway construction crews obliterated the lodge buildings in 1961. The precise location where those destroyed log structures once stood is well known, but not the specific site of the hydraulic ram-jet pump.

A young David Henson had seen the pump in operation back in the 1950s. He recalls how loud it was and that it was totally enclosed in a small rock structure. Years later, as he followed some dogs hot on a bear's trail, he ran across the pump site again. So, when we were at the Mt. Pisgah Picnic Area talking, David pointed toward a wilderness area where he remembered seeing the ram-jet pump in operation. Admittedly, the notion that the pump site still existed and might be found was intriguing. So intriguing, in fact, that I could not get the thought out of my head. I had to come back and find where that pump was located.

Crawling Through a Rhododendron "Hell"

Not long after receiving David's guidance, I found my way into that wilderness drainage area he had pointed to—where he remembered seeing the ram-jet pump. The setting was beautiful, and it must have taken nature's erosive forces and the waters of the small stream thousands of years to form such a deep gorge. However, besides a forest of towering hardwood trees, there were

---

[97] *Goulds Pumps for Every Service* by GOULDS MANUFACTURING COMPANY, Seneca Falls, New York, USA; copyright, 1895.

rhododendron thickets blanketing both sides of the stream for as far as the eye could see. The sounds of flowing water could easily be heard, but it was impossible to see the glistening water itself. Almost immediately, I wondered how David Henson and those bear dogs had penetrated such a rhododendron "hell."

Finally, I summoned the gumption to "ballhoot" down a steep slope, directly into the midst of the dense rhododendron growth. It was almost impossible to pass through. I had to contort my body every which way to slide between the mass of thick, tangled branches. Elderly men's bodies are not meant to endure such tortuous exercise, but somehow mine found a way to keep going.

Finally, after a few minutes of agonizing squatting, crawling, and sliding, creek water could be seen dead ahead. This little branch was much smaller than expected, and I could easily determine there were no signs of a pump installation anywhere around. Deciding to explore further upstream, I again began ducking rhododendron branches and wading uphill through the water and rocks.

The going was slow and tough, however. At times, it was necessary to scale up a rocky waterfall or climb the sheer creek banks and portage around a particularly difficult rhododendron thicket. It did not take long for the cold water to penetrate my "waterproof" boots. For seemingly an hour's time, I endured the discomfort of soaking wet and freezing feet, while continuing to make progress up the drainage gorge. Not even exhaustion or numb feet could prevent my being impressed with such closeness to nature or enjoying the excruciating venture. However, no signs of a hydraulic ram-jet pump installation were encountered anywhere, and it seemed more and more unlikely that one could have been installed on this rough little branch.

Then, finally, upon reaching an opening in the dense cover where an old Forest Service Road crossed the creek, I spotted something very peculiar upstream in the distance. It surely did not have a natural look about it—that thing poking above the tops of the rhododendrons, about 20 or 30 yards upstream. Actually, it looked too straight to be a bare tree trunk stripped of its branches and leaves. What could it be?

As fast as my weary legs and numbed feet could carry me, I plunged through the rhododendron growth ahead and, at last, burst into a wide opening. The day seemed to have gotten brighter, and the creek and everything around it was much more visible now. Suddenly, I could see that it was an old, cast-iron standpipe that had caught my attention. Like a lighthouse guiding sailors at sea, this iron pipe protruding straight as an arrow out of a rock pile and high into the air had led me to that spot. It was a spot, much to my surprise, where a man-made, stone dam was holding back the waters of the creek—a dam!

This must be it, I thought at once. *It has to be the place where the hydraulic ram-jet pump was installed.* And yes, that is exactly what it turned out to be. The stonework in the dam was as beautiful as the day it was laid. Over the years, however, the impoundment behind it had filled with silt, and the vegetation growth had gradually crept in from the creek banks such that it now resembled a broad and shallow stretch of the stream. Amazingly, though, water still flowed through a weir constructed at the top of the stone dam, spilling into the creek several feet below.

Considering that it is more than a century old, the dam is in astonishingly good condition. The stonework appears to be mostly intact, with the mortarless joints still fitting tight together. Approximately eight feet high, two feet thick at the top, and 50 feet across, bank-to-bank, the dam would have formed a reservoir in the creek that could easily supply water with adequate pressure and a constant flow to the hydraulic ram-jet pump.

David Henson had allowed the pump was enclosed in a little rock house close to the dam, and it had a door opening—with no door—and a dirt roof (probably overlaid on sheet metal). He remembers very well helping his Uncle Paul clean the leaves and silt out of the large pool of water behind the dam. Also, each year before the cold winds blew in from the North, he recalls his uncle stacking bags of leaves in the door opening, presumably to seal up the rock shelter and keep the pump from freezing up.

Intriguingly, David remembered seeing a tall iron pipe protruding out of the top of the pump house, while listening to the noisy pump operation. Surely, it had to be the same cast-iron standpipe which protrudes, to this day, from a pile of rocks that are obviously the remains of the pump house.

Although there are no signs of the old ram-jet pump—which almost certainly was salvaged during the Buck Spring Lodge demolition stage—we can confidently establish its location with the standpipe and rock pile, just below the dam. This arrangement allowed for the water supply line to pass through the bottom of the dam directly into the pump. It is surmised that the iron standpipe would have been attached to the supply line, and its function was to remove air and stabilize the water flow to the pump.

From this location, almost 300 feet lower than Buck Spring Lodge and half a mile away, the hydraulic ram-jet pump forced the "sweetest mountain spring water" all the way up to the highest point in the highest lodge building. David said that the iron discharge pipeline running from the ram-jet pump to the lodge was partially exposed in some places, and he believes it ran along the course of the old Vanderbilt Road for part of the way. Undoubtedly, evidence of this pipeline still exists, and I might try to find it one day—when my feet thaw out.

Conclusion

It is true what a noted local historian claimed 60 years ago—that the National Park Service had relegated Buck Spring Lodge into "the limbo of memory." Yet, the lodge site where George Vanderbilt, his family, and guests experienced the Pisgah Forest's wild mountains has been preserved and is easily accessible today. The same views can still be appreciated, the lodge grounds can be explored, and an intact log springhouse that has survived for almost 125 years can be visited.

Please, do not allow the memory of this western North Carolina historic treasure to remain in limbo any longer. Take a trip to the Blue Ridge Parkway's Buck Spring Gap Overlook at milepost 407.6 and ensure memories of Buck Spring Lodge remain alive for future generations. You will be glad you did.

This old photo shows how the Buck Spring Lodge grounds looked in 1935. Note the original steps leading up from the motor road junction to the lodge buildings on the hill. These cut-stone steps survive to this day. On the right side of the photo is the caretaker's house, located where the Buck Spring Gap Overlook parking area is now situated. (National Park Service digital archives)

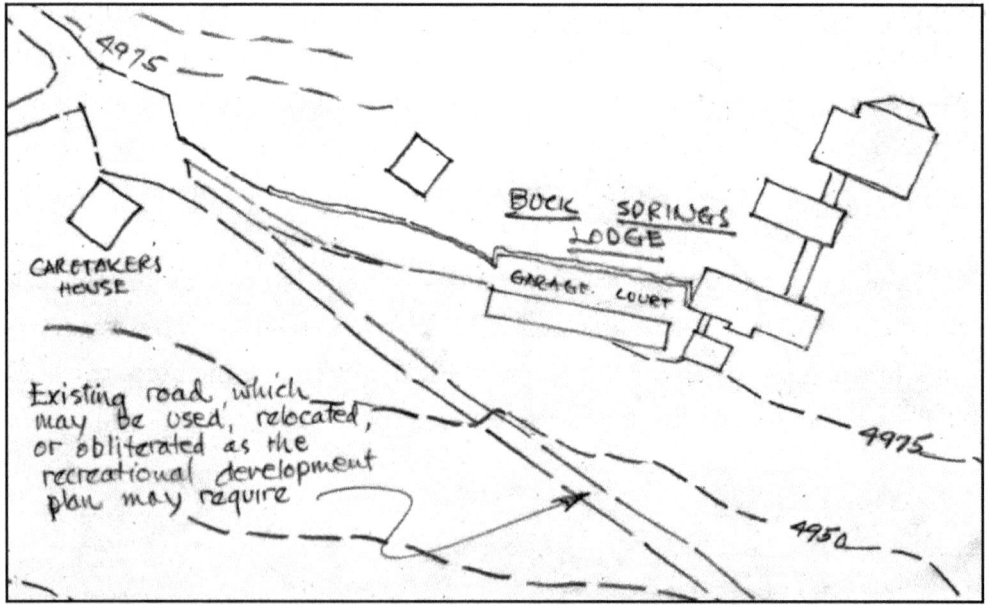

A Blue Ridge Parkway planning map, shown above, reveals the layout of the various Buck Spring Lodge buildings, circa 1960 and prior to their demolition. Note the "Garage Court" (courtyard) which still exists and can be seen and enjoyed today. (National Park Service digital archives)

The dining room porch is shown in this photo, located on the south side of the building. A covered breezeway connects the dining room to the next lodge structure above it, which was the guest cottage. (National Park Service digital archives)

Buck Spring Lodge is viewed from the south side in this photo. Note the sloping site and covered breezeways that connected the different lodge buildings. (National Park Service digital archives)

The interior of the main Buck Spring Lodge building is pictured here, looking to the east. Beyond the doorway, the main porch can be seen jutting out over the "1,000-feet deep chasm." (National Park Service digital archives)

This is a view of the interior of the main Buck Spring Lodge building, looking to the west. Note the large stone fireplace that was built to burn eight-feet-long logs. (National Park Service digital archives)

The main Buck Spring Lodge building sat on the highest point of the ridge, its massive stone chimneys reaching for the sky. This view from the western side barely shows the covered breezeway on the extreme left connecting with the other lodge buildings below. (National Park Service digital archives)

This is a recent view of the expansive Garage Courtyard terrace, where motor vehicles once parked and were serviced at Buck Spring Lodge. In the early days, prior to the advent of motor cars, stables were located here. Original stone retaining walls flank the courtyard on the upper and lower sides. (author's collection)

The original log springhouse still stands today near the Buck Spring Lodge site, just as it has for more than a hundred years. (author's collection)

FOLLOWING GREAT-GRANDFATHER'S FOOTPRINTS

A young Lt. William H. Hargrove

Captain Hack Hargrove – A Useful Citizen

Introduction

USEFUL CITIZEN FILLED WITH HONOR HAS GONE TO REWARD.

The above words from a long hidden obituary clipping caught my attention a few years ago as I rummaged through some old genealogy records. Reading further, it became obvious that the tribute was for my Great-Grandfather

William Harrison Hargrove.[98] Of course, I was not unfamiliar with him, having often heard my mother and aunts talk about their Grandfather "Hack" Hargrove. Certainly, I knew he was a Civil War veteran but details of his life and history were somewhat vague. As I continued to peruse William Hargrove's obituary and learn more about his life's occupations and achievements, the more intrigued I became.

Not only was he a veteran of the War Between the States, but at one time or other he had been a farmer, teacher, county surveyor, county board commissioner, state legislator, railroad agent, real estate agent, and newspaper editor—among other things. The writer of the obituary column recorded, "He has been closely identified with the affairs of the county, especially in the welfare and development of Canton." I finished reading the article, put it aside, and have since contemplated Hack's productive life and the breadth of his career and accomplishments.

My father once told me that everyone should strive to leave footprints behind as evidence of their existence and worthy achievements. Undoubtedly, Great-Grandfather Hack left many footprints, and I resolved to uncover them and discover where they might lead. The story that follows is a product of this quest and offers a brief history of William Harrison Hargrove, a man of more than ordinary ability and a "useful citizen."

Following Footprints into the Pigeon Valley

In the midst of the Blue Ridge Mountain Range, where peaks tower a mile high over western North Carolina's Haywood County, a fertile valley lies astraddle the upper Pigeon River. Known as the Pigeon Valley, it once hosted a pioneer settlement known as Forks of Pigeon where the east and west tributaries of the Pigeon River are joined. William Harrison Hargrove was born into this community of mostly farming homesteads in 1841.

The first pioneers reached the Pigeon Valley at the onset of the 1800s, as the white man's treaties forced the removal of the Cherokee Indians further

---

98   Sometime after the Civil War, William H. Hartgrove dropped the "t" in his name and began spelling it as we do today—"Hargrove." For consistency the "t" has been dropped in William's name throughout this article.

westward. Those original settlers laid claim to the rich bottomlands near the rivers, while the latecomers homesteaded on the mountainsides and in the coves along streams and creeks.

In the early years, pioneers built small log cabins to live in. They used great care in choosing building spots that were near a source of water, well-drained, and high enough to avoid the flooding waters of the river or nearby creeks. Axes were wielded to fell huge trees in the surrounding forest, and the downed timber was dragged to the house site by oxen, horses, and manpower.

First, the largest logs were carefully positioned across foundations of stacked rocks to provide a stable support for the structure. On top of these log "sill" beams, the cabin walls were laid up, one log stacked on top of the other. Using only an axe and froe, the builder shaped the logs and carefully crafted the corner joints to fit tightly together in an interlocking fashion.

An important element of the cabin was the fireplace, which was typically constructed using native stones held together with a muddy mixture of clay and straw. Not only was this hearth used for cooking meals and heating the small cabin during the cold winters, but it also provided a source of light at night when the family gathered and enjoyed each other's company.

Lastly, a roof was fashioned over the log structure. Poles spanning from one side to the other were covered with riven clapboards and/or thatch to keep the weather out. Animal skins and rough-hewn board shutters were placed over window and door openings, while the cracks, or "chinks," between the logs were packed with a mixture of mud, straw, and stone to keep the cold and critters out.

By today's standards, these homes seem crude and inhospitable, but for those pioneer settlers in the valley there were no better options. The log cabins provided a refuge from the elements and protection from the wilderness perils, thereby improving the settlers' chances of survival.

Farmers who owned tracts of bottomland were rewarded with its rich alluvial soil, which was easily broken and prepared for planting. Higher up on the mountainsides the settlers were not so fortunate. There, the soil was rocky, less productive, and more difficult to work. But no matter their lot, the pioneer farmers were a hardy and determined sort. They fretted little over hard work and through tremendous toil and exertions caused the Pigeon Valley to bloom with their precious crops.

Each spring, along about March or April, the valley gradually exchanged its dark grey shroud for a beautiful green veil, spotted with colorful blossoms of the serviceberry, mountain laurel, rhododendron, and dogwood trees. It was in this picturesque setting, with the scent of wild onion and damp earth in the air, that the early settlers exerted their energies to break the ground, using horses or mules to pull crude plows or by simply wielding hoes. Of course, these exhaustive efforts were aimed toward raising vegetables and grain crops to feed their families and livestock.

Surplus crops were bartered for vital necessities that could not be produced at home such as salt, sugar, iron tools, cloth, medicine, and other goods. And it was not uncommon in the day for the farmers to barter shares of their harvests for the services of a doctor, hired hand, blacksmith, traveling cobbler, teacher, or even a preacher. In this way, the crops were the Pigeon Valley's treasure and the key to local economics.

Travel and transportation would have been especially important to the early settlers and essential for commerce to exist. Crops, goods, and stock had to be moved into, out of, and throughout the Pigeon Valley to the mills and to markets. This would have been facilitated somewhat during dry weather by the existing crude roads, which all able-bodied men were required by law to maintain. In the winter months, however, these roads were often no more than narrow traces of ruts and muddy washouts that would have offered little advantage to farmers opting to use them.

Just after the formation of Haywood County in 1808, the newly elected county officials ordered two wagon roads to be "marked out and made" to connect the Pigeon Valley with outside communities. One road ran from Waynesville across Pigeon Gap into the Forks of Pigeon region (along present-day Hwy 276). Another road connecting Beaverdam (Canton) with the upper Pigeon Valley snaked along the Pigeon River, passing John McDowell's "flowery garden" (or Garden Creek) and connecting with the previously mentioned upper Pigeon Valley road to Waynesville.

The primary umbilical between Asheville and Waynesville and points farther west was called the Western Turnpike. Completed sometime around 1850, this important road passed near where the town of Canton is located today. It served the Pigeon Valley folk as the principal link to the Buncombe Turnpike at Asheville and, thereby, to the outside markets in Tennessee, Virginia, South Carolina, and Georgia.

A mill and a separate general store owned by "Colonel" Joseph Cathey were in operation in those early years at Forks of Pigeon, where the East Fork and West Fork Rivers converge to create the Pigeon River. Cathey has been described as one of the most capable and influential men of his time in the county, and his store was reportedly one of the largest and most successful around. It was stocked with a generous variety of supplies that the mostly self-sufficient farmers would have needed but could not produce or fashion for themselves. Integral with this mercantile business was the local post office, which occupied a small space within the store's walls and claimed the aptnamed postal address "Forks of Pigeon."

Nearby, on the bank of the East Fork of the Pigeon River, was Cathey's gristmill which was powered by a huge undershot wheel driven by water diverted from the river. The commerce and facility provided by the store and mill made these Cathey enterprises essential hubs of the local community. It was here that settlers brought their valuable corn and wheat crops to be ground into meal and flour, bought and traded for much needed supplies, socialized with their neighbors, and received news from the outside world.

As the Pigeon Valley settlement grew over the years, so did the requirements for social organizations and establishments to provide the settlers with spiritual and educational sustenance. At least three different churches were eventually organized in the valley, where the hardworking pioneer families faithfully received moral guidance. These churches, along with their camp meetings, were main focal points for religious and social congregations during the early days.

Camp meetings were always popular events, held usually in the late summer after the crops were planted and before harvest season. Entire families packed up belongings and traveled to the meeting grounds, where they along with their neighbors camped out and worshipped for entire weeks at a time. It was not uncommon for these epic religious revivals to be coordinated around the schedule of some renowned traveling minister or evangelist, in which case full advantage could be taken of these individuals' oratory and spiritual gifts.

In 1838, a fine two-room schoolhouse was constructed to serve the community on land donated by Elijah Deaver. This frame and board building was reportedly located near where the Masonic Lodge currently sits and was anchored with heavy brick fireplaces and chimneys at each end. William Harrison Hargrove's grandfather, William Manson Hartgrove, made the brick and helped build these two massive chimneys.

In addition to the public school, which was free to all students, subscription schools were not uncommon. These offered parents or guardians the opportunity to "subscribe," or contract, with the teacher for their children's education. In which case, the teachers' fees were often bartered for bushels of corn or wheat, sides of meat, days of labor, and the like.

Life in the valley during those early times was surely difficult and filled with challenges and hardships that simply cannot be appreciated today. However, residents found diversions from their daily work that tended to lighten their spirits and provide sparks of enjoyment and fun to keep hopes kindled.

Womenfolk, for example, could derive satisfaction from their laborious and vital homespun work. Significant amounts of their time and toil were exerted in spinning wool, cotton, and flax into yarn and thread. This, in turn, was woven, sewn, knitted, and fashioned into artful and practical clothing and coverings for their families. Though tedious and demanding, the vital work would surely have provided pleasure to the pioneer women, as well as given them a feeling of pride for their creations.

Hunting, trapping, and fishing were necessary activities for the valley's pioneers, providing food for the table, clothing for the family, and furs to shield off the cold. These pursuits also offered a welcome escape for the men and boys from their routine labors, just as visits to Cathey's store and mill tended to do. At these popular commercial enterprises, they took delight in passing time with friends and catching up on the latest news, gossip, and tales.

Everyone—men, women, and children—would have opportunities throughout the year to participate in community gatherings and activities. These events tended to introduce excitement and a bit of gaiety into their lives and included church gatherings and singings, fall corn huskings, hoe-downs, quiltings for the women and girls, barn raisings, molasses candy-pulling in the winter, square dances, and such.

This was the Pigeon Valley where William Harrison Hargrove was born almost two centuries ago. It was a typical rural mountain community that possessed the essential elements required for the citizens to work, worship, learn, and prosper. And it was the place where my great-grandfather's footprints led me.

William Harrison Hargrove's Formative Years

William Harrison Hargrove was born on January 31, 1841, to Augustus Columbus Hartgrove and Ellen Childress. His father, Augustus, was a native of Mecklenburg County and came to Haywood County in about 1824 with his parents, William Manson and Mary McKinney Hartgrove. William Harrison Hargrove's mother, Ellen Childress, was from Buncombe County and the daughter of Samuel Childress, who had relocated there from Tennessee.

Augustus Columbus and Ellen Hartgrove lived for a time in a small log cabin located in the Peter's Cove area of Forks of Pigeon. Over the years, they were blessed with the following children: William Harrison (1841), Joseph Franklin (1844), Mary (Mollie) (1848), Augustus Alexander II (1850), and Althea Caroline (1853). Another son, Thomas, died at the age of one, and a daughter, Amanda, died as an infant.

Much would have been expected of eldest son William Harrison, as his mother and father toiled to make the farm a productive and successful venture. The young man's labors and efforts were directed toward plowing, planting and harvesting crops, and hauling the harvests to the market or mill. Other responsibilities included feeding and caring for the livestock, cleaning out the barn and pens, spreading manure over the planting grounds, milking the cows, fetching water, building and mending fences, clearing fields, and chopping firewood.

He would have taken much delight in loading wagons and sleds with baskets of corn and then riding alongside his father to Cathey's grist mill. The marvelous workings of the huge water wheel driving hand-crafted wooden mechanisms surely piqued his fascination. It was these wonderful machines, after all, that produced the tremendous torque required to turn heavy granite millstones.

Wide-eyed young William, harboring a boy's insatiable curiosity, took in everything about the unfolding mill scene. He could hear the miller bark directions to men unloading and hefting baskets of corn and wheat to the very top floor, where the feed hoppers were located. Then, the youth looked on as the dust-covered miller threw a lever to open a sluice gate, feeding the Hartgrove's corn into the middle of the groaning millstones. With a practiced eye and trained ear, the miller set the gap between the top runner stone and the bed stone to grind the corn to the exact texture ordered by William's father. As the corn was ground into meal, it spilled out of the wooden vat surrounding the millstones and down into waiting sacks below.

Depending on how many customers were lined up ahead of them at the mill, it might have taken several hours to have their corn ground. If that were the case, William had plenty of time to wander over to Cathey's Store and discover all manner of things to be found there including farm tools, hand tools, hardware, rope, dry goods, spices, produce, flatware, silverware, colorful calico materials, clothing, hats, boots, and medicines. Without fail, hard and soft candies with wonderful fragrances and colors were always displayed in great abundance to tease customers' senses, including young William.

Eventually, though, he would get a look and nod from Augustus signaling it was time to head back and check on the miller's progress. As soon as their corn was carefully loaded in the wagon and the miller's toll was paid, William and Augustus would hop aboard the wagon and be on their way. Tired and hungry and with hopeful thoughts of a hot supper awaiting their return, the father and son hurried home.

Based on his later accomplishments, the youthful William must have acquired a satisfactory education. It is likely he attended the Bethel Academy for several years, with classes held in the schoolhouse that his Grandfather William Manson Hartgrove helped construct. After that, the records show his father sent him over to Waynesville to attend the private school of John M. McIver for more advanced study.

William would need all this learning and his innate reasoning capacity to make an especially important and far-reaching decision as his 20th birthday approached. It was a time when states' rights, slavery, and secession were contentious political issues in the United States. Consequently, one rebellious southern state after another was choosing to secede from their country and unite to form the independent Confederate States of America.

Throughout the South, young men were being asked to take up arms to defend their states and the "southern cause." Eventually, the debate reached into the remote mountain region of Haywood County where William was forced to contemplate these serious affairs and weigh his partiality. After North Carolina belatedly chose the path of secession, he and other young men in the Pigeon Valley were compelled to declare their allegiance to the Confederacy and defend their state's rights.

The Rebellion Joined

After wavering for several months, North Carolina finally voted to secede from the Union in May 1861. The sentiment in Haywood County was not completely pro-secession, with many sympathizers remaining loyal to the Union throughout the war. But the county moved quickly to form volunteer military companies. On July 18, 1861, William joined Captain Thomas Isaac Lenoir's Haywood Highlanders, a local militia group hailing from Forks of Pigeon. Soon, the Highlanders company was transferred to the service of the Confederate States in September 1861, becoming Company F of the 25th North Carolina Infantry Regiment.

During August of 1861, Private Hargrove and his company trained at Camp Patton, located in Asheville, North Carolina. Then, the mountaineer soldiers moved eastward and were outfitted with uniforms and muskets during a long march and train ride to the coastal town of Wilmington. After more training there, the 25th North Carolina Regiment was finally sent into action, engaging in crucial battles at Seven Pines, Malvern Hill, Harper's Ferry, Antietam, and Fredericksburg in 1862.

In the spring of 1863, the 25th N.C. Regiment was ordered back to North Carolina, where it mostly guarded against Union incursions in the eastern part of the state. However, the regiment was ordered back to Virginia in the spring of 1864. During the greater part of that year, the 25th N.C. was involved in the fighting around Petersburg, Virginia. It was near there where Grant's Union army with its overwhelming advantage in manpower, weapons, and food had laid siege to the city and was gradually encircling General Robert E. Lee's Army of Northern Virginia. In this theatre and until the final surrender at Appomattox Courthouse in April 1865, William and his regiment would fight their last battles at Ream's Station, Fort Steadman, Amelia Courthouse, and finally Five Forks.

Throughout the long war, William was hospitalized twice. On March 21, 1863, First Sergeant Hargrove's name appears on the register of the C.S.A. General Hospital, No. 4 in Wilmington, N.C. He was taken with dyspepsia, a malady associated with poor digestion, and it appears he was out of action for several months. Part of this furlough time was spent back at Forks of Pigeon.

The second hospitalization was around August 15, 1864, when First Lieutenant William Hargrove's name shows up again on the hospital records of General Hospital, No. 4 in Richmond, Virginia. Records confirm that he was again suffering from chronic diarrhea with emaciation and dyspepsia. He was given a 30-day furlough, allowing his return to Forks of Pigeon to get well. Muster rolls confirm that in October 1864, after recovering from the illness, William made his way back to the front lines.

Undoubtedly, he was on duty in the Petersburg trenches in July 1864 when Grant's huge mine exploded, triggering the famous Battle of the Crater. The 25th N.C. Regiment played a critical role in this confused affair by helping hold the Confederate line and ultimately protecting the city of Petersburg. In the horrific conflict, William's close friend from Forks of Pigeon, Captain James Madison Cathey, the son of "Colonel" Joseph Cathey, was killed.

William entered the Civil War as a private, working his way up to First Sergeant in March 1862 and to an officer's rank in August 1864. From then until the end of the war, he was sometimes listed as captain and at other times as first lieutenant on various muster rolls and in the company records.

Local Haywood County author W. C. Allen gave the following account of "Captain Hargrove" in his book titled *The Annals of Haywood County, North Carolina*:

> "During the battle of Five Forks he (Captain Hargrove) rescued Lieutenant G. S. Ferguson, who was desperately wounded. In the affair, however, he was himself captured and sent as a prisoner to Sandusky, Ohio. He was released in June 1865 and returned to Haywood County."

So it was that during one of the last major battles of the Civil War, and after having saved his friend, Lt. Garland Ferguson, William was captured by the Union troops during the Battle of Five Forks. This occurred less than two weeks before General Lee's Army of Northern Virginia surrendered at Appomattox Court House.

Records show that Lt. Hargrove was captured on April 1, 1865, and sent first to City Point, Virginia and then on to Old Capitol Prison in Washington, D.C. From there, he was transferred to Johnson's Island, Ohio, a prisoner-of-war camp for Confederate officers near the town of Sandusky, where he was imprisoned until war's end.

William signed the Oath of Allegiance to the United States on June 18, 1865, and was released from Johnson's Island prison—free at last to return to the Pigeon Valley for good. After four terrible long years, William's life-and-death struggle on behalf of the Confederate States had finally come to an end. The trip back home to the mountains from the Northern Ohio prison must have been an arduous undertaking. An account in William's personal diary sheds light on his journey.

- *Left Sandusky, OH, on June 19th on train and traveled by train through Newark, OH, to Bellairs, VA, to Martinsburg, VA, and then to Baltimore, MD, arriving on 20th*
- *Left Baltimore on 21st on a stock boat and Traveled on stock boat down Chesapeake Bay to Fort Monroe, VA, arriving on 22nd*

- *Left Fort Monroe on 23rd on stock boat and Traveled on stock boat up the James River to City Point, VA, and then to Pittsburg Landing, VA, arriving on 23rd*
- *Stopped off in Petersburg, VA, to look in on friends in hospital. Found all OK except G. S. Ferguson who was improving. (William stayed over in Petersburg waiting for his friend Garland Ferguson to get well so that he could take Ferguson home. After waiting until July 5th and then finding out that it would be another 3 weeks before Garland could be released, he decided to go home alone.)*
- *Left Petersburg on July 5th on train and Traveled by train to Danville, VA, arriving on July 5th*
- *Left Danville on July 6th on train and Traveled by train to Greensboro, N.C., and then to Salisbury, N.C., arriving on July 6th*
- *Left Salisbury on July 7th by train and Traveled by train to Morganton, N.C., arriving on July 7th*
- *Left Morganton on July 7th at 9 p.m. and arrived home on July 10th at 3 p.m.*

The trek home consumed about three weeks' time, and William mostly relied on trains and stock boats to make his way from northern Ohio to Morganton, North Carolina. From there, where the rail lines ended, it can only be surmised that he hitched rides on wagons and hiked on foot the rest of the way into the Pigeon Valley.

It is a testament to William's character that he stopped off in Petersburg, Virginia, to check on friends convalescing in the hospitals. He steadfastly remained there for almost two weeks waiting to assist his wounded friend, Garland Ferguson, and take him home. No sacrifice was too great for those brave young southern soldiers who had shared such terrible horrors for four long years. They had fought side by side, slept and eaten together, looked after one another, and, in fact, had grown closer than blood brothers.

In writing this account of William Hargrove's Civil War experience, it has been exceedingly difficult to hold back personal sentiments and thoughts. However, William did open his own heart and mind to share frank opinions about the war. The diary that he kept at the time includes later reminiscences of the war years, from which the following short excerpts are respectfully taken:

In this war just ended I have known many who did not want to enlist or volunteer, but were influenced by some of the above illegitimate influences (newspapers of the day and big mouth politicians) and now their bones are bleaching far from home or friends and their graves erased, not even a board to mark the lonely spot, and now many of those same persons who influenced them into war are now condemning those poor unfortunate creatures and branding them as hot-headed rebels. This is the pay you get for not saying No.

Arrived home from this bloody ruthless and unjust war with a very sad heart with the thought of leaving so many dear friends behind me, never again to return.

These heartfelt reflections represent only a small portion of what William wrote and left behind for later generations to read. They clearly illustrate that he returned home from the war with bitter feelings towards those who had led the South into a civil war. He did not believe there had been just cause on either side to take up arms against fellow countrymen, fathers, sons, and brothers. And he would feel that way for the remaining years of his life.

Beginning Afresh

William Hargrove returned from the war in July 1865 to a Pigeon Valley that was much changed from the one he had left four years earlier. Fields were fallow and overgrown. Roads had not been maintained and were in deplorable condition. Homes and barns were either deserted or in a state of neglect and disrepair. All of this affected by the extended absence of the many brave young men who had left their families and the Pigeon Valley to fight the war just ended. But they were all back now—those who had survived the war—and they quickly began making the farm fields productive again and rebuilding their community and their lives.

The Augustus Columbus Hartgrove homestead would have gleefully welcomed William and his younger brothers Joseph Franklin and Augustus Alexander (who had been conscripted at about age 14) back from the war. Surely, William's mother, Ellen, cried joyous tears as she pulled her sons against her bosom, embracing and feeling them and knowing that they were now at home and safe.

There was so much catching up to do and getting reacquainted, but that would all be in due course. Almost immediately, William and his father and brothers would have begun working the fields back into shape and tending to roads, buildings, and equipment long neglected and in dire need of repair. Although backbreaking, William could embrace this hard work as if there were no tomorrow. He was alive and with his family again. He was where he should be.

Over the next few years, William not only helped with the family chores, but he involved himself with other work such as teaching school and regularly hauling farm crops to distant markets. An old pocket notebook of his, passed down from Granddaughter Nannie Hargrove Smathers, reveals many noteworthy things about William's life around this time.

Interestingly, the little notebook is identified on the front with the title "Wm. H. Hartgrove's Book, Lexington, Ky, Nov 9th, 1866." Apparently, William intended to dedicate the entire notebook to a trip he was making to Lexington, Kentucky, but only about eight of the approximately 40 pages have recordings associated with the trip. There are no clues in the ledger illuminating the purpose of the trip or who might have accompanied him. However, other records indicate it was probably a stock drove sponsored by Captain Thomas Isaac Lenoir, who was a large landowner on the East Fork of the Pigeon River.

William begins his notes as follows:

Kentucky Campaign – Left home on 9th Oct. 1866, Traveled by way of Asheville, Pt. Rock (Paint Rock) & the Greenville road to within 8 miles of Greenville (Greeneville) Tenn.

The notes continue and list all the towns and river crossings that he encountered on the trip up to Kentucky, with distances denoted. William arrived back home from Lexington around Nov. 23, 1866, making the "campaign" about 45 days in duration.

The rest of the space in the "Wm H. Hartgrove's Book" is crammed full of other notations that record expenses on other trips to distant markets, track attendance of scholars in the schools he taught, account for money he owed and was owed to him, and document numerous other things.

There are records of at least two treks to markets in Augusta, Georgia. His notes record expenses for tolls, corn and fodder, horse collars, a wagon axle tree, sugar and cheese, and more. One of these trips in 1870 began later than usual on November 18th and William did not arrive back home until December 16th.

It appears that the drovers' route to Georgia was always the same, traveling from Beaverdam (Canton) down Hominy Creek and over to the Buncombe Turnpike. Then turning southward, they followed the turnpike to Flat Rock and down Saluda Mountain into Greenville, South Carolina. From there, other roads led southwesterly to Augusta, Georgia. These market adventures normally took about a month's time, and William made several of them over the years until the railroad finally penetrated the mountains.

Many of the pages in the "Wm H. Hartgrove's Book" are comprised of attendance records for the subscription and public schools that William taught. Additionally, he used it to keep accountings of the money owed to him by the sponsors of his subscription school scholars. The record shows that he opened and taught one subscription school session at "Chincapin" (Chinquapin) Grove in 1867. In August 1869, there are recordings for another three-month subscription school at the Chinquapin Grove schoolhouse.

Apparently, William began teaching three classes at the public Bethel Academy on November 22, 1869. He calls these classes "Class 1st," "Class 2nd," and "Minor Class." A total of approximately 30 "head" (William's word) of scholars attended this school session, including his sister, Althea. William's schedule was very demanding during the latter part of 1869, with one school session following close behind another. Somehow, though, he squeezed in enough time to carry on a romance, as will soon be revealed.

Interestingly, William's notebook offers evidence of his membership in a curious organization. At the very top of one of the pages was written "Ben Franklin's" and under that heading, along with the date of Feb 6, 1867, were listed names of club members along with credits and debits for initiation fees. It is surmised that William and several of his young friends had founded a Ben Franklin's Club, following the lead of the famous Ben Franklin himself. Franklin had fashioned his own club with friends many years before to discuss topics of the day.

That club was dedicated to mutual improvement, which may also have been the inspiration for William and his friends, including Jo. F. Cathey, A.J. Long, D.B. Nelson, and R.A. Sentelle. The Reverend D.B. Nelson was the first Grand Master of the Masonic Lodge in Waynesville and a principal at Bethel Academy. R.A. Sentelle became the first County Superintendent of Schools. It is likely that William's novel club offered a forum for these up-and-coming young leaders of the community to discuss politics and other mutual topics of interest.

Throughout William's notebook, there are many other interesting and revealing notations, including the ones listed below.

- *Boar had a calf July 20th, 1870*
- *Disease took the Jack*
- *Rose took the bull Aug. 17th, 1870*
- *Christmas Day Dec. 25th, 1866*
  - *Frost bitten snow last night & cool today*
- *Christmas Day 1867*
  - *Nice & pleasant spent part of the day at Mr. Chambers and the night at Col. J. Cathey's*
- *Deliver the mules to John Summey if he will receive them & the money $475.00. Two one hundred dollar bills U.S. legal tender & at least $175.00 in small bills. (William's math is interesting.)*
- *On April 14th, 1870, Jimmie Brown set in to work for a period of one month beginning at 12:00 at a salary of $4.50 per month.*
- *Mr. Brown sent two head of cattle here January 5th to winter at 50 cts/per head per month. Took them away March 25th.*

The wonderful old personal notebook opens a window into William's personal affairs during the period immediately following the Civil War. Farm work, droves to far-away markets, teaching school, and even a social organization tagged the Ben Franklin's Club helped bridge the gap between the fury of war and another life-changing event.

A Hargrove and Cathey Union

On November 9, 1869, William Hargrove married Nancy Louisa Cathey, who was 21 years old at the time. Nannie, as she was known later, was the daughter of William Burton and Lucinda Moore Cathey, and the granddaughter of "Colonel" Joseph and Nancy Alice Hyatt Cathey. Five children would be born to the couple over the next ten years as follows: James Burton (1870), Florence Leona (1872), Joseph Alexander (1874), Theodore Augustus (1877), and William Walter (1879).

The young married couple immediately moved in with Nancy's mother (who had been widowed three years earlier) and commenced to forge a life together. Mrs. Lucinda Cathey's two-story frame house was situated on the west side of the Pigeon River, near the Moore's farm where Lucinda was raised. During that first growing season, William and a hired hand by the name of Jimmie Brown raised crops on a piece of the Moore's property. And it seems that the fall harvest did not stop there. Nancy produced the fruit of her and William's love with the birth of their first child, James Burton, on October 26, 1870.

One of William's diary accounts reveals his building "some" cabins on the Moore place and moving into them during the winter of 1871 and 1872. The use of the word "some" in William's narrative might refer to a stable and hog pen that would have been needed, in addition to a small log cabin. Apparently, he had not completed the house nor was there a stable to shelter livestock when they moved to the cabin. The diary offers the following glimpse of this tough winter:

> ...moved to them (the cabins) on 29th of Feb. 1872 and then fell a snow 15 in. deep which found us in poor condition to receive it as we had no stables nor cracks filled in our cabin.

It is difficult to appreciate the hardship that William and Nancy undoubtedly suffered during that cold winter—especially poor Nancy. Being a dutiful wife and companion, she faithfully moved with her husband, amid the cold winter, into a log cabin which had no mud-filling in the log chinks. During the late February blizzard mentioned in William's diary, Nancy—caring for one-year-old James and expecting at the time—would have been exposed to freezing wintry blasts and blowing snow inside her cabin. But the young family survived somehow, and come spring, there was more than warmer weather to be thankful for. On April 15, 1872, Florence Leona was born into the world in a small rustic log cabin perched on a mountainside overlooking the Pigeon River.

William made a crop that year on the Moore property and managed to find some land to purchase. Those facts are revealed in the following diary entry:

Made a crop on the Moore place but in fall found myself a good deal in debt for land & no visible means to get out.

It is evident that William is worried about paying off a debt incurred from buying a piece of land. The solution to the dilemma was to begin working for his wife's Grandfather "Colonel" Joseph Cathey, earning a wage of $16.00 per month. On December 4, 1872, he and the family moved back to Lucinda Cathey's place, while he commenced work for Colonel Cathey.

A little more than a year later, during the spring of 1874, William moved the family back to their little log cabin and tended a crop on the Moore's bottomland. It must have been a bumper crop, because he was prompted to record the number of bushels of corn and wheat made and the fact that it was a nice income.

That same year was marked by at least two significant family events. The more pleasant being the birth of a third child, Joseph Alexander, on April 12, 1874. But on a more somber note, William and his family, along with the entire Forks of Pigeon community, would mourn the loss of the Pigeon Valley's most revered citizen. "Colonel" Joseph Cathey died on June 1, 1874.

The property that William acquired in 1872 was likely carved out of William

Moore's large tract, and it could have been the same piece of land where his crude log structures were built. Nancy's mother Lucinda was a Moore herself, and she must have helped the young couple obtain the property. In fact, county property records reveal that in September 1874 Lucinda deeded a 43-acre tract of land to Nannie (Nancy was going by the name "Nannie" by then), which surely had once been Moore property.

It is believed that William and Nannie continued to inhabit their small log cabin for a short while. In 1875, William again raised corn and wheat crops. That winter he made two trips to the market in the company of his brother-in-law, James Webster Cathey (sister Althea's husband and Nannie's brother). When they returned from the second of these trips in late January 1876, William found his father gravely ill. Sadly, Augustus Columbus Hartgrove died on February 18, 1876.

William wrote that in June of 1876 heavy rains and a Pigeon River "freshet" flooded the whole valley and did tremendous damage to the crops and fields. Undeterred, he was able to replant the crops and make them in three months, barely completing his harvest in late September ahead of the first white frost that crept down from the mountain tops.

That winter was one of the worst in memory for the Pigeon Valley folk. A temperature of 20 degrees below zero was recorded—the coldest on record for the valley. It was during this Arctic spell that William made a journey to Texas on January 15, 1877. The records are silent on the reasons for the trip, but he probably went to visit younger brother Augustus Alexander, who had recently moved to Texas from Haywood County.

Also, there were likely affairs of their father's estate to be discussed. William may have gone there to obtain a signature or deliver property proceeds from the settlement of the estate. It would not be unreasonable to think that, while in Texas, he paid a visit to his Uncle Lawson Hartgrove who had relocated there as well. William's diary shows that he returned home on February 5, 1877.

With the births of Theodore Augustus on June 6, 1877, and William Walter on September 18, 1879, William and Nannie Hargrove's family was complete. By then, the Hargroves had outgrown the small log cabin and William would have built an addition or a new house to accommodate the growing family. Although farming and making crops was still an essential source of the family's livelihood, William's role in county political affairs was growing and becoming more important to him and to the county.

A Useful Citizen

Ever since William returned from the Civil War, friends, neighbors, and acquaintances were addressing him by the interesting moniker "Hack." Personal letters still exist from the period immediately following the war in which he signed his name "Hack." Although the origin of this name is unclear, it is notable that as the years passed more and more people began reverently addressing and referring to him as "Captain Hack," acknowledging his officer's rank in the Confederate army. Accordingly, hereafter in this biographical account, William Harrison Hargrove will respectfully be referred to as either "Hack" or "Captain Hack" while recounting his affairs.

Weather and farming were not the only matters of interest and pursuit for Hack Hargrove in 1876. The county records for that year show he was serving on Haywood County's Board of Commissioners. Interestingly, it is recorded that he voted against one Commissioners' order to grant a spirituous liquor license. Hack's vote demonstrates a devotion to the interests of temperate behavior, which would be manifested later when he became a leader in the Sons of Temperance brotherhood. Eventually, he would hold the highest office in the State of North Carolina with this organization, which was dedicated to the temperance movement prohibiting consumption of alcoholic beverages.

In 1879, these same records tell of Hack's appointment by the County Commissioners to a five-person committee "whose duty it should be to devise a plan on which to build a courthouse." By this time, Hack had obviously established an excellent reputation for himself, and the county fathers looked to him to ensure that a good and reasonable plan for the erection of a new courthouse was produced.

As a result of this committee's efforts, the county's third courthouse, constructed of brick, was completed in 1883. In retrospect, it was an incredible responsibility and undertaking for William, a Pigeon Valley farmer who just a few years before was dwelling in a tiny log cabin and struggling to make a living and escape indebtedness.

The Commissioner's Court archives indicate that in 1879 Hack went before the Board of Commissioners to "renew his bond as County Surveyor." The bond, in the amount of $500, ensured that Hack would reliably and professionally fulfill the responsibilities of the position. Since he was renewing the surveyor's bond, it is evident he was already working as the County Surveyor and likely started in 1877.

At that time, the most common role of the land surveyor was to determine the boundaries and area of a given piece of land. Surveyors would measure and describe the property boundaries using metes and bounds (distance and direction) measurements. The most difficult part of the work was representing property metes and bounds geometrically and accurately on a map, as well as in a narrative description that could be used in legal property documents. Also, the surveyor had to possess sufficient knowledge of mathematics and geometry to calculate the area, or acreage, within his boundary descriptions. Hack obviously had the qualities and skills to handle this technical work, because he performed in the County Surveyor position for many years.

In 1881, he was once more approved to conduct the County Surveyor's responsibilities for an additional two-year term. However, the Court records show that Hack resigned from this position in 1882. Although not mentioned in the record, there was a particularly good reason that he forfeited this prestigious and coveted job. Another employment opportunity had presented him with a challenge and reward potential that was simply too good to pass up.

In the year 1882, the Western North Carolina Railroad finally arrived in Haywood County. No longer would the farmers depend on long droves down the turnpikes to Greenville, South Carolina, and Augusta, Georgia, to reach markets hungry for their grain products, cattle, and swine. The railroad allowed easy access to the markets beyond the mountains in North Carolina's Piedmont, South Carolina, and Virginia. Additionally, local industries such as logging and tanning found the railroad a perfect outlet for their products. The rail service also provided opportunities for more merchants to enter the western mountains and for tourists to travel to Haywood County and experience the area's beauty and climate.

The coming of the railroad proved to be an economic boon and blessing to the county as well as to the small town of Pigeon River (Canton), which was the western terminus of the railroad for a few months until construction progress extended the line westward to Waynesville and beyond. One can only imagine the level of excitement and activity around the Pigeon River railroad station, as it quickly became the focus of commerce for the entire county. Construction of warehouses and other infrastructure to support the passenger and freight services was hurriedly completed and a railroad depot readied for the arrival of the first trains.

Of course, someone had to run the railroad's business at Pigeon River—someone with a good business head, adequate supervisory skills, and proven credibility and influence in the community. Who, then, did the WNC Railroad Company choose for this important station agent position? They found all these necessary qualities in a local native: Hack Hargrove.

Hack had been the County Surveyor for at least five years when he resigned the position in 1882 and became the first Agent for the Western North Carolina Railroad in Pigeon River. A statement of account dated October 1882 from the Western North Carolina Railroad auditor's office in Salisbury, N.C., has been found, and it is addressed to "W.H. Hargrove, Agent Pigeon River, N.C." This statement shows the monthly credits and debits for all passenger, freight, and telegraph services at the Pigeon River railroad station. Obviously, being the railroad station agent at Pigeon River, Hack was the person in charge and responsible for all the railroad services and related financial matters.

Agent Hack Hargrove held the important railroad job for about five years. The circumstances or reasons for his leaving the railroad are unclear. However, it is known that the railroad company was undergoing a time of turmoil after its arrival at Pigeon River in 1882. Not long after the railroad's completion to Pigeon River, another company, Richmond & Danville Railroad, acquired ownership. For the next few years, they were embroiled in a dispute with the North Carolina State Legislature over the ownership rights to the railroad. This distracting situation could possibly have influenced Hack's final departure from the railroad business.

All the while Hack was working for the county and then the railroad companies, Nannie continued to support him and take care of the family. She provided counsel and encouragement to her husband and sought to lighten his burdens by taking care of the household, supervising daily farming activities, and raising their children. Yet, after bearing five children in a period of less than 10 years, this hardy woman succumbed to illness. On February 13, 1883, Nannie Hargrove met her maker at the relatively young age of 34 years. Undoubtedly, her passing would leave family, friends, and the entire community grieving for a long time to come.

It must have been an extremely sorrowful and challenging period for Hack, likely the lowest ebb of his very eventful life. The children's ages ranged from three to 12 years old at the time. It is believed that his mother, Ellen, or mother-in-law, Lucinda, moved in with the family and helped fill the void occasioned by Nannie's unfortunate fate. Certainly, the older children, James, Florence, and Joe, would share increased responsibilities around the farm and help mind Theodore and Walter. Extreme sacrifice from the entire family was required to endure and overcome such a tragedy, but they managed somehow.

County Commissioners' Court records reveal that in 1885 Hack was re-elected to the Board of County Commissioners. Also, in June 1885, the commissioners appointed him and two other members to constitute a Board of Education, possibly the first to be formed in Haywood County. These responsibilities along with his familial duties and the railroad agent job at Pigeon River surely made it an extremely demanding and hectic period for Hack.

County records for June of 1887 declare that "Hack Hargrove came into Commissioner's Court and took the oath of County Surveyor." It seems Hack had given up his railroad employment and was able to regain the County Surveyor position rather quickly, demonstrating not only his skill level in this occupation but his influence in local county politics and with the Pigeon River town officials as well.

The county records also indicate that in 1888, Hack again resigned from a position to which he had been appointed by the Commissioner's Court.

This time he resigned from the Board of Education which is noted as follows in the record:

> *Honorable W. H. Hargrove tendered his resignation as a member of the County Board of Education which resignation was accepted with the thanks of this Court in behalf of the educational interest of this County for his valuable services.*

Hack's resignation became necessary upon his election in 1888 to represent Haywood County as its representative to the Lower House of the 1889 North Carolina State General Assembly. The government was in session from January 9 through March 11, 1889, in which time he was able to renew old friendships with veterans from the rebellion who were met there in assembly. No matter the initiatives or work taken up during that session, Hack would have immersed himself in the legislative business after overcoming some degree of awkwardness and unfamiliarity with the process.

Sometime around 1890 or 1891, Hack's oldest son James (Jim) Burton, about 20 years old at the time, fled the mountains for the West. Jim travelled to Townsend, Montana, where his Uncle Alfred Franklin Hargrove and a party of 43 related persons from Haywood County had moved in 1880. His motivation for leaving the family and the Pigeon Valley are still unclear, but it is known that Jim spent more than two decades prospecting for gold in Montana, Nevada, and California.[99] To his brother Joe fell most of the farming responsibility. Florence would continue in her role, with Ellen's and Lucinda's assistance, managing the household and seeing that the family was properly fed and cared for.

Masonic records show that in December 1894, Hack belonged to the Pigeon River Masonic Lodge. Although little publicized, the Masons had a strong influence on the educational, political, financial, and religious development in the county. It was in 1866 that the first Masonic Lodge opened in Waynesville with the Rev. D.B. Nelson elected as the first Master. Joseph Franklin Hargrove, Hack's brother, was one of the founding members of the

---

[99] Jim Hargrove, the author's grandfather, returned to the North Carolina mountains after a couple of decades of gold prospecting out West.

Waynesville Masonic Lodge. From this first Waynesville lodge sprung other lodges in Pigeon River, Clyde, and Sonoma (Pigeon Valley or Bethel).

In 1894, Hack voted in favor of forming a new Sonoma Lodge in the Pigeon Valley area. It is probable that he was one of the early members of the Waynesville Lodge, and, as the newer lodges were formed, moved first to the Pigeon River Masonic Lodge and then to the Sonoma Lodge when it was created about 1895.

Hack's involvement with the Masons, a fraternal organization which professed to "seek to make good men better and thereby make the world a better place in which to live," offered yet another avenue to improve the welfare of the community. Throughout most of Hack's adult life and until he was buried with Masonic honors, he devoted his energies through this organization to better those around him.

During the last decade of the 19th century and into the 20th, Hack Hargrove continued his political and professional pursuits. He served other terms as a County Commissioner and continued surveying, as evidenced by existing survey and land plats drafted by his own hand. It is also known that Hack worked as a surveyor in helping lay out and construct a huge pulp mill in the village of Canton (formerly Pigeon River) during the years 1905 to 1908. The Champion Fibre Company soon became one of the world's largest pulp mills and transformed Canton into a thriving industrial town.

An old newspaper clipping, found stuck between the pages of a weathered book, exposed another of Hack's professions and contributions to his community. The clipping is from a 1908 *Canton Vindicator* newspaper, and it reveals an intriguing fact about Hack Hargrove. By that time, the Champion Fibre Company had just begun production of wood pulp, and the *Vindicator* was one of the first, if not the first, newspapers in Canton. And who do you think was at the helm publishing this fledgling rag? That's right—it was Hack Hargrove feeding the news and stories of human interest to the citizens of Canton and the Pigeon Valley.

Further investigation shows that in 1908, Hack helped found still another newspaper named the *Haywood Enterprise*. He was an associate editor of this weekly publication which was dedicated to the support of the platform and activities of the Republican Party. So, it can be said that he was devout in his politics and not afraid to express his political beliefs and thoughts.

It seems Hack remained very active and influential in the latter years of his life, being involved in politics, publishing newspapers, farming, and continuing his surveying work. Yet, it has been learned there was still another profession that he was dabbling in and seeking to derive an income. One of the early *Vindicator* editions had a promotional advertisement for "W.H. Hargrove—Real Estate Agent," in which Hack was offering great deals on lots in the booming mill town of Canton for $100 to $300, including generous financing terms. There is apparently no end to Hack Hargrove's professional pursuits and interests, likely limited only by our inability to discover them.

On April 20, 1909, William Harrison (Hack) Hargrove, age 68 years, departed the world of the living and his beautiful Pigeon Valley. After an extraordinary and productive life, he now belonged to the ages. Hack was buried with Masonic honors at Bethel Cemetery and his funeral was widely attended, with the notable exception of eldest son Jim, who was still prospecting for gold out West in California.

Jim was immediately notified of his father's death by a telegram from his brother, Dr. Theodore A. Hargrove. He responded with a letter of his own that is still in the possession of the family. The following short passage is taken from that letter:

> ...what makes me feel so bad about it is that I didn't write to poor old Pa oftener. He certainly had a hard time of it through life but if I was only as good a man as he always was, I would feel that I was ready to go any time.

Jim was not alone in wishing that he "was only as good a man" as Hack Hargrove. Many of Hack's contemporaries wished the same, and today there is one more person who entertains that hope—that would be Hack's great-grandson and Jim's grandson, the author of this article.

Conclusion

It has been an extremely rewarding personal experience to discover the old footprints left behind by my Great-Grandfather Hack Hargrove—clues that revealed a trail of his many contributions to Bethel, Canton, and Haywood County. They clearly show he was a man with more than ordinary abilities and certainly a "useful citizen," as his obituary writer opined many years ago.

This story includes information from the following sources:

- *The Annals of Haywood County, North Carolina* by W. C. Allen, 1977
- *The Early History of Haywood County* by W. Clark Medford, 1961
- *The Middle History of Haywood County* by W. Clark Medford, 1968
- *The 25th North Carolina Infantry Regiment* by Carroll C. Jones, 2009
- *Western North Carolina: Its Mountains and Its People to 1880* by Ora Blackmun, 1977
- *Haywood History 1809 – Civil War* by Kathy Ross and published by *The Waynesville Mountaineer* Publishing Company
- *Diary and Reminiscences of W. H. Hargrove* printed December 1938 by Hattie Rue and Dale Campbell, Sweetwater, Texas
- *Thomas Erwin History* by Thomas Erwin
- The Bicentennial Edition of *The Mountaineer*, Waynesville, N.C., July 1976
- US Census Records
- William Harrison Hargrove's personal notebooks, diary, and other family records
- Records from Haywood County Commissioners' Court
- Cathey and Hargrove genealogy records compiled by Tony Jones
- *Canton Vindicator* newspaper editions from 1908 and 1909
- An old newspaper obituary clipping (newspaper unknown)

First Lt. William H. Hargrove of the 25th North Carolina Infantry Regiment, Co. F, Confederate States of America served throughout the entire American Civil War. (author's collection)

This photograph taken in 2013 shows the remains of the old Chinquapin Grove schoolhouse where Hack Hargrove taught youthful scholars after the Civil War. (author's collection)

Hack Hargrove (right) is posing with a workmate in front of a surveyor's tent, circa 1906. At the time, he was about 65 years old and was working as a surveyor on the Champion Fibre Company pulp mill construction project at Canton, N.C. (courtesy of Canton Historical Museum)

A distinguished looking Hack Hargrove is shown here in his later years. (author's collection)

When A Trip to the Market Took a Month's Time

Introduction

Today we think nothing of jumping into our car and making a quick trip to the supermarket. However, for our ancestors who settled in these mountains of western North Carolina, a trip to the market was not such a simple proposition.

Back in the mid-19th century, many Haywood County farmers sold their livestock and produce at markets outside of the mountains. These trips, which involved driving livestock over miles and miles of poor dirt roads, were called "droves" back then and normally occurred in the fall after the crops were harvested and the apples picked. Grueling droves to Greenville, South Carolina, or as far away as Augusta, Georgia, could keep Haywood's mountaineers away from their families for a month's time or longer.

During that era, William Harrison Hargrove, or simply Hack as he was called by acquaintances, lived in the community named Forks of Pigeon (Bethel), and he made several such droves during his lifetime.[100] Fortunately, Hargrove left behind personal hand-written records that give some insight into these annual market trips. From his accounts and other historical sources, it is possible to gain an appreciation for what those epic treks must have been like in the period immediately following the Civil War.

The Buncombe Turnpike

In about 1827, the Buncombe Turnpike was completed linking Greeneville, Tennessee, and Greenville, South Carolina. This wagon road, which passed through the Buncombe County town of Asheville, North Carolina, served

---

[100] Sometime after the Civil War, William H. Hartgrove dropped the "t" in his name and began spelling it as we do today—"Hargrove."

for more than 50 years as the primary north–south artery for transportation in western North Carolina. It immediately opened the mountains to outsiders wishing to engage in commerce in a region hitherto inaccessible. Of more importance to the local mountaineer farmers, this road provided a means by which their surplus farm crops and livestock could be transported and either sold or bartered at distant lowland markets.

Before the Civil War, Hack Hargrove used this fine road on numerous occasions to reach the markets in South Carolina and Georgia. He must have relished the opportunities as a teenager to venture to those far-away places. However, Hack's life was abruptly interrupted in 1861 by the American Civil War, as were the lives of many young men throughout the country. Upon his return to the Pigeon Valley after four long years of fighting for the Confederate States, "Captain" Hack resumed the market droves down the Buncombe Turnpike.[101]

In the Reconstruction Era following the war, Hack found the road in extreme disrepair and the conditions deplorable compared to the pre-war state. Sections of the turnpike south of Asheville that had once been corduroyed, or covered over with thick timber planks, were now filled with washouts and deep ruts. The wood pavers had, for the most part, deteriorated or rotted away. State and local government treasuries were depleted, and money was not available to repair the ruined infrastructure. Yet, the importance of the Buncombe Turnpike to the mountain regions remained as it was prior to the war, if not more so.

Just after the rebellion, Hack made his living teaching and farming. He and his young wife, Nannie Cathey, raised corn and wheat crops on a patch of bottomland next to the Pigeon River. Currency was extremely scarce during those hard times, and farmers like them were obliged to use a portion of their livestock and surplus corn and wheat yields to barter for goods and services locally.

However, the returns and rewards for these valuable products were much higher outside of the mountains, so much so that Hack Hargrove and his neighbors could justify long arduous trips to lowland markets each fall and winter.

---

101 Although Hargrove's rank at the end of the Civil War was first lieutenant, he was addressed as "Captain" by family, friends, and acquaintances after the war.

In 1870, Hack made a trip to the market in Augusta, Georgia, jotting notes of daily expenses along the way. Thankfully, his valuable record has survived, and we can use it to illuminate much about those grueling market droves.[102]

A Grueling Drove to the Augusta Market

On November 17th, 1870, Hack Hargrove and a few friends and kinsmen set out with a covered wagon loaded with grain products and apples. Accompanying them was an eclectic herd of livestock including swine, cattle, and turkeys, which the men drove along the roads with them.

From Forks of Pigeon, Hack would have led his procession down an existing county roadway until the Western Turnpike was encountered. This junction was just east of the Pigeon River fording spot on the Western Turnpike, near today's Town of Canton.

The Western Turnpike was the primary east-west route through North Carolina's western mountains. It was a vital thoroughfare that was completed around 1850, connecting Asheville with Waynesville and other points further to the west, including Webster, Franklin, Murphy, and beyond to Ducktown, Tennessee, and into Georgia.

Snaking eastward and away from the Pigeon River, the turnpike road followed the course of a small stream named Hominy Creek through a gap in the Newfound Mountains.[103] It meandered by John C. Smathers' roadside drover's inn located at the Buncombe-Haywood County border and then passed through the territory where today's communities of Candler and Enka are located.

Beyond the present environs of Enka, the Western Turnpike led the Haywood drovers in an easterly direction until running up against the French

---

102   This little notebook was passed down to the author's aunt, Nannie Hargrove Smathers, who was a granddaughter of William Harrison Hargrove. It is approximately 4" x 6" in size and has 43 existing pages, all in poor condition. The cover page has been torn from the binding and is loose, but it has not been lost. On the top of this page is written "Wm H. Hartgrove's Book." The pages are filled with William's—or Hack's—handwritten notes and records in pencil and ink.
103   It is thought the Pigeon River once flowed through this "water gap" on its way to the Atlantic Ocean. (See this book's article titled "The Pigeon River Once Emptied into the Atlantic Ocean.")

Broad River at Sandy Bottom, just south of Asheville. Hack's notes indicate that on November 18th he paid a toll of 50-cents at Hominy Creek, and the next day paid another toll of 65-cents at Sandy Bottom. After fording the French Broad at Sandy Bottom, he and his party of men and beasts soon came upon the Buncombe Turnpike and headed due south.

Hack's notes reveal that on November 19th he purchased corn and fodder for $1.40 at "King's," which was likely the first drover's station they encountered on the Buncombe Turnpike. These stations, or inns, were located every few miles along the entire length of the turnpike to accommodate the traveling farmers and their livestock.

In addition to providing a place of respite for the drovers, the stations were veritable commercial enterprises. Proprietors procured grain, produce, and hog's meat from local farmers, and, in turn, sold these vital goods to the transient trekkers driving their agrarian capital to the marketplace.

Large pens associated with the drover's stations were used to corral the livestock overnight—except for the turkeys. These unpredictable creatures usually found their own roosting accommodations in nearby trees. Corn, fodder, chestnuts, and acorns purchased at the stations or taken directly from the drovers' wagons were fed to the animals each evening.

From Asheville, the Buncombe Turnpike ran a mostly southward course, passing through the villages of Hendersonville and Flat Rock and then across the Green River, where Hack was obliged to pay another toll of 60-cents. At that point, the road began its treacherous descent out of the mountains through Butt Mountain and Saluda gaps, and then on down by Traveler's Rest before reaching Greenville, South Carolina.

Hack's party chose not to sell their goods and livestock at the Greenville markets. Instead, they aimed to drive another hundred miles or more to Augusta, Georgia. This last leg of their journey was facilitated by much better roads with gentler slopes. According to Hack's notes, they reached the river town of Augusta on December 3rd.

Finally, after 17 days of grueling conditions and tedious plodding along the Buncombe Turnpike and sandy-clay roads of South Carolina, the little band of mountaineers reached their Augusta market destination located astride the

Savannah River. Wasting little time, the livestock and grain would have been sold for rare US legal tender or bartered for commodities that could not be produced or easily obtained at home. Certainly, sugar, salt, coffee, and specified textile goods were high on the take-home lists of their families, friends, and sponsors.

Once the bargaining and haggling was done and the strange sights and sounds of the bustling river town looked at and listened to, the band of mountain men loaded up and headed back to the hills. Their pockets were full of money, the wagon was loaded with precious foreign goods, and thank God, they were rid of those smelly hogs and independent turkeys.

On the return trip, Hack parted with some of his hard-earned cash to pay the toll operators and drover's station proprietors for debts incurred on the outward leg of the journey. According to the record he left, their wagon broke down somewhere short of Saluda Gap, on the steep climb back into the mountains. He noted a payment of $4.00 for a new axel tree to repair the wagon.

However, it would take more than a broken axel tree to dampen Hack Hargrove's spirits on the homeward stretch. There was someone very special waiting for him back at Forks of Pigeon. Of course, Nannie would be proud to see him home again, safe and sound. But that "someone special" was their infant son, James Burton Hargrove, who was born just three weeks before Hack departed for Augusta.[104]

Hack and his teamsters arrived back in the Pigeon Valley on December 17th, 1870, a full month after setting out for Augusta. One can only imagine the wonderful reunion and joyful Christmas that must have been had in the Hargrove home.

Coming of the Railroad

William H. Hargrove continued to make these trips to the lowland markets every fall or winter. Unbelievable as it might sound, in the winter of 1875-1876, he and his brother-in-law, James Webster Cathey, had the gumption and stamina to make two trips to the market.

---
104   James Burton Hargrove is the author's grandfather.

But not long after that remarkable feat, the long market droves along the Buncombe Turnpike to South Carolina and Georgia would no longer be necessary. With the coming of the Western North Carolina Railroad to Asheville in 1880 and to the settlement of Pigeon River (Canton) in 1882, the farmers were able to exploit this more efficient and economical means of transportation to access the markets beyond the mountains.

Hack Hargrove lived to see the day when he did not bid farewell each fall to his family. As a matter of fact, the Western North Carolina Railroad Company hired him as their first Railroad Agent at Pigeon River in 1882. He surely would have been relieved at not having to make those long droves to the market and, for sure, not having to fool with those danged hogs and turkeys.

Note to Readers: William H. Hargrove (Hack) is the author's great-grandfather. Research material for this article was taken from Hargrove's surviving notebook that is filled with handwritten records in pencil and ink. Other sources include the books *Western North Carolina: Its Mountains and Its People to 1880* by Ora Blackmun and *Rooted Deep in the Pigeon Valley* by Carroll C. Jones.

HACK HARGROVE'S DROVE TO MARKET 1870

Droves by farmers from Forks of Pigeon, North Carolina, to the markets in Greenville, South Carolina, and Augusta, Georgia, followed the route shown on the map above. These droves could take a month's time or more. (author's collection)

The pigs are leading the way in this mid-19th century scene of a "drove" to a distant market. (Painted by Elizabeth Cramer McClure and taken from Ora Blackmun's book titled "Western North Carolina: Its Mountains and Its People to 1880.")

William Harrison Hargrove (Hack Hargrove or Captain Hack) hailed from Forks of Pigeon (Bethel) in Haywood County, North Carolina. As a teenager before the Civil War and a veteran following the war, he participated in many mid-19th century droves to lowland markets in Greenville, South Carolina, and Augusta, Georgia. (author's collection)

Captain Hargrove's Diary Discovered Amongst Attic Plunder

One morning a few years ago, I found myself prowling through a trove of attic plunder in a beautiful old farmhouse in Bethel, North Carolina. It was cold and dark up there, and the unfinished flooring was so rough I had to carefully shuffle my feet from one board to the next. Spider webs hanging from the sloping roof rafters glistened in the flashlight's dim beam, and the heady smell of things old and forgotten was overpowering.

I was in the historic Plott house on Garden Creek, located between Canton and Bethel, because this rare survivor of the early 20th century was being sold. The owner had requested a few of us from the Bethel Rural Community Organization to come and make an inventory of the sundry items that had been packed away in the attic over the last century or more. For that reason, I was rummaging through the musty contents of steamer trunks, wooden and cardboard boxes, paper bags, reed baskets, and wood barrels when, suddenly, my light shone on an item of immense personal interest to me.

Squatting in an extremely uncomfortable position with my head ducked under the steeply pitched roof, I fished out a small, tattered journal from the bottom of a box. The first words that stood out in the poor light were *W.H. Hartgrove's School*, and a quick scan of the yellowed pages revealed at once what I had discovered. It was an old diary, more than 150 years old, and it had been scribed by my own Great-Grandfather Hargrove!

William Harrison Hargrove was a Civil War veteran who had served in the Confederate Army for the entirety of the war. He was one of the hundred or so volunteers from Forks of Pigeon (present day Bethel) who formed a company named the Haywood Highlanders in June and July of 1861. On July 18th of that first year of the war, those nervous and excited mountain boys led by Captain

Thomas Isaac Lenoir marched to Asheville to join the fray. Soon thereafter, they were mustered into the service of the state of North Carolina as Company F of the 25th North Carolina Infantry Regiment.

Hargrove and the 25th N.C. Troops fought with General Robert E. Lee's Army of Northern Virginia at the Battle of Sharpsburg (or Antietam) in Maryland—the bloodiest single day of the war. About three months later, in December of 1862, he was also on hand when General Lee's army battled and whipped the Yankees at Fredericksburg, Virginia, in what was to be the greatest Confederate victory of the war.

During the last year of the Civil War, when the size of the Rebel army was greatly diminished by death and desertion, Hargrove fought and suffered for nine long months in the muddy trenches in front of Petersburg, Virginia. Just two weeks before the Confederate Army surrendered at Appomattox, First Lieutenant Hargrove was captured at the Battle of Five Forks when the Yankees finally drove the stubborn Rebel troops out of their Petersburg defenses.

He ended up in a prisoner-of-war camp at Sandusky, Ohio, located on the shore of Lake Erie, and there he remained until the conclusion of the war. After the final surrender of the last Confederate armies in the field and after Lieutenant Hargrove had signed an oath of allegiance to the United States, he was released and allowed to return to his home. Travelling on foot and by stock boat, train, and in wagons, he finally reached Forks of Pigeon three weeks later.

The diary I had stumbled upon in the attic was filled with Great-Grandfather Hargrove's cursive writings. After the war, he taught school for a time and recorded in the diary the names of all the scholars attending his "Chincapin [sic] Grove" school, along with the number of days they attended and the amount of money their parents owed him. Also, recorded in their own hand, were the names of other Confederate officers who were imprisoned with him at the Ohio prisoner-of-war camp. And that was not all!

Hargrove's four years of service with the Confederate States had apparently affected a significant change in his attitude toward the war. It can be reasonably concluded, based on many of the reminisces and recordings contained in the diary, that he bore extreme mental burdens from his wartime experience.

His disillusionment with the entire affair is manifest, as is the anger he harbored toward the men of the South—and the North—who led the country into a Civil War and incited boys like him to join the fight.

Below is one haunting rant from the diary that strongly reflects his sentiments.

> *Released from there (the prisoner-of-war camp) June 18th, 1864 (actually it was 1865), arrived home from this bloody, ruthless, and unjust war July 10th with a very sad heart with the thought of leaving so many Dear friends behind me, never again to return. And with what I have seen of war have become so much disgusted that I wish to admonish my friends and relatives to stop when the war cry is sounded by the news papers [sic] & a few of the Big Boys of the land, and consider well the merits of said cry and never engage in any way with the least shadow of doubt in your minds.*

Besides the "Big Boys of the land," Hargrove placed blame where it was not expected. As can be deduced from the expression below, his wrath even extended to those fire-eater preachers—or "enthusiasts of the pulpit"—who had supported the Southern cause.

> *And if you cannot engage in it without doubts as to the merits of the cause be firm in it & not be drug in against your will; and not be influenced by the patriotic appeals of enthusiasts of the pulpit pretending to be ministers of the most High God, but in deed & in truth useful Agts (agents) for the Devil's work wearing the cloak of divine hypocracy [sic], or "white sepulchers."*

William Harrison Hargrove admonished his own sons to not be "influenced in this cruel and dirty work because the news papers [sic] of the day says it is right or some big-mouthed politician full of demagougerism [sic] & enthusiasm appeals to your passions or sympathies & uses every possible means to incite you to action."

There were other heartfelt feelings about the war expressed in the diary, but none more palpable or powerful as the following:

I have known many who did not want to enlist or volunteer, but were influenced by some of the above illegitimate influences & now their bones are bleaching far from home or friends & their graves erased, not even a board to mark the lonely spot & now many of those same persons who influenced them into the war are now condemning those poor unfortunate creatures & branding them as hot headed rebbels [sic]. This is the pay you get for not saying no.

After the war, Hargrove overcame his dark Civil War memories and forged an impressive professional career. He never said "no" to hard work when it involved supporting his family or rendering beneficial services in favor of his fellow men and women. "Captain Hargrove," as he came to be called, farmed, taught school, served as a Haywood County Commissioner and County Surveyor, was elected to represent Haywood County at the State General Assembly, held the state's highest office in the Sons of Temperance organization, worked as the railroad's first station agent when it reached Pigeon River (Canton) in 1882, was a surveyor for the Champion Fibre Company during its original construction, and briefly managed and edited the *Canton Vindicator* newspaper. Finally, in 1909, his eventful life ran its course.

It is no wonder that an obituarist at the time felt inclined to describe "Captain Hargrove" as a "useful citizen." And it is no wonder I was so thrilled to discover my great-grandfather's long-lost diary buried in the attic plunder at the old Garden Creek Plott house.

Shown in this photo is the old Plott house overlooking the Garden Creek farm fields and archaeological site, midway between Canton and Bethel. While searching through the house's attic plunder, the author discovered his Great-Grandfather Hargrove's long-lost diary, which is more than 150 years old. (author's collection)

Several years ago, the author discovered Captain William H. Hargrove's diary (shown in photo) in the attic of the Plott house located at Garden Creek. Its 80-some yellowed and frayed pages contain notes inscribed with pen and pencil from 1865 until June of 1877. The names of Hargrove's fellow captives at a prisoner-of-war camp on Lake Erie in 1865 were recorded in it. Also, other things of manifest importance to Hargrove show up in his notes including weather observations, farming events, student records, and the births of his children. (author's collection)

Confederate Flag Waving

I wonder what my Great-Grandfather William Harrison Hargrove would have allowed about all the Confederate flags being brandished about these days. He was a Confederate veteran of the Civil War, serving with distinction from the summer of 1861 until finally being captured at the Battle of Five Forks on April 1, 1865.

Along with his regiment, the 25th North Carolina Troops, he fought at the Battle of Sharpsburg in Maryland, the bloodiest single day of the war. He was also on hand when General Robert E. Lee's troops battled and whipped the Yankees at Fredericksburg, Virginia, in what was to be the greatest Confederate victory of the war.

During the last year of the Civil War, when the size of the Rebel Army was greatly diminished by death and desertion, Lieutenant Hargrove fought and suffered for nine months in the muddy "ditches" in front of Petersburg. Just two weeks before the surrender at Appomattox, he was captured when the Yankees finally drove the Rebel troops out of their Petersburg defenses. Yes, my great-grandfather would certainly have seen his fair share of waving Confederate flags during America's devastating Civil War.

Recently, I had the good fortune of stumbling across a diary hidden away in the attic of an old house in Bethel, North Carolina. It was one that my Great-Grandfather Hargrove had kept and was filled with writings in his tiny cursive hand. Knowing that he had taught school for a time after the war, I was not surprised to find a list of his scholars (students) with the number of days they had attended his Chincapin [sic] Grove school and the amount of money their parents were indebted to him. Also recorded in the diary were many names of other Confederate officers who were imprisoned with him at Johnston's Island Prison in Sandusky, Ohio. And that was not all!

Undoubtedly, his four years of service to the Southern cause had affected a significant change in his attitude toward the war. When it was all over and Great-Grandfather Hargrove finally found his way back home from Ohio, he was terribly disillusioned with war. Not only that, but he was also filled with hard feelings toward those who had incited boys like him to join the fight. The following writings in his diary reflect those sentiments.

Released from there (Johnston's Island Prison) June 18th, 1864 (actually 1865), arrived home from this bloody, ruthless, and unjust war July 10th with a very sad heart with the thought of leaving so many Dear friends behind me, never again to return. And with what I have seen of war have become so much disgusted that I wish to admonish my friends and relatives to stop when the war cry is sounded by the news papers [sic] & a few of the Big Boys of the land, and consider well the merits of said cry and never engage in any way with the least shadow of doubt in your minds.

Besides the "Big Boys of the land," my great-grandfather even placed blame where it was not expected.

And if you cannot engage in it without doubts as to the merits of the cause be firm in it & not be drug in against your will; and not be influenced by the patriotic appeals of enthusiasts of the pulpit pretending to be ministers of the most High God, but in deed & in truth useful Agts (agents) for the Devil's work wearing the cloak of divine hypocracy [sic], or "white sepulchers."

Great-Grandfather admonished his own sons—including my grandfather—to not be "influenced in this cruel and dirty work because the news papers [sic] of the day says it is right or some big-mouthed politician full of demagougerism [sic] & enthusiasm appeals to your passions or sympathies & uses every possible means to incite you to action."

There were other similar sentiments expressed in the diary, but none so palpable or powerful as the following:

I have known many who did not want to enlist or volunteer, but were influenced by some of the above illegitimate influences & now their bones are bleaching far from home or friends & their graves erased, not even a board to mark the lonely spot & now many of those same persons who influenced them into the war are now condemning those poor unfortunate creatures & branding them as hot headed rebbels [sic]. This is the pay you get for not saying no.

Confederate 1st Lieutenant William Harrison Hargrove's passionate feelings were hard-won from four long years of deadly warfare against fellow Americans. Without a doubt, he would be unimpressed by the Rebel flags being bandied about these days for political, hate-filled, and other misdirected reasons.

A Rebel soldier is waving a Confederate battle flag during the Civil War. (artist unknown)

A Confederate battle flag is being brandished about by an insurrectionist inside the US Capitol in January 2021. (Getty Images)

CANTON MEMORIES

An early glimpse of the railroad running through Canton

How, Why, and When Did Canton Really Get Its Name?

Many western North Carolinians have probably wondered at one time or another **how, why,** and **when** the Town of Canton got its name. These are questions that should not be too difficult to answer—one might think. Yet, when this engineer/historian began sleuthing and endeavoring to learn more about the old iron-truss bridge that once spanned the Pigeon River in Canton, North Carolina, a host of conflicting facts, dates, and fanciful tales about the naming of Canton were revealed.

Stories and accounts written over the years vary greatly regarding when that original pedestrian/vehicle bridge was actually built and when the town acquired the name "Canton." To get to the bottom of the iron-truss bridge construction mystery, a trip to the Haywood County courthouse in search of old records seemed to be in order.

Once discovered, the minutes from a May 5, 1890 session of the Haywood County Commissioners' Court were enlightening with the following order recorded: "Ordered that notice be given that sealed bids will be received until the first Monday in June for the construction of two stone abutments or piers for the purpose of erecting an iron bridge across Pigeon River at the ford near Pigeon River Depot, the work to be done in first class ruble (rubble) masonry with cut corners and coping. The same to be advertised two successive weeks in the *Waynesville Courier* and *Asheville Democrat*."

Sure enough, a search of the newspaper archives uncovered notices posted in three May and June 1890 editions of the *Asheville Democrat* newspaper. From the evidence available in the commissioners' minutes, it appears that W. M. Smith Stone Contractor built the cut stone abutments to support the original bridge. In the last months of 1890, a total of 800 dollars was paid to the Smith masonry company from the "Special Bridge Fund."

Being clueless regarding this Special Bridge Fund, another records source was uncovered and gleaned for enlightenment. Come to find out, the 1889 session of the North Carolina General Assembly had passed a law authorizing the Haywood County Commissioners to levy "a special tax on the property and polls...in the year 1890, a sufficient amount to build a bridge across said river (Pigeon River) at or near the Penland ford." This, of course, made it absolutely clear that Canton's old iron bridge was not a municipal project. All of the citizens of rural Haywood County, farmers included, funded the bridge and other spans being proposed throughout the county out of their own pockets.

Unfortunately, no existing minutes or other records have been discovered that can definitively establish the date the bridge contracts were let or when the construction work was initiated—nor do we know the exact completion date. However, there is other extant information that frames the timing of the bridge work.

Again, the county records indicate that a contractor—M. F. Renno (Reno)—was paid $337.05 in January of 1891 for filling the Pigeon River bridge abutments. This is, indeed, a good indication that the foundations were completed and awaiting the superstructure in early 1891. More than a year later, on July 1, 1892, one of the town's prominent citizens advertised in the *Raleigh News and Observer* that the little town of Pigeon River had changed its name to "Canton." Based on this report and bedrock local lore that the town borrowed its new name from the bridge company's hometown of Canton, Ohio, it is very likely the new wrought iron-truss bridge was erected across the Pigeon River between January of 1891 and July of 1892.

Certainly, it is a well-known fact that the bridge was purchased from the Wrought Iron Bridge Company in Canton, Ohio. Although the old trusses and single-lane roadway structure were demolished in or about 1962, the plaques bearing the bridge company's name and adorning each end of the bridge were saved and can still be found at the Canton Historical Museum.

From the photos of the bridge that have survived, it can be reliably determined it bore a particular architectural style known as a single-intersection, Pratt through-truss bridge. The structure was likely made of wrought iron as opposed to steel, which had yet to be proven a superior construction material. When completed in 1891 or early 1892, this bridge immediately eliminated the difficult river crossing at the nearby Penland ford. Wagons, coaches, horses, livestock, and pedestrians were now blessed with a safe, reliable, and dry method of crossing the Pigeon River on the primary east-west turnpike joining Asheville and Waynesville.

During the first months of 1891—while the bridge was probably under construction—the North Carolina General Assembly passed a law incorporating Haywood County's village of Pigeon River, henceforth to be known as the "Town of Pigeon River." However, it was not a popular name and did not sit easy with many of the local businessmen and dignitaries, especially a railroad ticket agent named Mr. C. S. Mingus, who went by the name Cash. The previously mentioned notice in the *News and Observer* on July 1, 1892, about the town's name change to Canton was authored by Cash Mingus and is given in its entirety below.

> *Pigeon River, the pretty little town situated on the far-famed river bearing the same name, in the county of Haywood, has been changed to Canton. The necessity for the change arose from the confusion arising from different places having Pigeon prefixed to their names as well as the river, which extends from the foot of Mt. Pisgah to the Halston (Holston) in Tennessee.*
>
> *Almost everyone, especially the tourist, the angler and the admirers of dame nature will remember the little town so picturesquely situated and so well and favorably known, and many will be glad to know that instead of Pigeon River it is now Canton. Other papers may copy.*

Many believable and other far-fetched stories have been repeated over the years about certain town citizens, such as Cash Mingus, being inspired by the new bridge's nameplate bearing the name "Canton, Ohio." Undoubtedly, there is some truth in these tales, but how much will never be known. However, it is known that in January of 1893 the General Assembly of North Carolina acted to officially change the name of the "Town of Pigeon River" to the one that persists to this day—the "Town of Canton."

It seems that Cash's artfully composed newspaper notice has given us at least a plausible reason for the town dropping the Pigeon River tag and adopting "Canton" as its new one. All those place names with Pigeon prefixed to them would surely have made life somewhat difficult for a railroad ticket agent like Mingus. After all, having to patiently explain to the multitudes of arriving passengers which Pigeon River destination they had reached would have gotten old in a hurry. And, certainly, there were no other Canton names around to confuse his patrons, except for that one up in…now where was that iron-truss bridge fabricated?

> Note to Readers: For those who might be interested, stop by the pretty little gazebo park on the east side of Canton's present-day Main Street bridge and direct your gaze across the Pigeon River toward the century-old brick building occupied by the Riverview Farm and Garden Store. Believe it or not, the remains of one of the cut-stone bridge abutments laid up in 1890 by men working for W. M. Smith Stone Contractor can still be spotted hugging the west bank of the river. The 1892 iron-truss bridge that was fabricated in Canton, Ohio, and spanned the Pigeon River was once supported on both sides of the river with cut-stone abutments.

Men on horseback and in a horse-drawn carriage are shown in this photo crossing the Pigeon River at a spot known as the "Penland ford". In 1891-1892, an iron truss bridge fabricated in Canton, Ohio, was erected at the ford, just upstream from the railroad bridge that can be seen in the photo. The North Carolina General Assembly changed the name of the nearby settlement from "Pigeon River" to "Canton" in 1893. (courtesy of Canton Historical Museum)

This is a very early 1900's view looking eastward at Canton's original iron-truss bridge spanning the Pigeon River. (courtesy of Canton Historical Museum)

In the mid-1950s, Canton's old iron-truss bridge still spanned the Pigeon River, as seen in this photo. Motor vehicle drivers were obliged to wait and make sure the single-lane bridge was clear before crossing the river. (courtesy of Canton Historical Museum)

This photographic view looks through Canton's original iron-truss bridge structure toward a brick building in the background (date unknown). The building has resisted recent river floods and still stands on the west bank of the Pigeon River. (courtesy of Canton Historical Museum)

In the center of this 1960s-era photo, Canton's brand-new concrete bridge can be seen carrying Main Street's vehicular and pedestrian traffic across the Pigeon River. Just to the right of the new bridge, you might note that the old iron-truss bridge is gone, having been demolished in 1962. Today, a historical marker on the near side bank of the river memorializes the original bridge. (from Tony Jones collection)

Adorning the two portals of Canton's original iron-truss bridge structure were plaques recognizing the bridge-builder. Both were saved and can be found in the Canton Historical Museum's collection. (courtesy of Canton Historical Museum)

Colonel Silas A. Jones' Pipeline Dream

Introduction

All of us living in these beautiful western North Carolina mountains are aware of the shuttered paper mill located in Canton. It was an enterprise fixed in our minds and, seemingly, had always been here. In fact, that factory started up in early 1908 and converted wood into pulp and paper for more than a century, right in the heart of Canton.

Prior to the chaos of the Champion Fibre Company's physical creation and the eruption of billowing smoke from its giant concrete smokestack, founder Peter G. Thomson entertained conflicting thoughts about where to build his mill. He had been practically convinced that Canton was the perfect site for his pulp mill because of several advantages, which included the following: it had an adequate supply of water from the Pigeon River; pulpwood from Thomson's extensive timber holdings at the Pigeon River headlands could potentially be sluiced through a water flume down the river to Canton; and, importantly, the Southern Railway's tracks passed through the small town.

However, even those compelling reasons did not deter some challenging notions. As a matter of fact, Thomson was lobbied by many entrepreneurs and politicians to build his Champion Fibre Company plant elsewhere. Waynesville, Clyde, Sylva, Bryson City, Andrews, Murphy, Asheville, and even Newport, Tennessee, were among the places where town-fathers' hopes were high that Peter Thomson would favor their communities instead of Canton.

An article posted in the Asheville newspaper at the time revealed one local lawyer's fervent hopes of securing Thomson's pulp mill for that place. "When one considers the immense advantages to be gained by the addition of 1,000 workmen to our city population, it would seem that no stone should be left unturned to secure the plum which threatens to drop. I don't want to wish Canton any bad luck, but that particular spot can't outdo Asheville when it comes to facilities for factories."[105]

Not to be outdone, Waynesville had its own gospeler expounding the virtues and logic of building the pulp mill in that fair town. His name was Silas Armistead Jones, and the following account explains the extraordinary proposal he made to Mr. Thomson for constructing the new pulp mill in Waynesville.

The Coming of Thomson's Pulp Mill

Silas Armistead Jones, or Colonel Jones, as he was called, was not a native of Haywood County. He was born in Kentucky and apparently spent some teen years galloping on horseback across the great plains of Texas delivering the US mail. His daughter, Lura Jones Smathers, described him as being "six feet two without his shoes" and had "kind blue eyes and a genial smile."[106]

Much later, when he came to Waynesville in 1894 from Tampa, Florida, he was completely "broken down from over-work from the upbuilding of that state, with nervous prostration complicated with kidney and bladder trouble." Western North Carolina's mountain climate, pure water, and fresh air apparently worked wonders to restore his health, and he decided to make it his home.[107]

In early 1905, Col. Jones and most everyone else in western North Carolina were aware that a mammoth pulp mill was going to be built somewhere in the mountains. Jones would also have known that an Ohioan by the name of Peter G. Thomson had met with more than 20 local businessmen in the little railroad town of Murphy, located in Cherokee County, to discuss the matter of timberlands and possible sites for his mill. He would have learned that Thomson was particularly interested in locations that had an abundant supply of water and easy access to forests capable of supplying the manufacturing facility with pulpwood for 25 years.

Throughout 1905, Peter Thomson worked to secure spruce and hardwood forests that could provide the specific wood needed for his mill's pulping

---

105   *Asheville Citizen-Times*, Asheville, N.C. (Jan. 06, 1906)
106   Lura Jones Smathers, *Silas Armistead Jones: The Story and Biography of My Father* (1970)
107   *The Wilmington Morning Star*, Wilmington, N.C. (Nov. 24, 1907)

processes. A woodsman by the name of Samuel Montgomery Smith guided him to the headwaters of the Pigeon River where bountiful tracts of the desirable timber existed. Additionally, Smith was very persuasive in explaining how pulpwood from these same headlands could be conveyed by a water flume to Canton, located some 15 miles or so downriver on the banks of the Pigeon River and astraddle the Southern Railroad.

Certainly, Col. Jones was mindful of these goings-on and understood that it was very likely the pulp mill would be built in Canton, unless he could persuade Thomson otherwise.

Waynesville Valley

Col. Silas A. Jones had spent a large part of his professional career in "upbuilding" Florida's Gulf harbors and "getting the railroads into Florida." The man was a far-sighted entrepreneur and, upon relocating to Waynesville, he continued to actively promote visionary business ideas for improving the community and, of course, personal enrichment. He wrote in a letter to the popular magazine *Manufacturer's Record* that "I located at Waynesville believing...it to be the center and heart of a section of the Appalachian Mountains having tributary to it more resources to build it up as a desirable place to live and as a manufacturing industrial center than any location in the Appalachian range."[108]

In late 1904, Jones was responsible for the incorporation of The Waynesville Factory Site and Electric Power Company. This new company was chartered with $300,000 capital to "develop electric power for manufacturing purposes and induce enterprises to locate" in Waynesville.[109] An intriguing map dated May 26, 1905, and issued by the Waynesville Factory Site and Electric Power Company depicts Waynesville and "its vicinity within a radius of twenty-five miles."[110] County Engineer and surveyor J. N. Schoolbred was the mapmaker—or "Delineator" as he was

---

108   A letter to the "Manufacturer's Record" from Silas A. Jones, courtesy of Alex Mckay
109   *The Charlotte News*, Charlotte, N.C. (Nov. 25, 1904)
110   The map can be found online at North Carolina Maps, https://library.unc.edu/wilson/digital-collections/.

tagged, and he produced the map working under the close direction of Col. S. A. Jones.

They very carefully attempted to highlight the Waynesville environs on this map by charting all the notable geographical features, towns, roads, and railroads. Every bit of spare space along the borders and in the corners of the map was filled with information and statistics that shined a favorable light on Waynesville, surely intended to gain the attention of potential investors, businesses, customers, and visitors.

At the very center of the map is a shaded area labelled "Waynesville Valley." This was the term chosen by the mapmakers to designate where the Waynesville Factory Site and Electric Power Company reportedly "controls about 1,000 acres of land joining the city." It was the preferred spot along the Southern Railway's tracks with a water source named Richland Creek where factories and industry were bound to bloom.

Imprinting on the map describes how Waynesville Valley is a "splendid location for a Chautaugua (a center for activities aimed at intellectual and moral self-improvement and civic involvement), cotton factories, textile factories, furniture factories, paper and pulp mills, tanneries, acid plants, and fruit and vegetable canneries." It was even promoted as the finest location for a "Female College."

In case there were any doubts as to the benefits of locating an industry in Waynesville Valley, there were other considerations illustrated by the mapmakers. One very prominent message just below the map's title offers the bold statement that Waynesville Valley is "absolutely protected from Cyclones and Floods." To reinforce this idea, there is an illustration at the bottom of the map demonstrating how Waynesville Valley is shielded from nature's destructive forces by the surrounding high ridges and peaks.

Other claims on the map invite one to wonder how well Col. Jones and Mr. Schoolbred vetted their facts. For example, they suggest in bold text that there is "MORE PULP WOOD, TANNIC ACID WOOD & FURNITURE TIMBER IN EASY REACH OF THIS VALLEY THAN ANY OTHER POINT IN THE UNITED STATES." Another one asserts that "Twenty-five Billion feet of timber" can be found within a 25-mile radius of Waynesville Valley. Yes, that is billion with a "B."

As previously mentioned, the Southern Railroad's tracks ran right through Waynesville Valley. However, Col. Jones must have believed more railroad infrastructure was required for the "upbuilding" of western North Carolina. So, he had Schoolbred delineate the "proposed" new railroads that were being promoted at the time. One of these was an extension of the existing North Carolina & Tennessee Railroad from Waterville up the Pigeon River gorge to Waynesville Valley.

Another interesting "proposed" railroad was the Waynesville & Asheville Electric Railway, one in which Col. Jones had a vested interest. This road was incorporated by the 1905 North Carolina Legislature and, not surprisingly, was intended to extend from Waynesville Valley to Asheville. The planned route generally followed the Pigeon River to Canton, but from there, it veered away from the existing Southern Railway's tracks. Strangely, it now seems, Col. Jones and his advisors chose for the railroad to take a northeasterly course from Canton, crossing Newfound Mountain to reach Asheville.

Near the center of the map, Schoolbred scribed in bold, capital letters the word "PIPELINE" to delineate a long water supply structure extending from the Pigeon River headwaters, above where Lake Logan was later impounded, all the way to Waynesville Valley. It is notable that the word "proposed" is not associated with "PIPELINE," as it is with the two proposed railroads previously mentioned. There is reason to believe this proposed water supply pipeline was added to the map for a singular purpose—to demonstrate to Peter Thomson that Waynesville Valley could potentially satisfy a large pulp mill's demand for water.

Colonel Jones' Pipeline Plan

Colonel Silas A. Jones knew very well that the quantity of water flowing in Waynesville Valley's Richland Creek was insufficient to support Peter Thomson's pulp manufacturing processes. The property controlled by The Waynesville Factory Site and Electric Power Company offered easy access to the railroad and had ample electric power supplied by an enormous 40-feet-high stone dam and new power generation station on the Pigeon River. Yet, there remained the crucial problem of meeting the pulp mill's demand for millions of gallons of water every day.

The solution that Col. Jones and Mr. Schoolbred came up with was simple. East of Waynesville Valley, just on the other side of Lickstone Ridge, was a good-sized rushing stream known as the West Fork of the Pigeon River. It was a tributary to the larger Pigeon River and Jones must have judged its flow sufficient for his purposes. He could simply construct a pipeline and divert water from this stream to Waynesville Valley.

Actually, the map itself offers one option on how Jones and Schoolbred intended to accomplish this feat. It appears they planned to dam and impound the West Fork of the Pigeon River stream just below where the Left Hand Prong, Middle Prong, and Right Hand Prong tributaries of the Pigeon River converge to form the West Fork (near the present-day Sunburst campground). The captured water would be carried through a large pipeline running alongside the West Fork River to the outskirts of the Bethel community. From there, the route of the pipeline turns westward, away from the West Fork, and runs across "Davis Gap" (known as Pigeon Gap today) all the way to a storage reservoir at Waynesville Valley. This long and undoubtedly iron pipeline would traverse through the countryside for almost 15 miles.

It was as easy as that to draw on a map. Whether or not this straightforward and simple approach to supply water for a huge pulp mill would suit Peter Thomson—or could even be done—remained to be seen. Jones intended to seek a conference with Thomson and lay out the options he saw so that the Ohioan could understand this great opportunity.

A Fateful Meeting

Fortunately, there exists a primary source account of the meeting which took place between Col. Silas A. Jones and Peter Thomson. The unpublished memoirs of Thomson's attorney, George H. Smathers of Waynesville, captured the essence of the meeting and, certainly, the outcome.

When Smathers first mentioned to Thomson that Col. Jones had requested a meeting to talk about building the pulp mill in Waynesville

Valley, Thomson immediately responded that the meeting would be "useless." He stated that "Richland Creek did not have a sufficient supply of water for (pulp) washing purposes." Smathers respectfully reported back to Col. Jones and communicated Thomson's doubts and reluctance to meet. Undaunted, Jones replied that "he would be able to overcome that objection" and insisted on having the meeting.

Smathers wrote that he "finally arranged for the conference" between the two men, which was held in Canton. When Peter Thomson "reiterated the reason why he could not entertain Waynesville for the location of the plants" and stated his belief that there was not sufficient water in Richland Creek, Col. Jones spoke up.[111] He "proposed to meet this objection by cutting a tunnel through the Balsam Mountains dividing Richland Creek from the west fork of the Pigeon River and conveying the water from the west fork of the Pigeon River through the tunnel to Richland Creek."

Mr. Thomson's reply to this idea was blunt and clear. The "expense of doing this would be prohibitive, but even if feasible, that from what he knew of the elevation of Richland Creek and the west fork of the Pigeon River that the water supply would not be sufficient."

Attorney Smathers joined in at this point and voiced his opinion that "the land owners below on Pigeon River would object to the diversion and would have a right to enjoin (stop) the same."

Smathers' memoirs reveal that shortly afterward Col. Jones "yielded gracefully and decided that in-as-much as Waynesville could not get the plants, he wanted to see Canton get them. Jones told Mr. Thomson that he would do everything in his power to aid in the location of the plants at Canton."[112]

---

111   In the quoted material, Smathers refers to Peter Thomson's "plants" more than once. In addition to the pulp mill, he is also including the tannin extract plant that Thomson later built within the confines of the Canton pulp mill.
112   Smathers, George H., *Memoirs of Geo. Smathers* (unpublished manuscript edited by Allen Roudebush), Canton Area Historical Museum

Conclusion

George Smathers remembered that Co. Silas A. Jones' proposal was to capture the West Fork of the Pigeon River waters by cutting a tunnel through the Balsam Mountains. Clearly, that is not what is shown on the Jones and Schoolbred map. Attorney Smathers' memoirs were recorded more than 30 years after Thomson's pulp mill was built, and there is a good chance his memory might have betrayed him in this instance.

Then again, if his recollection was correct, there is a distinct possibility that Jones could have revised his plan, soon after the fateful meeting with Thomson, to reflect conveying water to Waynesville Valley through a pipeline. Although the record left by Attorney Smathers is silent on the matter, there might have been another conference to discuss the newly proposed pipeline, in lieu of a tunnel through the Balsam Mountains. If so, we know that nothing became of it. Peter Thomson did build his pulp mill in Canton, and Col. Jones' pipeline, as well as the forementioned proposed railroads, were simply "pipeline" dreams that never came true.

Colonel Silas A. Jones, shown here in an 1899 newspaper rendering, led the unsuccessful effort to convince Peter Thomson to build his new pulp mill in Waynesville. (courtesy of Alex Mckay)

Colonel Silas A. Jones led the unsuccessful effort to bring Thomson's pulp mill to Waynesville. (photo from the book "Silas Armistead Jones: The Story and Biography of My Father" by Lura Jones Smathers and courtesy of Alex Mckay)

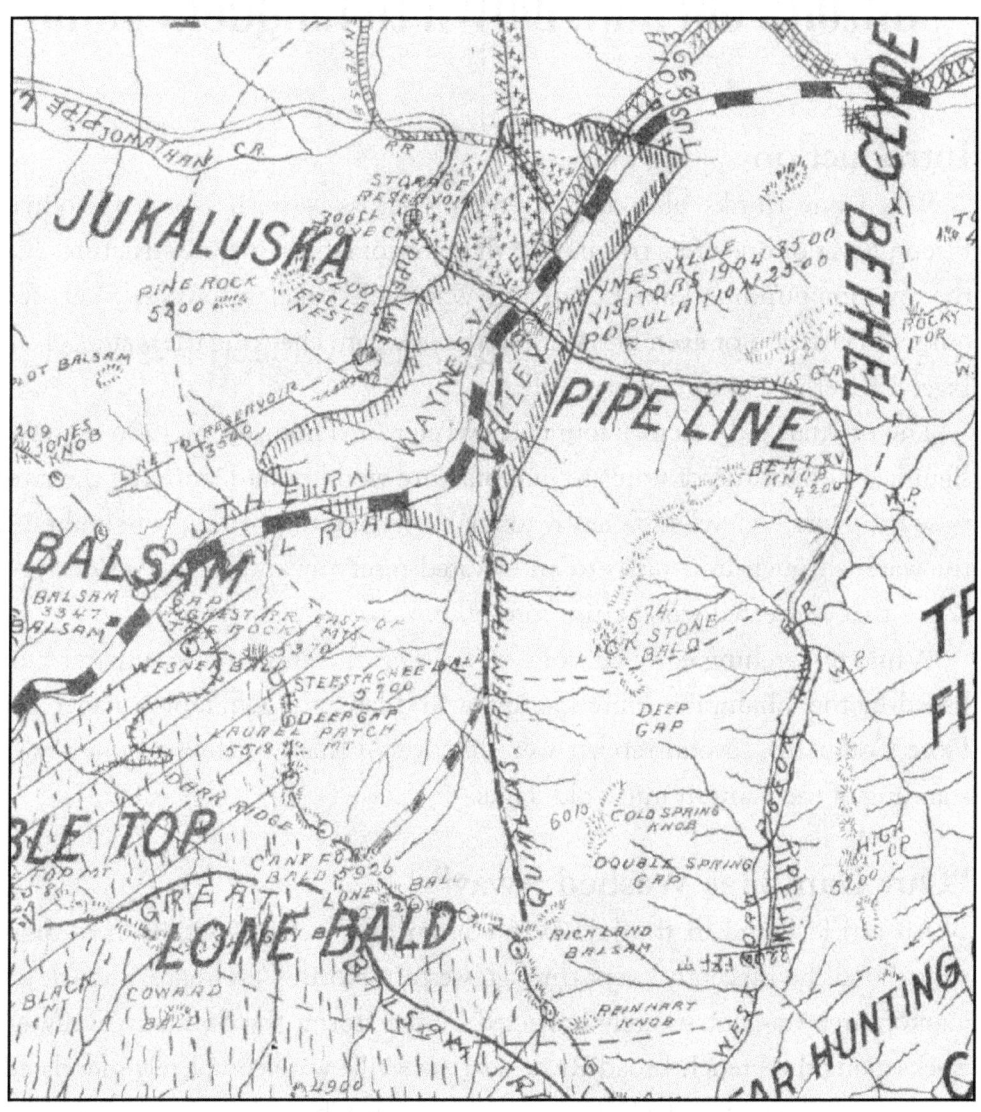

This cropped section from J. N. Schoolbred's larger map shows the "PIPELINE" running from the upper West Fork of the Pigeon River to Waynesville Valley. (N.C. Maps)

Canton's Old Dam Blown to Kingdom Come

Introduction

When one thinks of a dam stretching across western North Carolina's Pigeon River or one of its tributaries, thoughts of large concrete structures like the ones impounding Lake Logan and Waterville Lake are invoked. Very few folks will envision or even know about the low dam checking the waters of the Pigeon River at Canton's paper mill.

The original pulp factory founded by Peter G. Thomson in 1906 required significant quantities of water to manufacture wood pulp. Damming the river raised the surface level sufficiently to enable large pumps to capture and push the water through iron pipes to an elevated reservoir and to the various processes that converted wood chips into pulp.

While researching early editions of *The Log* (the employee newsletter published by the Champion Fibre Company and later the Champion Paper and Fibre Company), several reports were uncovered that enlightened our understanding of the Canton mill's old dams.

"Our Dam Has Washed Away"

An article found in the July 1916 edition of *The Log* describes how disastrous floods had recently swept through western North Carolina. Although the Canton area was not severely impacted by the storm, the Southern Railway's tracks along the French Broad River near Asheville were completely inundated. This caused the editor of *The Log* to predict, "The Champion Coated Paper Co. at Hamilton, Ohio, may suffer from a shortage of pulp due to the retarded shipments from Canton."[113]

---

113   The wood pulp manufactured at Peter G. Thomson's Champion Fibre Company in Canton was used at his Champion Coated Paper Company in Hamilton, Ohio, to produce coated paper, a premium paper product at the time. The pulp was shipped up there by train over the Southern Railway Company's lines, and sometimes railroad problems were encountered.

Whether Peter Thomson's Coated Paper Company in Ohio was affected by the railroad delays is unknown, but the same report also included this interesting piece of news: "It is true that a section of our dam has washed away…"

Yes, a section of the original 1906 low dam across the Pigeon River had indeed washed away. We can be certain of that because a follow-up report in *The Log*, dated August 1916, describes repairs made to it. "Charles Westmoreland, who has been making repairs to the dam at the Pump House with his crew, recently loaded by hand onto flat cars more than 600,000 pounds of stone. These stones ranged in weight from five to 2,500 pounds."

Mr. Westmoreland and his men must have done a pretty-good job filling the breech in the dam with those stones, because the repair lasted for more than 30 years.

A New Dam to Withstand "Devastating Flood Waters"

More sleuthing into the dam story uncovered a September 1947 issue of *The Log* that revealed a new dam was being contemplated by Champion. A very brief statement announced the impending project: "Work will soon start on installing a concrete Dam across Pigeon River, just below the site of the old Dam. This is something which has been badly needed for a long time."

It seems that the Champion Paper and Fibre Company did not waste any time with the project. A report in the January 1948 edition of *The Log* states, "Champion Canton's new intake dam across Pigeon River has been placed in operation. The new dam, a weir type, was constructed to withstand the most devastating flood waters."

Construction began on the reinforced concrete dam on September 15, 1947, and was completed in less than two months. The new project extended approximately 205 feet from abutment to abutment, was five feet high, and contained more than 4,400 bags of concrete and approximately 75 tons of reinforcing steel.

Although the dam was built in less than two months by Champion's own employees, it has survived until this day, holding back the waters of the Pigeon River and resisting the "most devastating flood waters" for the past 75 years.

Well, the Dam is Gone Now"

In the September 1949 issue of *The Log*, Mr. J.E. Slaughter wrote, "On July 5th the old dam, located just a little way upstream from the new concrete dam, was demolished. After having a lot of dynamite strung along the old dam, wires were attached and then a battery was used to set off the blast." A wonderful photo taken in 1949 and included in *The Log* captured the powerful forces of the dynamite explosion that demolished the old dam.

Mr. Slaughter also observed, "There must be something like a million bags of sand distributed along the upper side of the old dam, put there to stop leaks from time to time." Attempting to ease his readers' concerns, *The Log*'s reporter wrote, "Well, the dam is gone now, and our worries are over in regard to the old dam..."

So, it has been determined by searching through *The Log* newsletters that Champion's original 1906 dam structure is long gone, blown to kingdom come in 1949. Makes you wonder (not worry) whether some of those huge rocks that Charles Westmoreland's boys used to repair the dam in 1916 or some of the sand from those "million bags of sand" are still at the bottom of the river, somewhere.

I'll bet they are, and many Pigeon River brim and red-eye bass are happy to call them "home."

In late 1947, the Champion Paper and Fibre Co. constructed a new concrete intake dam across the Pigeon River. Shown here just after completion, the dam was approximately 205 feet wide, abutment to abutment, and five feet high. (courtesy of Canton Historical Museum)

On July 5, 1949, the Champion Paper and Fibre Co. used dynamite to demolish the mill's original 1906 dam across the Pigeon River. This photo of one of the explosions was made by Bob Anton from the Engineering Department and presented in The Log newsletter. Reportedly, more than 150 sticks of dynamite were used in the demolition effort. (courtesy of Canton Historical Museum)

Champion Paper and Fibre Company's Tabulating Office

Many of you readers are too young to know about the tabulating offices that large businesses and factories had in the mid-1900s. Even those who are old enough to remember them probably have no idea what went on in a tabulating office, or what they tabulated. Perhaps a closer look into a so-called tabulating office is in order.

Champion Paper and Fibre Company's monthly newsletter, *The Log*, was published for many decades, regularly reporting the goings-on in the Canton, North Carolina mill's various departments and offices. Included in these several areas of operation were pulp and paper production, finishing, maintenance, laboratory, accounting, and **tabulating**. That's right—there was a tabulating office in Champion's Canton mill at one time.

A chance conversation with Jewell Lipham of Canton shed some light on the mill's former Tabulating office. Jewell, all of 95 years young at the time, related to me how she and her late husband, Woody, moved from Atlanta to Canton in 1946. Woody, who had been working as an accountant at the First National Bank of Atlanta, was hired to establish a new tabulating office associated with the Champion mill's Accounting Department.

Jewell allowed that she had no idea what her husband's tabulating work entailed, other than she remembered it involved moving pegs connected to electrical cords from hole to hole on a "peg board." Although that certainly sounds intriguing, it reveals little about what the actual tabulating work was all about.

You might be wondering if we will be left to our own imaginations about the tabulating services Mr. Lipham founded at the Canton Mill, just after World War II. Well, it just happens that an article found in *The Log* newsletter gives a friendly and informative report about the Tabulating section of the Canton Division's Accounting Department.

As an aside, a notice in an earlier edition of *The Log* shared the following unrelated news of the birth of a daughter to Jewell and Woody:

> "Jean Elizabeth Lipham arrived recently at Norburn Hospital. Her dad is that pleasant fellow who runs Tabulating, and although we haven't had the pleasure of meeting his wife, from what we hear, Jean Elizabeth has a charming and talented mother."

While Jewell was surely busy at home with her baby daughter, it seems that Woody was making headlines at the mill. His Tabulating office was featured in *The Log's* March 1948 edition along with a photograph of the "amiable Supervisor." This enlightening article relates that Woody graduated with an accounting degree from the University of Georgia. Immediately afterward, he joined the U.S. Army and served four years in the American and Pacific theatres during World War II, while rising to the rank of captain. In 1943, Woody married Jewell White, who by his own account was the loveliest girl on the University of Georgia campus when they were studying there.

Although the article does not expose how Supervisor Lipham used those pegs attached to cords that Jewell still remembers, it does divulge the many functions that were handled by the Tabulating office. One responsibility of singular importance was using data furnished by the Time Office to calculate and prepare the mill's giant payroll.

Jewell even recalled the manner in which employees were being paid when she and Woody arrived in Canton. Each payday, two men would ride the train to Asheville, collect enough cash from the bank to meet the payroll, and then return to Canton in time to pay the workers. She remembers that a fellow named Letch Worley would hand out envelopes filled with money to the tired mill workers as they filed out the gate at the end of their shift.

Preparing the payroll was not the only task performed by the Tabulating office. Woody Lipham's team also tabulated the plant's ledger figures, labor distribution numbers, cost statements, sales analyses, and earnings records. Additionally, they were tasked with the responsibility of organizing and supplying specified information to the various departments and management, as well as the several government reports that were regularly required.

This was the important work of Champion Paper and Fibre Company's Tabulating office from the late 1940s until the 1970s. Durning this period, before the advent of huge electronic data-processing computers, the tabulating business was accomplished using electro-mechanical machines that punched, read, and sorted cards; and made complex calculations as fast as the information could be fed into them. It was a technology first invented in the late 1800s and further developed by companies like IBM and Remington Rand in the first half of the 20th century.

Many people were required to constantly and carefully operate and monitor these machines. But getting the correct solutions out of them was not as simple as feeding in a bunch of punched cards and pressing a button. Each different type of operation required precise arrangements, and the control mechanisms of sophisticated calculating machines had to be re-wired for each job. The "set-up" of these mechanisms had literally thousands of possible variations.

At Canton, data recorded by foremen and supervisors throughout the plant was submitted to Supervisor Woody Lipham's Tabulating office. Then, men and women working at card-punching and calculating machines—the computers of that era—and at sorting tables and desks processed this vital information into assorted documents and reports.

The information computed and compiled by the Tabulating office was then used by mill management to keep the plant running as smoothly and productively as possible. Thus, it is plain to see the significant role played by the Tabulating section of Champion's Accounting Department in the mill's day-to-day operations. But how in the world were pegs connected to electrical cords employed in this tabulating process?

It is likely that Jewell recalled the operation of a new machine Champion began using in about the year 1950—the IBM No. 604 Electronic Calculating Punch. The new "brain," as it was called, could solve complex arithmetic and algebraic problems as fast as information could be introduced into the machine's circuitry.

Found in yet another edition of *The Log* published in 1950 is a wonderful description of this computing machine: "It contains over 1,200 tubes and numerous skillfully wired panel board assemblies. Problems and computations are put into the machine by means of plug boards into which cable plugs are inserted to correspond to the particular information desired."

For at least a couple of decades, these electrical cable plugs of the IBM 604, and later enhanced versions of it, would facilitate the many addition, subtraction, multiplication, and division computations and tabulations involved in payroll, production, accounting, and other areas of Champion's operations.

So, as it turns out, Jewell Lipham's memory was spot-on regarding her husband's Tabulating office. Those pegs attached to electrical cords actually did exist! They were the cable plugs that were inserted into plug boards to program the calculating machines. The function of these "pegs and cords" played a key role in the running of the Tabulating office, as well as the Champion Paper and Fibre Company's Canton mill.

In January 1960, Woody Lipham braved the wintry weather and drove to work on his farm tractor. It appears that a group of employees have gathered outside the Tabulating office to welcome him upon his safe arrival. Back then, Champion's Tabulating office was located on Main Street, near the railroad tracks and depot building. (The Log newsletter dated February 1960)

In this photo, Champion employees can be seen hard at work in the Tabulating office using the latest computing machines. (courtesy of Canton Historical Museum)

A Tabulating office employee (Gudger Worley) is shown here using one of the tabulating machines. (courtesy of Canton Historical Museum)

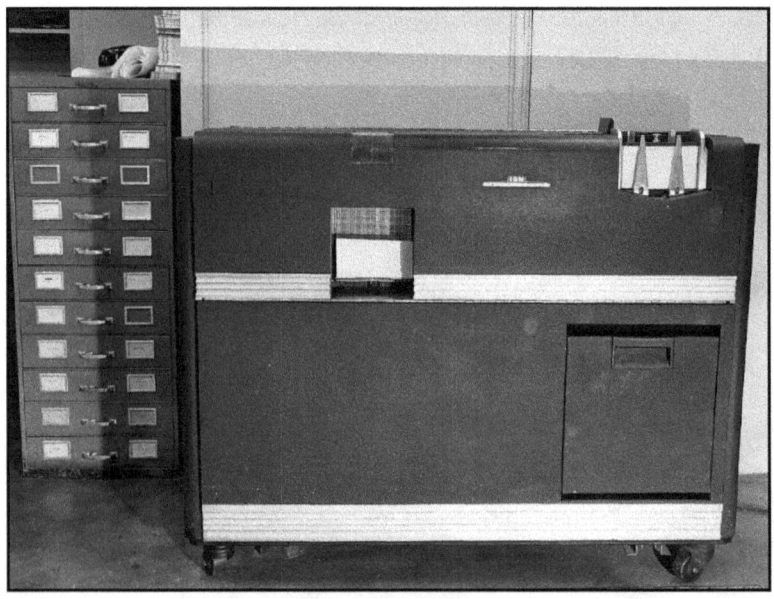

Champion's IBM "Calculating Punch" machine played a key role in the operation of the Tabulating office. (courtesy of Canton Historical Museum)

Canton's Original Bucket Factory

In the 1950s and '60s, I grew up within a football field's length of an old concrete block building that we recognized as Cochran's woodworking shop. It was certainly a substantial structure, located on Penland Street where it sat on low-lying ground along the river and next to the Little League baseball field. To me, this lonely old shop building was just another edifice that I hurried past every day on my way to either the ballfields, swimming pool, river, or school. Never did I pause to consider the historical legacy of that old building or realize it was originally a factory that manufactured lunch buckets, of all things.

The town of Canton, North Carolina, was a legitimate industrial boom town in the early 1900s. Champion Fibre Company's mammoth pulp mill had started up in 1908 and, as a result, the town's population exploded, growing from a few hundred citizens to several thousand in very little time. In support of the mill's manufacturing processes, logging and sawmill enterprises in the surrounding western North Carolina mountains were determined to harvest every old-growth evergreen and hardwood tree that could be "got out" of the highest ridges and wild river valleys. At the same time, the Southern Railway Company was hauling tons of supplies and pulp wood into Canton every day, while carrying out many tons of manufactured wood pulp and lumber. It was truly an exploding industrial economy, and one that seemingly aroused the inventive imagination of a local man.

Calvin Filmore Christopher, a Bethel resident, was touted as North Carolina's most prolific inventor during his lifetime. Prior to 1915, he had patented a turntable lock and an automatic switch for the railroads, several improvements to steam engine drive mechanisms, a new-fangled "rotary steam engine", various types of automatic computing scales, an innovative "metallic-clothesline," and even a "dinner-pail."

Christopher's unique dinner-pail—or lunch bucket—was described thusly in the patent documentation:

> This invention relates to dinner pails, its object being to provide a novel arrangement of compartments formed within sections which are movably connected so that, when the pail is opened, the said movable sections can be shifted to positions where the contents thereof are readily accessible.
>
> A further object is to provide a device which, when closed, presents a neat appearance and is compact.
>
> A further object is to provide means whereby the drinking cup, which is mounted on the pail, will cooperate with members on the pail for holding said pail in closed position.

Calvin Christopher received a patent for his novel dinner-pail in April of 1914. Shortly thereafter, in 1915, the Union Manufacturing Company was organized and incorporated for the specific purpose of manufacturing Christopher's lunch buckets. After raising $50,000 in authorized capital, the company promptly purchased a parcel of land from Jodie Smathers and his wife Minnie. The property was located in Canton on the west bank of the Pigeon River and next to the Tennessee and North Carolina Railroad (T&NCRR) tracks.

At that time, the T&NCRR railroad line ran up the "backside" of the river, connecting the logging and sawmill operations at Sunburst (where Lake Logan is located today) with Canton. In late 1915 or early 1916, Union Manufacturing proceeded to construct a concrete-block factory building on the Smathers tract, near where Felmet's Garage building (recently occupied by the Riverview Farm and Garden store) was located and just a hundred yards upstream from where an iron-truss bridge spanned the Pigeon River. Also, the new factory building was located immediately adjacent to the T&NCRR tracks.

Mostly local men were elected as officers and directors of the company, including T.L. Gwyn, W.T. Sharp, J.O. Plott, G.L Hampton, T.J. Wooldridge, and T.J. Bailey. The financial arrangement between Calvin Christopher and the Union Manufacturing Company is unknown. However, it is suspected that he sold his dinner-pail patent rights to the company. One thing is obvious, though. Christopher and the company's investors believed there was a huge market for dinner pails in boom-town Canton, as well as other places across the country with industries supported by lots of hungry employees. Sometime in 1916, the Union company began manufacturing the Christopher lunch buckets.

A contemporaneous publication (the *Carolina Mountaineer's Haywood County Industrial and Resort Edition*, dated December 1916) stated that "anyone who makes a careful study of the dinner pail will become convinced, not only of its superiority, but of its ultimate success financially upon the market." This same source also predicted that "there would come a time when the 80x40-feet (factory) building will have to be much larger."

Apparently, the Union bucket factory building was not expanded and made "much larger," nor did it generate the overwhelming success anticipated by the local press and company investors. In fact, records show that the company fell into receivership and was sold in 1919 to C.V. Hampton. Interestingly, this sale also included the patent rights to the dinner-pail.

The following year, Mr. Hampton turned around and sold everything to T.C. Lancaster, who was the secretary of a South Carolina textile company known as Crescent Manufacturing. This time, there was no mention in the deed of the conveyance of dinner-pail rights. In 1921, the title to the property was turned over to the Crescent Manufacturing Company, whereupon a hosiery mill was established in the concrete-block factory building. Over subsequent years, the substantial structure would host, in addition to the hosiery mill, several businesses including a fraternal organization and a woodworking shop.

Sadly, the old Union bucket factory building was demolished at the turn of the twenty-first century after suffering a catastrophic fire. However, some "friends" of the Canton Historical Museum have made sure the old concrete-block factory is not forgotten. A historical marker with a photo and brief history of the bucket factory has been installed near the site, along the walking trail beside the Pigeon River.

Now, the history and location of the Union Manufacturing Company's bucket factory will once again be remembered and pointed out to younger generations, new Canton citizens, tourists, and those of us who paid little attention to that old building back in the day.

This is the Union Manufacturing Company's "Bucket Factory" as it appeared in about 1916. Note the railroad tracks running in front of the concrete block building that once joined the Sunburst logging industry on the upper reaches of the Pigeon River with Canton. (courtesy of Canton Historical Museum)

In the mid-1950s, the original bucket factory building shown here was occupied by J.R. Cochran's Canton Woodworking business. Interestingly, the paved Penland Street can be seen in front of the concrete-block building. The road sits on the old railroad grade where trains once passed back and forth between Canton and the Sunburst logging village. (from Tony Jones collection)

CANTON MEMORIES | 263

Calvin Christopher patented this "dinner pail" that was manufactured at the Union Manufacturing Company in Canton. (courtesy of Canton Historical Museum and Roland Osborne)

Calvin Christopher's novel "dinner pail" is shown here with its compartments opened and its drinking cup ready for a hungry and thirsty worker. (courtesy of Canton Historical Museum and Roland Osborne)

Champion YMCA's Gra-Y Program

Peter Gibson Thomson was the man who founded the Champion Fibre Company in Canton, North Carolina, in 1906. The new pulp mill started up in 1908, and 12 years later he rode down a familiar train route from his home in Cincinnati, Ohio, to Canton. This time he aimed to do something different, yet special, for his Champion Fibre Company's employees.

In 1920, Thomson dedicated a magnificent brick edifice in Canton as the new Champion YMCA. Said to be the finest YMCA building ever built at an industrial plant in the South, it was intended to benefit not only Canton's young Christian youth but the pulp mill employees and the entire community. In very little time, this Champion "Y" became the town's center of physical fitness as well as cultural and civic activities of every description.

As a young boy in the 1950s, I can remember climbing up the wide flight of stairs at the huge building's entrance and hustling into the grand "Y" lobby. The sounds of a dribbling basketball and a referee's whistles from the gym could easily be heard. And there was a distinctive noise of billiard balls crashing and clattering on the pool tables. All of this was grasped instantly, as soon as I walked through the Y's huge front doors. But lingering in the lobby was never an option.

Usually, I would head toward the gym to play basketball or bound down the stairs toward the swimming pool—or maybe the locker room to put on the pads for yet another grueling football practice. It is amazing how these memories have been hiding away in the back of my mind. Now, with this recent shallow dive into the YMCA's Gra-Y program, I have been able to recall them very clearly.

At the 1920 dedication ceremony, Peter Thomson presented the building to the employees of the Champion Fibre Company and to the International YMCA to operate. In his dedication speech he said, "Wonderful changes have taken place in these 15 years (from 1905 when he began acquiring property to build the pulp mill). The town's population has increased from 200 to about 4,000 or 5,000, and the entire western North Carolina has benefitted from our enterprise. It is my wish and hope that you will be able to enjoy the benefits of this building for many years to come." He declared his expectations for the International YMCA to operate the facility in the traditional manner other facilities were being operated across the United States.

The Young Men's Christian Association's work was not new in the 1920s. It started in England in the mid-19th century to meet the practical and spiritual needs of the young men who were flocking to London during the Industrial Revolution. Soon after, the YMCA movement arrived in the United States just before the Civil War. The railroad and industrial towns began partnering with the YMCA to not only look after the spiritual and physical needs of employees but to also lodge and feed them.

Interestingly, over the years the games of volleyball and basketball were invented or developed through the YMCA's activities and leadership. Also, the YMCA inspired the formation of the U.S.O. (United Service Organization), Peace Corps, and even Father's Day.

By now, you are probably wondering what the Gra-Y organization had to do with the local YMCA. References to the Gra-Y program in Canton have been discovered going back to 1932. It turns out, the Gra-Y program was one of four programs that the national YMCA developed to promote Christian character through speech, sportsmanship, and scholastic achievement. The other three programs were the "Hi-Y" for high school boys, "Jr. Hi-Y" for middle schoolers, and "Tri Hi-Y" for girls and young ladies.

The Gra-Y organization aimed to fulfill the spiritual and physical needs of grade-school boys and develop their characters as they grew into manhood. In Canton, the Gra-Y program encompassed grade-school boys all the way through what we refer to today as middle schoolers—or until they entered high school. Administering these programs was Grover Suttles, who served as the secretary of Canton's YMCA for many years, and he was followed by Jack Justice.

In the 1950s, when I was of Gra-Y age and participating in almost every sport or activity the "Y" had to offer, I can distinctly remember Jack Justice. He was held in very high esteem by all the parents. Of course, us young kids knew little about his vast responsibilities, but we certainly looked up to him as a guiding light in that huge YMCA building and on the ballfields.

There were other guiding lights, or men and women we looked up to, including German (Nazi) Miller, George Price, Elizabeth Thompson, Wade Garrett, and Paul Rogers to name a few. They coached our Gra-Y football and basketball teams and umpired three baseball leagues: the Farm League, Little League, and Pony League (which eventually became the Sr. Little League). When school was out, we were around them constantly, and they literally became parental figures, teaching and guiding us through our athletic endeavors.

One successful local man whose father had died in World War II told a reporter that he "didn't know what would have happened to him, what kind of future he would have had, without the interest and attention that he received from men involved with the YMCA, especially Jack Justice. They didn't hesitate to initiate one-on-one conversations with us young boys, if they felt some guidance was needed. It seemed that someone was always keeping an eye on you," he said.

Undoubtedly, those same sentiments were held by many young men who grew up in Canton and participated in the YMCA's Gra-Y program. This program simply gave hundreds upon hundreds of Canton boys the foundation to cope, compete, and survive in today's society.

Many photographs taken through the years of Canton's Gra-Y activities can be found in the Canton Historical Museum. A few of these are presented here in these pages, courtesy of the Museum.

In this 1950s-era photo, Canton Gra-Y football players are huddled and listening intently to their coaches. Coach Wade Garrett (on the right) was an All World Fastpitch Softball player for the Champion YMCA team. (courtesy of Canton Historical Museum)

Coach German (Nazi) Miller is giving instructions to a few Gra-Y football players on the practice field, located where the former Roberston Memorial YMCA building still stands today. In the 1950s and early 1960s, this was where the Gra-Y football teams practiced and where Farm League baseball games were played. (courtesy of Canton Historical Museum)

The 1962 Gra-Y midget football team shown above had an undefeated season and was invited to Vineland, New Jersey, to play in the Glass Bowl game. These Canton Gra-Y boys bettered the northern home team on that memorable Thanksgiving. (courtesy of Canton Historical Museum)

A late 1940's or early 1950's Gra-Y football team is posing for a photo at the practice field located along Park Street, where the former Canton Fire Department and Town Hall buildings are still located. The coaches were German (Nazi) Miller on the left and Jack Justice on the right. (courtesy of Canton Historical Museum)

An early photo (late 1940s or early 1950s) shows Canton's Gra-Y football team posing at the practice field located where the former Robertson Memorial YMCA stands today. Note the absence of faceguards and the baggy padded pants. (courtesy of Canton Historical Museum)

An early photo (late 1940s or early 1950s) shows a Canton Gra-Y football team lined up and waiting for the snap. A few of downtown Canton's buildings along Park Street can be seen in the background. (courtesy of Canton Historical Museum)

At the beginning of each Gra-Y football season, the coaches issued equipment to each player. Shoulder pads and pants are stacked on the table to the left and helmets were staged on the table behind the players. (courtesy of Canton Historical Museum)

It is a jump ball at the Champion YMCA gym in the 1950s. To distinguish the competing Gra-Y basketball teams, the uniforms (or no uniforms) used were simply "skins" and "shirts." (courtesy of Canton Historical Museum)

These early 1950s-era Gra-Y basketball players are posing in the original Champion YMCA gym for a photo-op. (courtesy of Canton Historical Museum)

Proud youthful players on a 1950s-era Gra-Y basketball team have been awarded badges for their team's performance at the original Champion YMCA gymnasium. (courtesy of Canton Historical Museum)

A Champion Y Little League baseball team poses for a photo at the field near the old Canton High School (today's Canton Middle School) on Penland Street. (courtesy of Canton Historical Museum)

A 1950s-era Gra-Y basketball team is boarding the "Y" bus for an away game, as Coach German (Nazi) Miller keeps the boys in line. (courtesy of Canton Historical Museum)

The Gra-Y boys sold Christmas trees every year to raise funds to support their various activities. For many years, these holiday tree sales took place on Park Street across from the old A&P Supermarket. Flanking the young salesmen are coaches German (Nazi) Miller (on right) and George Price (on left). (courtesy of Canton Historical Museum)

A Canton Boy Through and Through

Introduction

Way back during my childhood in the 1950s, Canton was a progressive town situated at the entrance to the Blue Ridge Mountains. This once small village had been founded on the banks of the Pigeon River, next to the railroad and an important turnpike penetrating the mountains.

It was the town's location and the bountiful forestlands surrounding it that attracted and caused an Ohio-based company to construct a huge pulp mill in Canton. The Champion Fibre Company founded by Peter Gibson Thomson started pulp manufacturing operations in 1908, immediately increasing the town's size, population, and importance.

By the mid-20th century, Canton's city streets thrived with small retail stores and service businesses. The center of the business activities was located primarily along Main and Park Streets and a couple of short streets connecting them. These enterprises supported the lively commerce generated by the paper mill and the local mill workers, Pigeon Valley farmers, and mountain tourists.

Closely surrounding the small business district and mostly within walking distance were the churches, elementary schools, high school, and residential neighborhoods. That was Canton in the 1950s, a busy mill town tucked away in the mountains and populated with friendly working-class citizens. Certainly, my parents, who were both Champion employees, fit comfortably into that category. And so did my brother and I, who were born-and-raised Canton boys.

The Beginnings of an Engineering Career

Thinking back on those youthful days in Canton brings back memories of playing ball—any kind of ball. Whether kicking, throwing, catching, shooting, batting, or driving and putting the balls, it did not seem to matter. That was all I wanted to do—play ball. Eventually, the pursuit of sports at the Champion

YMCA and the local high school earned this young man a football scholarship at the University of South Carolina in Columbia.

After four years of playing football with the USC Gamecocks and earning a degree in civil engineering, I returned to Canton in the mid-1970s to begin an extended professional career in the paper industry. It was the start of a journey that would eventually lead me far away to the South American country of Brazil; then to Pensacola, Florida; back to Canton; and eventually to Pensacola again.

One of the first engineering assignments that came my way at the Champion paper mill was to determine the amount of water contained in the mill's reservoir. That would be the beautiful Lake Logan located a few miles up the West Fork of the Pigeon River. The lake had practically filled up with sediment, severely reducing the volume of water captured behind its massive concrete dam.

A co-worker and I proceeded to measure the depths of the lake at many points and plot this data on a map. We then were able to calculate the quantity of water contained in the lake and determine the amount of sediment to be removed from the lake bottom. After obtaining approval and funding for a project to dredge the lake, a local contractor was hired to excavate and haul the sandy material away.

Surprisingly, when most of the water was drained, several old concrete foundations were exposed at the upper end of the lake. As we soon learned, the Champion crews tasked with cleaning up and removing what was left of the old Sunburst logging village and sawmill in the late 1920s—before the lake was impounded—had simply left these massive concrete structures in place. And that is exactly what I instructed our modern-day excavation contractor to do—leave the old concrete foundations alone! We left them for the next generation of young engineers and archaeologists to discover.

Still another Lake Logan project was awarded to me in those early days when my engineering experience was extremely raw. I was asked to install "flashboards" along the top of the concrete dam over its entire length. It was yet another measure to increase the volume of water impounded behind the dam by increasing its height.

We simply set short pipe columns along the concrete dam's crest and secured sturdy wooden boards—called flashboards—between them. The dam's height was raised a couple of feet with the flashboards, thus increasing the volume of water impounded behind it by millions of gallons. It was as simple as that and now, 50 years later, it appears the flashboards are still holding back the waters of the West Fork.

The Chance of a Lifetime

A decade or so after these early Champion ventures of mine, another project at the Canton mill came along that was indirectly related to the Lake Logan water reservoir. This one happened to be a little larger in scope and held a much higher level of importance.

Previous assignments in Brazil and Pensacola, Florida, building new paper mill facilities had seasoned me for this greater challenge. I was asked to lead the Canton Modernization Project, a $300,000,000 engineering and construction endeavor having the manifest goal of bringing the Canton paper mill into compliance with the latest air and water environmental permit requirements.

One of the project's most challenging objectives was to reduce the mill's daily amount of water usage from more than 50-million gallons per day to approximately 30-million gallons per day. Project engineers and technical specialists analyzed every use of water in the mill, and many modifications were made to the pulping and paper-making processes to achieve the required reductions.

The fact that the mill succeeded in achieving this water reduction goal in the 1990s, along with meeting the other air and water permit requirements, allowed it to continue operating for years to come. It is an accomplishment this local Canton boy will forever be proud of.

Retirement and Literary Endeavors

Those who know me may have wondered about my late plunge into writing, of all things, upon retirement from the paper industry. Certainly, this civil engineer did not take up writing books and shorter articles about our local history for financial gain. Trust me, hopes of a bestseller or even monetary rewards were never motivational factors. My dives into the past were mainly driven by a want to learn more about western North Carolina's history, share this knowledge with others, and preserve the history for generations to come.

Initial works of non-fiction, including the books titled *The 25th North Carolina Troops in the Civil War* and *Captain Lenoir's Diary*, were founded on extensive research of primary and secondary sources. Both books, in my opinion, are extremely valuable additions to our written knowledge base of western North Carolina's history. Although extremely laborious and time consuming, these writing projects filled me with purpose and, eventually, a feeling of satisfaction and accomplishment.

More recently, I have delved into historical fiction efforts that will also require some explanation. Turns out, it was a rather impulsive notion that got me started down this path of make-believe. The true circumstances that brought a man named Thomas Isaac Lenoir to the Haywood County mountains prior to the Civil War—as covered in meticulous detail in *Captain Lenoir's Diary*—intrigued me greatly. In fact, I was inspired to invent and write a fictional story based somewhat on the challenges Lenoir faced while trying to survive and make a living on the East Fork of the Pigeon River. This story became the first novel in my *East Fork Trilogy*.

Seemingly out of the blue, my pen (actually, my computer) created a young fictional character named Basil Edmunston who was set loose in the rural East Fork region of the Pigeon River Valley in the years leading up to the Civil War. Neither Basil nor I looked back after that as we conceived stories and crafted the pages of three books comprising the trilogy: *Master of the East Fork*, *Rebel Rousers*, and *August's Treasure*.

It was indeed a learning experience to develop interesting characters, write dialog for the first time, and dream-up meaningful adventures. The fact that I became so emotionally caught up in these tales was truly unexpected. For example, *Rebel Rousers* is a story about two young Rebel soldiers who could not stay out of trouble during the Civil War. I became quite attached to both of them while writing the book, and there was one scene that especially got to me.

During a fierce battle with the Union troops, a young Private Hartgrove dropped his Mississippi Rifle and ran as fast as his skinny legs would carry him toward the fallen banner of his regiment. Ignoring the lethal gunfire whizzing all around him, he reached down and took up the tangled flag from the dead flag-bearer's corpse. Raising the Rebel colors high into the air, he overcame fearful instincts and began moving directly toward the enemy lines. Upon seeing their flag advancing once again, the Confederate colonel and his re-inspired troops began following behind Private Hartgrove as he held the regimental colors high and led a successful charge against the Yankee line.

While writing this intense scene, I was overcome with emotion and respect for the bravery demonstrated by the young soldier. Indeed, it was so emotional that more than once I had to stop writing and wipe away the teardrops on my computer's keyboard. Believe it or not, this truly happened!

After satisfying myself with that three-year, or so, immersion into fiction, I did not have to look far to uncover another subject of interest regarding Haywood County's history. A friend shared with me a trove of photographs taken during the construction of Canton's original pulp mill (Champion Fibre Company) between 1905 and 1908. These wonderful old photos that had been passed down through his family kindled a fire in me, and there was only one way it could be doused. I had to learn and tell the true story of how Canton's paper mill came to be, through these photos and my writing.

The resulting book is titled *Thomson's Pulp Mill: Building the Champion Fibre Company at Canton North Carolina – 1905 to 1908*. By writing this story, that burning fire inside of me was very effectively extinguished. And for a Canton boy whose great-grandfather helped build the mill, whose mother and father worked there, and who himself worked at the mill, nothing could have been more fulfilling than helping Mr. Peter Gibson Thomson build that mill again.

Conclusion

Unfortunately, recent events have dampened the significance of my engineering and literary experiences. After more than 30 years working in the paper industry and, afterward, writing and publishing seven books about our local history, a much more significant fire in Canton has apparently been extinguished forever.

In early 2023, Pactiv Evergreen, the owner of the paper mill in Canton at the time, made the fateful decision to shut the mill down after 115 years of continuous operation. Never in my own lifetime did I expect this would happen. But it has happened, and there is no doubt the impact of the mill's closure on Canton and Haywood County is significant. Somehow, those of us who have chosen to live here will have to find a way to patch this huge hole in the road and continue life's journey. Afterall, it is up to us to make sure our future and the future our children remain bright.

Very faint memories from long ago still remind me of the time when I grew up in Canton on Pearl Street, just a few blocks from the paper mill. Included in these recollections are the opportunities my brother and I had to "help" Mother hang and gather clothes on the clothesline, while listening to her fuss about the black fallout from the mill's smokestack contaminating the clothes. Little things like that, however, would never have diminished our appreciation for the smelly, smoke-spewing paper mill across the river where the family's steady income was won.

Clearly, this Canton boy can remember when his hometown was a smelly place. It smelled like home then, and it still does today.

The author and his younger brother, Rego, are enjoying a snowy and smoky day in Canton during the 1950s. (from Tony Jones collection)

Plumb Proud of My Mountain Dialect

Almost immediately upon arrival at my chosen college campus, I began to notice something very peculiar happening. It seemed that other students, teammates, and even the football coaches with whom I interfaced and engaged in dialogue would look at me in a curious manner and with a slight grin. I still remember that more than once new acquaintances would query, "Where you from, anyway?" Still others might remark, "Man, you talk funny. Say something else."

So it was that I quickly came to realize, upon that first venture outside the western North Carolina mountains to the capital city of Columbia, South Carolina, there was something unique or special about me that other people seemed to enjoy. My distinct mountain accent and dialect set me apart from everyone else. In fact, it would become a personal badge that I would proudly brandish as I grew into manhood and made a life for myself beyond the mountains.

Living and growing up in Canton, North Carolina, in the 1950s and '60s and with roots firmly embedded in the Pigeon Valley, I naturally acquired the speech of my family, neighbors, and the local mountaineers without ever appreciating it. By that time, more than 150 years had passed since the first Indian traders and later Scotch Irish, English, and German settlers penetrated the remote mountain fastnesses of western North Carolina. Over this time span, their archaic dialect, which included vestiges of an Elizabethan language and incorporated the use of a distinctive clipped speech, unusual colloquialisms, and concocted words and contractions, had been drastically watered down through a long evolutionary process.

Improved roads, railroads, and the timber industry opened up the vast western North Carolina mountains and valleys and brought the mountaineer farmers into more frequent contact with outsiders—or "furiners." The mountain farms themselves grew larger while producing surplus grain crops and livestock. These farm products could be hauled, or "drove," to faraway markets in Charleston and Greenville, South Carolina; Augusta, Georgia; or nearby towns and rail hubs to be sold and bartered. Other commercial activities and industries such as selling "sang" (ginseng), animal skins, and even distilled corn liquor began to gradually bring the mountain highlanders closer to the civilized folk. This was to have a profound influence on their culture and speech.

The Pigeon Valley region followed a similar progression. In the early days, there were only a few farms lying along the Pigeon River where the rich silty soil was fertile and easily tilled. This choice land was claimed by those brave pioneers who arrived in the Valley first, likely finding the hearth fires of the retreating Cherokee Indians still warm. The vast majority of the settlers who followed found property along tributary streams and creeks and on the hillsides and ridges bordering these small water courses. In these mountain venues, they cleared away forests, constructed small log cabins, and hauled rock out of the fields in order to cultivate the land, feed themselves, and make a go of it in the wild mountain frontier.

As time went by and generation followed generation, the farming enterprises began to prosper and to evolve into larger and more productive farms. Taken in aggregate, the output of surplus crops and livestock from the river farms and those smaller ones located in the hollers and astraddle the hills began to stimulate the local economy. Demand for these surplus goods created an increasingly vigorous commerce between the Valley farmers and the nearby settlements, including the little hamlet of Pigeon River (Canton), and more distant marketplaces such as Augusta, Georgia.

In the time frame spanning from the 1880s through about 1920, the arrival of the railroad, the invasion of the Blue Ridge Mountains by timber barons, and the construction of a huge pulp mill in Canton further diversified the economy and provided for even more contact between the Pigeon Valley farmers and the merchants, factory workers, and citizens of Canton, Bethel, Clyde, and Waynesville.

There is no doubt this interaction with people considered to be outlanders, or outsiders, tended to dilute the ancient mountain dialect of our Pigeon Valley ancestors—but it did not kill it outright.

Horace Kephart, in his noteworthy study of the North Carolina mountaineers titled *Our Southern Highlanders*, promoted a belief that the mountain women are the primary reason the unique dialect and speech of the highlanders persisted. From his perspective living among the Southern Highlanders in the early 1900s, he observed that the mountain men traveled to the mills, villages, logging camps, and railroad towns regularly to trade and transact business. Consequently, they tended to adapt their speech and habits to that of the outlander.

On the other hand, the "penned-at-home" nature of the women's existence precluded their venturing beyond the surrounds of the tiny homesteads they inhabited. For this reason, they remained insulated from the influence and infection of outsiders, and the integrity of their native dialect was protected. The faithful, dependable, and sturdy mountain women preserved much of the original mountain dialect for generations, until the schools and technological advances made it virtually impossible to be "penned-up" or isolated from the modern world.

However, there are still hints and strains of the mountain accents and dialect left in our speech today. As I observed when I went off to college, this unusual speech is still very obvious to those who are not native to the Valley and not accustomed to hearing it.

My mother was born and raised in the heart of the Pigeon Valley, and her ancestry can be traced back to the first Hargroves, Shooks, Moores, and Catheys who began settling along the Pigeon River in the early 1800s. Some of the colloquialisms and expressions she routinely used are so familiar to me today that I unconscientiously speak them from time to time. For example, when I'm surprised or just plain puzzled with something, I might declare, "Well, that beats a henaroot." The definition of "henaroot" has escaped me thus far, but I know when and how Mom used the expression, and I tend to employ it occasionally under similar circumstances to the delight of my wife and daughters.

Another expression that Mother sometimes used to add emphasis to an articulation was "bigger than Pete." To show her surprise, she might exclaim, "Why, that man just up and left the country *bigger than Pete.*" Again, I'm not aware of the origins of this idiom but I repeat it anyway, just as she did, to accent something I have said or simply extract a chuckle from an outlander.

By listening to and mimicking my mother, aunts, and grandmother, I unknowingly acquired from them a treasure trove of dialect, colloquialisms, and words that are remnants of the language spoken by their pioneer ancestors following the Revolutionary War.

Some of the old mountain expressions and words that remain with us today come to mind readily. A sampling of these is listed below along with an attempt to define them or add meaning. Hopefully, these expressions will never be forgotten or, better yet, go unspoken.

Selected Words and Idioms from our Pigeon Valley Ancestors

- *fair-to-middlin* > means about average and derives from a grading measure of the old cotton merchants – "I'm feeling *fair-to-middlin* today."
- *turn-o-meal* > means one's turn and derives from the fact that each man had to wait his turn to have the corn meal ground at the mill – "It's his *turn-o-meal* to work the roads."
- *laid off* > means postponed – "I've *laid off* and *laid off* until I ain't got no choice now 'cept plow that field."
- *layed by* > means put aside or put up or finish – "He's done got the crops *layed by.*"
- *lit out* > means set out or took off – "He *lit out* of here like a scalded dog."
- *feathered into them* > means attacked and derives from the Old English expression of burying an arrow up to the feathers. Horace Kephart wrote that this expression was used long ago "before villainous saltpeter supplanted the long bow."
- *edzact* > means to cipher or figure out – "Let me study it over a spell and then I can *edzact* it."
- *plunder* > means junk – "Nothin' in that old shed 'cept a bunch of *plunder.*"

- *mess* > refers to a quantity of one-feeding of the family – "Let's string a *mess* of beans for tonight."
- *nare or nary* > means none or not any – "Ain't *nary* apple ain't got no worms."
- *yander* > means over there – "He's out *yander* in the field."
- *peart* > means almost or near – "She's *peart* near finished with that thar quilt piece."
- *leather-britches* > means beans dried in the pod and then boiled hull and all
- *fling* > means to throw – "He can *fling* a rock clear across the river."
- *heerd* > means heard – "I ain't *heerd* hide nor hair of him again."
- *churched* > means getting kicked out of church for not living by the accepted standards and rules. Old timers would get a couple of warnings before being *churched* for offenses such as drinking or not attending church regularly. For example, "Old John got *churched* for sampling the shine too much."
- *fixin'* > means getting ready – "She's *fixin'* to feather into him."
- *hit* > corruption of the preposition "it" – "*Hit* just ain't right, no ways."
- *fetch* > means to get – "Go *fetch* the molassey sugar for Paw."
- *tol'able* > means tolerable or endurable – "She's getting along *tol'able* well."
- *smidgen* > means a bit or morsel and more than a mite – "Give me a *smidgen* of tobaccer snuff."
- *bodaciously* > means bodily or entirely – "I'm *bodaciously* hungry."
- *peckerwood* > means a woodpecker
- *stove* > means jammed or jabbed – "He *stove* up his neck bad."
- *carry* > means take – "I had to *carry* her over to town to see the Doc."
- *troublin' stick* > means the wooden stick or paddle used to stir the clothes when washing them in a kettle of boiling water and lye soap – "She *troubled* the water hard as can be with that *troublin stick* of hern."
- *battling paddle* > means a wooden paddle used to beat and hammer the wash during the scalding and washing process – "She wielded a mean *battling paddle* on Monday wash days."

- *infare* > means a celebration or wedding feast put on by the groom's parents
- *tote* > means to carry – "Let's *tote* the corn over to the mill and get it run."
- *poke* > means a paper bag or bag – "Fill up this here *poke* plumb to the top."
- *holler* > means to yell or is another word for valley – "He *hollered* so loud that they heerd him plumb to the top of the *holler*."
- *airish* > means conceited or proud and derives from putting on airs – "That boy is a mite *airish*."
- *boomer* > means a type of mountain squirrel also known as a red squirrel or pine squirrel
- *josh* > means to kid or jest – "He's just *joshing* you."
- *plumb* > means all the way or completely – "Fill my poke *plumb* to the top."
- *allow* > means think or figure – "Don't know what to *allow* about that kind of carrying-on."
- *afeared* > means afraid – "I ain't *afeared* of him."
- *haint* > means has not or have not – "He *haint* got no right to that land."
- *you'uns (u'ns)* and *we'uns* > corruptions of the plural pronouns "you" and "we" – "Let's *you'uns* and *we'uns* jest saunter over thar and see what they allow."
- *young'uns* > means young children – "Tend to the *young'uns* while I'm gone."
- *tobaccer* > means tobacco – "Need to mosey over to Cathey's mill to get me some chaws of *tobaccer*."
- *tater* and *mater* > means potato and tomato – "We'uns going to have *taters* and *maters* with a mess of beans fer dinner today."
- *reckon* > means to think or know – "I don't *reckon* I knowed him."
- *helve* > means the handle of a tool such as an ax or hammer – "Ain't nothing better than hickory for an *ax helve*."
- *toddick* > means small measure or portion of meal given to the miller as a toll for grinding corn – "The miller earned his *toddick* today turning that wormy corn."

- *slut* > means makeshift candle made by filling saucer with fat and using a cotton cloth wick – "Better light up that *slut* to see by."
- *comeuppance* > means to awaken or make aware – "A man that sips on ol' Jed's cider is in for a real *comeuppance*."
- *quair* > means the same as queer – "Ol' Jed sure has been acting mighty *quair* here lately."

A Canton Boy's Hometown Memories

Canton in the 1950s and '60s was a small progressive town located on the Pigeon River in Haywood County, North Carolina. It was situated around Champion's huge paper mill sprawled along the river and beside an important railroad artery and turnpike running through the mountains. At that time, before the advent of shopping malls, huge chain discount stores, and medical centers, Canton's city streets thrived with small retail and service businesses and a few professional offices.

These enterprises supported the commerce generated by local factory workers, Pigeon Valley farmers, and tourists visiting the mountains. The center of the business activities was located primarily along Main and Park Streets. Closely surrounding the small business district, and mostly within walking distance, were the churches, elementary schools, high school, and residential neighborhoods.

It wasn't much more than that—just a little incorporated village tucked away in the mountains and populated with friendly working-class citizens. That includes my younger brother and me, who were born and raised in Canton during the above-mentioned period. Although more than 50 years removed now, I still consider Canton my hometown and the source of a goodly portion of my life's memories.

Most of these recollections are pleasant with a few bittersweet ones mixed in for good measure. Unpleasant experiences have been forgotten, for the most part, as the years flew by. Often, when I think back on those youthful times, Canton seems to take on an almost idyllic fantasy.

Let me take you back in time to the small town of Canton and share a few personal flashbacks and thoughts of those days gone by. I remember…

- the large, red-brick YMCA building before it was torn down to make room for Champion's new paper machine,

- learning to swim at the old YMCA under the watchful eyes of Paul Rogers,
- selling Christmas trees on Park Street for the "Y" under Nazi Miller's direction and freezing to death in the little shack where we took refuge from the cold,
- fishing off the old iron-truss bridge that carried Main Street's automobile and pedestrian traffic across the Pigeon River,
- walking back and forth from our home on Pearl Street to Pennsylvania Avenue Elementary School, and crossing the old iron-truss bridge and making that arduous hike up "Steep" Street (Mears Avenue),
- practicing youth football on the field across from Charlie's Restaurant and running laps around the horseshow ring,
- shopping for sports equipment at Stone's Paint and Wallpaper Store on Park Street, including baseball gloves and golf clubs,
- playing golf from dawn until dark at the nine-hole Mountain View Golf Course with my brother, Rego, and our buddies,
- having a coke in the drug store below Dr. Carey Wells' dental office at the corner of Main and Park Streets,
- playing basketball in that "cracker-box" gym at the original YMCA and threading long set shots through the roof trusses,
- going to Saturday-night dances at the old YMCA gym and sitting along the wall and waiting to see if the girls might consider me for a dance partner,
- square-dancing (clogging) with the "Y" team in front of real live audiences,
- going to summer camp at Camp Hope and all the fun things associated with that opportunity, including nighttime campfires and storytelling, archery lessons, making crafts, and swimming in the cold waters of the East Fork River,
- going to high school football camp at Camp Hope and how much fun it **was not**,
- standing on the Park Street bridge among huge crowds of spectators and watching the Labor Day parade pass by,

- enjoying the Labor Day "rides" and selling food and drinks out of makeshift booths for the Gra-Y ball teams,
- the real "Labor" Day when our Gra-Y football team, toiling under Nazi Miller's close supervision, cleaned up the mess after the Labor Day celebration was over and the carnival "rides" had moved out,
- swimming at the Canton Recreation Park and diving off the high diving board,
- playing farm league, little league, and senior little league baseball for managers of the likes of Barton Ray, Claude Ford, and Tony Jones,
- playing football and basketball for the Gra-Y teams with Nazi Miller and George Price coaching and running the show,
- wading and fishing the Pigeon River all summer day long and catching brim, red-eye bass, horny-heads, silversides, and hogsuckers,
- buying fishing tackle at Bill Schull's Nantahala Hardware store,
- climbing the mountain behind our house on Pearl Street and standing on top of the Town's concrete reservoir while looking down on the Canton folk,
- riding inner tubes down the Pigeon River in the summertime,
- wanting to go inside the old pool hall on Main Street—next to "Steep" Street—that Mother forbade us to enter,
- going to the Colonial Theatre to see movies like *Old Yeller*, *Davy Crockett*, countless westerns, and certainly a "scary" movie or two,
- shopping with Mother at the old and new Smathers' Market grocery stores,
- how Daddy smelled like the mill when he got home from work in his old rusty work car and with pulp caked on his shoes,
- playing football, basketball, baseball, and golf for the Canton High and Pisgah High School teams coached by Boyd Allen, Bill Stamey, Bob Holcomb, and other fine mentors,
- the public library, cinema, bus station, post office, Charlie's Restaurant, Stone's Paint and Wallpaper store, Ford car dealership, gas stations, and A&P grocery store located along Park Street,
- when, prior to the construction of I-40, Main Street and Park Street

- each had two-way traffic and all the regional east-west traffic passed through Canton,
- getting shots and polio vaccines at the Health Department above the old Town jail on Main Street near the railroad,
- Mom and Dad buying gas at Gregory's ESSO station and charging it,
- admiring the latest car models at Murphy's Chevrolet on Main Street and the Ford dealership on Park Street,
- going to Charlie's restaurant after church and having a hot dog and my favorite soda—a Grapette,
- when Mother would take us to the dime store to check out the toys, Jack Feingold's Army Store to get fitted for PF Flyer tennis shoes and dungarees, and Winner's Department Store to buy fancier apparel,
- visiting the Canton Library next to the post office and Mrs. Avery's summer reading programs,
- buying a "Western Flyer" snow sled at the Western Auto store on Main Street,
- attending Pennsylvania Avenue grammar school and playing under huge trees at recess, dusting erasers against the school's brick walls, enjoying the milk breaks, eating lunch in the cafeteria, dreading the fire and atomic bomb drills, and learning the multiplication tables and verb conjugation,
- the swimming, diving, and archery contests held on Labor Day at the Recreation Park,
- lifeguarding during the summers at the Recreation Park, while getting sunburned and listening to WWIT on the radio,
- working for the Town of Canton during college breaks collecting garbage, cleaning the streets, cutting grass, manicuring the ball fields, and umpiring little league games,
- the new Main Street bridge and enormous Robertson Memorial YMCA building under construction,
- the temporary YMCA, which was located next to Sluder's Furniture Store on Main Street, with pool tables on the ground floor and ping pong tables on the upper floor,

- watching the Champion "Y" fastpitch softball teams play on Friday and Saturday nights during the summer and idolizing players like Nazi Miller, Clyde Miller, George Price, Wade Garrett, Bill Bearden, Charlie Poindexter, Ron Peterson, Red Ivester, Bob Holcomb, and Bobby "Snake" Moore,
- "Peaches night" at the fastpitch softball games when the team from Spartanburg, South Carolina, would hand out peaches to all the fans.

These are just a few Canton memories from the early years that have found hiding places in far nooks of my mind. Thank goodness they were not lost, and I can still reflect on them. But enough of that. Let me stop here, and I'll leave you to feast on your own hometown memories. Hope you enjoy them!

Canton's Champion YMCA building was constructed by the Champion Fibre Company and dedicated to the town's citizens in 1920. For 40 years, the "Y" was the center of sporting and cultural events for young and old folks alike in Canton. In the early 1960s, this wonderful old "Y" building was demolished to make room for the mill's new paper machine. (from Tony Jones collection)

The author remembers when the annual Labor Day celebration was the biggest event of the year for the citizens of Canton. Shown here are the parade onlookers lined up along both sides of the Park Street bridge watching a local high school band as it marches by. (from Tony Jones collection)

In the 1950s and '60s, Canton's Labor Day parade-goers hustled over to the carnival "rides" after the last band and float had passed them by. The Ferris wheel, merry-go-round, rollercoaster, and other delightful contrivances along with refreshment and game booths were usually set up on the carnival grounds between the Pigeon River and the National Guard armory building, which is still standing. (from Tony Jones collection)

Memories of Canton's Labor Day celebrations must include the refreshment and game booths that competed with the carnival rides for customers' business. Shown here on Penland Street are these two ladies vending snowballs to a thirsty celebrant. Behind them are contestants wielding bows and shooting arrows at targets in hopes of hitting the bullseye and winning a prize. (from Tony Jones collection)

The Colonial Theatre located on Park Street was where young kids, such as the author and his brother, could go and watch movies like Old Yeller, Davy Crockett, and countless westerns and "scary" movies. The brick building to the right of the theatre and partially in view once housed a bus station and café, among other things. (from Tony Jones collection)

Playing sports was the most important thing in our lives while growing up in Canton in the 1950s and '60s. In this photo, a farm league baseball game is underway on a field located where the former Robertson Memorial YMCA building still stands today. Note that the umpire is standing behind the pitcher and, in this case, happens to be the infamous Bobby "Snake" Moore. Snake was an outstanding third baseman for the world-class Champion "Y" fastpitch softball team. (from Tony Jones collection)

Smathers Super Market was the store in Canton most frequented by the author's mother and her two young sons. In this photo, a rooftop Christmas tree and Santa Claus welcome customers to the grocery store. Just across the street are two other retail businesses the family often visited—Jack Feingold's Army Store and Winner's clothing store. (from Tony Jones collection)

Faint memories still exist of the author's mom and dad filling up their cars with gasoline at Gregory's Esso station, located where Main and Park Streets merge into Hwy 19-23 on the west side of town. They would tell the attendant pumping the gas to "charge it" and settle their bill at the end of each month. In this photo, Mrs. Marjorie Gregory assists a notable customer—Mr. Hazel Ramsey—who was Canton's mayor. (from Tony Jones collection)

The author and his younger brother were benefactors of wonderful parents (Jimmie Hargrove and Tony Jones), and they had an unforgettable childhood growing up in Canton. (from Tony Jones collection)

PREFACE FOR "THOMSON'S PULP MILL"

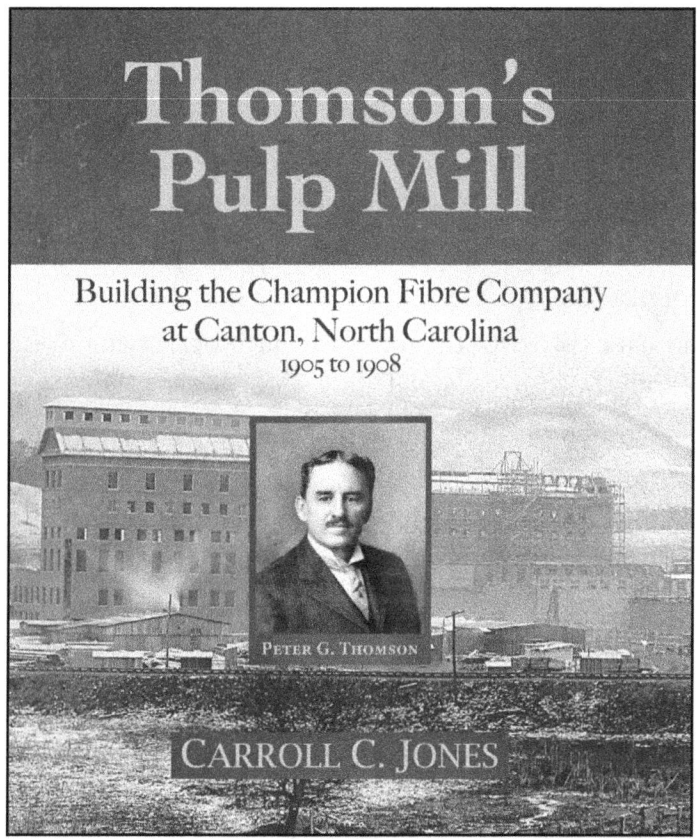

The book *Thomson's Pulp Mill: Building the Champion Fibre Company at Canton, North Carolina – 1905 to 1908* offers a concise and illustrated account of the construction of Peter Gibson Thomson's pulp mill in Canton, North Carolina, more than a century ago. Originally known as the Champion Fibre Company, it later evolved into the Champion Paper and Fibre Company, International Paper, and other concerns through latter years. Not only will the reader discover a very practical reason that drove Mr. Thomson to build the mill, but also why the tiny town of Canton was chosen as its location, what that original mill entailed, and how tremendous challenges were overcome to construct the mill's immense brick buildings. More importantly, many wonderful and rare old photographs that have come to light are presented in this book. These serve to illuminate the construction project from the driving of the first timber piles into the muddy bottomland to the spewing of smoke from the mill's signature towering chimney.

Fresh out of college, I went to work for Champion International as an engineer, unaware of the wetness that still dripped from behind my ears. Thank goodness there were experienced co-workers in the Canton paper mill's engineering department who covered for me while I became accustomed to designing and building projects—first small maintenance jobs and, gradually, larger and more sophisticated projects. During that initial year or so, I was able to explore every dark corner of the mill's vast facilities, trying to figure out how things were built, how they worked, and, most of all, where I was. Those first impressions of timber framing, brick masonry construction, and an ancient steam engine driving a paper machine with pulleys and leather belts remained with me through the coming decades while I worked in the paper industry.

Lately, a good portion of my time has been dedicated to either historical writing projects or to fly fishing. In pursuit of knowledge and local history—not the local wild trout—it has been my pleasure and good fortune to become acquainted with the important resources held at the Canton Area Historical Museum. These holdings, along with lively conversations with the museum's curator and friends of the museum, have served to revive nearly forgotten memories of the Canton paper mill. I discovered in the museum unpublished memoirs of two principal men in the history of the Champion Fibre Company: Reuben B. Robertson, Sr., who for many years helmed the mill operations and later the affairs of the entire company, and attorney George H. Smathers, who played an instrumental legal role in the development of the original pulp mill.

These men's documented memories—such as the one about the "Rooshian" workers (the name given by locals to foreign workmen from Bulgaria), and another about attempts, through hypnosis, to persuade a local widow lady to sell her land to the Champion Fibre Company—kindled my desire to write about the construction of the original mill. However, even these rich typewritten memoirs did not provide enough source material to record the true construction story. So, I abandoned that literary dream as a mere fancy and one that would never come to fruition. There simply was not enough extant information to do a proper job—or so I thought.

Then one day, I ran into an old high school friend for the first time in many years. He was a Canton boy and, like me, had spent most of his professional career away from our hometown. As we caught up and resumed our acquaintance, he offhandedly mentioned some old mill construction photos in his possession. Well, as it happens, his late mother's Uncle Thomas Marr played a vital role in the construction of the original mill's tannin extract plant and the employee village known as "Fibreville." Later, Mr. Marr became the superintendent in charge of the entire extract department, which was a highly profitable operation for the Champion Fibre Company, even carrying the company through some problematic growing times. These old photographs of the construction work had been passed down through Mr. Marr's family, ending up in the appreciative hands of my friend.

One look at this immense trove of rare photos convinced me that they should be preserved and shared somehow. Admittedly, the quality of some of the images is poor, but, even so, they offer a glimpse into the obscure past and show the pulp mill under construction—a sight almost lost to us forever. The notion of presenting the photographs in a book format so that they could be interpreted, understood, and appreciated became too strong to ignore. My friend agreed with the idea and has very graciously allowed them to be included in *Thomson's Pulp Mill*.

Therefore, I have endeavored to associate these photographs with a narrative story about the construction of the Champion Fibre Company pulp mill at Canton. Detailed captions accompany most of the photos, offering as much insight as I have been able to glean and understand. There are also a few other photographs from the Canton Historical Museum's collection that have been used to supplement the visual treasures contained within this book.

It will become obvious to the reader where the source material for the story comes from. Footnotes and the bibliography will show that much of the historical information is derived from either the Robertson and Smathers memoirs or newspaper articles published at the time of the mill's construction. In every case, I tried to find more than one newspaper account to authenticate some of the reported facts. For those who might wonder, many instances of inaccurate reporting—or "fake news"—indeed came to light.

Likewise, I did not take the memoirs at face value. Both men recorded their memories many years after the fact. Mr. Robertson even wrote in a foreword to his memoirs that since "none of those who carried responsibility in Champion's infancy are with us today… one's style is not therefore in any way cramped by the fear of the carping criticism of those who might want meticulous accuracy."[114*]

Due consideration was given to these words as I crafted *Thomson's Pulp Mill*, using the "facts," stories, and tales from the Robertson and Smathers memoirs. Where deemed necessary, readers are reminded that these were the men's recollections, and memories are not infallible. However, the dated type-written memoirs are rich beyond description, providing us invaluable information as well as interesting tales of the history of Thomson's pulp mill.

Actual details of the original mill and machinery are exceedingly scarce. A foundation plan drawn by George F. Hardy, the mill's architect/engineer, was discovered in the archives of the Evergreen Packaging Company's Canton mill. This document provided the foundation details of the pulp mill, but excluded the extract plant structures, two other large wood preparation buildings, the river pump house, and a water reservoir situated high on a hill above the mill. Although the poor condition of this old print made it barely decipherable, it proved extremely helpful in determining the layout and size of many of the original buildings. Not only that, but it also showed the piling details under each building, so that the true scope of the piling work can be fully understood and appreciated.

For example, various reports at the time of the construction work stated that the mill's huge concrete smokestack was built on top of either 400 timber piles or a thousand piles, depending on the source of information. However, both counts can be disputed with confidence, since the Hardy drawing very specifically shows that approximately 200 piles were actually used.

An edition of *Manufacturer's Record* published at the time of construction contains a very descriptive article of Thomson's enterprise, including details of the mill's various buildings and some of the mechanical equipment housed

---

114   *Vol. II, Reuben Robertson Memoirs* (unpublished); "Foreword."

within the brick walls. Yet, much is not known about many of the specific machines employed in the mill—their make, size, and how they functioned and were operated. Nevertheless, I describe the original mill's pulping and extract processes in sufficient detail to satisfy most readers' appetites for such things. Also, a listing of all the different buildings, along with the size and contents of each one, is included. And to better orient readers with these facilities, a plot plan of the mill buildings is presented as well.

This story and the descriptions of the original Champion Fibre Company mill are surely important, and undoubtedly readers will find the information interesting and enlightening. But it is the rare old photographs that demonstrate in magnificent detail how the mill site looked just prior to construction, during the construction period in 1906-1908, and after the 1908 start-up. Only to the discerning eye will the challenging conditions in which the men worked, the sheer massiveness of the structures and equipment they erected, and much more be comprehended.

I hope you will have an opportunity to read *Thomson's Pulp Mill: Building the Champion Fibre Company at Canton, North Carolina – 1905 to 1908*. It would be my great privilege to escort you back into a mill town's past, where the story of Peter G. Thomson's pulp mill can be revealed at last.

Construction began at the Champion Fibre Company pulp mill in the spring of 1906 with the pile-driving work. Shown here are three steam-powered pile-driving rigs hammering huge timber piles deep into the ground. These piles would eventually support the concrete foundations and brick buildings that housed the mill's machinery and operations. (from Sellars collection)

In this fall of 1907 view of Peter G. Thomson's pulp mill under construction, the pile driving and bricklaying work appear to be almost complete. (from Sellars collection)

This early photo shows the Champion Fibre Company's pulp mill in full operation. (from Canton Historical Museum's collection)

A GLIMPSE OF THE AUTHOR

Carroll C. Jones was born and raised in the mountains of Haywood County, North Carolina, in the small paper-mill town of Canton. He is a direct descendant of the Hargrove, Cathey, Shook, and Moore families who pioneered the Forks of Pigeon region of Haywood County (present-day Bethel, N.C.), the setting for several of his books. After attending the University of South Carolina in Columbia, where he played football for the USC Gamecocks and earned a degree in civil engineering, he began an extended career in the paper industry lasting more than three decades.

Carroll's professional work led him out of the Carolina highlands to Brazil, South America, and then back to the US. In the late 1980s and early 1990s, he managed the Canton Modernization Project, which brought Champion International Paper Company's Canton mill into compliance with the EPA's environmental water and air standards. Upon the successful completion of that three-hundred-million-dollar endeavor, he moved to Pensacola, Florida, and worked in various mill and corporate management positions for the Champion and International Paper companies.

Now retired and living in the heart of the mountains once again, Carroll juggles his involvement with community organizations, fly fishing, and his interest in local history and writing. To his credit, all seven of the books he has written have been honored with awards from the North Carolina Society of Historians. These books are listed below.

The 25th North Carolina Troops in the Civil War
Rooted Deep in the Pigeon Valley
Captain Lenoir's Diary

East Fork Trilogy fictional series:
Master of the East Fork
Rebel Rousers
(winner of the prestigious 2016 President's Award
From the North Carolina Society of Historians)
August's Treasure

Thomson's Pulp Mill:
Building the Champion Fibre Company
at Canton, North Carolina – 1905 to 1908

www.ingramcontent.com/pod-product-compliance
Lightning Source LLC
Chambersburg PA
CBHW050548160426
43199CB00015B/2579